Preface Books

A series of scholarly and critical studies of major writers intended for those needing modern and authoritative guidance through the characteristic difficulties of their work to reach an intelligent understanding and enjoyment of it.

General Editor: MAURICE HUSSEY

Samuel Johnson, c. 1775, by Sir Joshua Reynolds

A Preface to Samuel Johnson

Thomas Woodman

Longman, London and New York.

Longman Group UK Limited,
Longman House, Burnt Mill, Harlow,
Essex CM20 2JE, England
and Associated Companies throughout the world.

Published in the United States of America
by Longman Publishing, New York

First published 1993

ISBN 0 582 08666 3 CSD
ISBN 0 582 08665 5 PPR

British Library Cataloguing-in-Publication Data

A catalogue record for this book is
available from the British Library

Library of Congress Cataloging-in-Publication Data

Woodman, Thomas M.
    A preface to Samuel Johnson / Thomas Woodman.
        p.   cm. – (Preface books)
    Includes bibliographical references and indexes.
    ISBN 0-582-08666-3 (CSD). – ISBN 0-582-08665-5 (PPR)
    1. Johnson, Samuel, 1709-1784 – Criticism and interpretation.
I. Title.
PR3534.W66 1993
828'.609 – dc20 828.609 92-46734
                                      CIP

Set by 50 in Baskerville

Produced by Longman Singapore Publishers (Pte) Ltd.
Printed in Singapore

Contents

Contents

List of illustrations

Acknowledgements

It is proper to begin this book by acknowledging the help of the late Maurice Hussey, former general editor of the series, who was most encouraging in the early stages of this project. The staff at Longman have also been very encouraging throughout. I owe a special debt of gratitude, of course, to my mother and to my wife Rosemary.

For permission to reproduce illustrations and photographs we are grateful to the following:

Lord Beaverbrook, The Beaverbrook Art Gallery, Fredericton, N.B., Canada, page 207; The British Museum, pages 9, 17 and 79; Haverford College, Pennsylvania, page 39; Houghton Library, Harvard University, page 93; Dr Johnson's House Trust, page 210; Longman Group UK Ltd, page 137; National Monuments, pages 49 and 113; Scottish National Portrait Gallery, page 31; Yale University and the Edinburgh University Press, pages 212 and 213 (maps redrawn for the *London Journal* by Harold K. Faye). We have been unable to trace the copyright holder of the illustration which appears as the frontispiece (print supplied by Paul Mellon Centre), and would welcome any information to help us to do so.

Introduction

James Boswell's *Life of Johnson*, by common accord perhaps the greatest biography in any literature, was until comparatively recently a popular bedside book, well thumbed by every person with any claims to education. Samuel Johnson – or 'Doctor' Johnson as he is popularly known – is still a very famous man. The number of entries under his name in dictionaries of quotations is only likely to be surpassed by the Bible and Shakespeare, and he is frequently referred to and quoted in the higher levels of the media. Thousands of people visit the Johnson Birthplace museum at Lichfield every year and the London house at Gough Square where he worked on the *Dictionary*.

Yet times have changed as far as students coming up to university today are concerned. Most of them seem to start with no more than a hazy feeling of some link with a dictionary and perhaps a recollection of Johnson's memorable appearance as a character in one episode of the television series *Black Adder*.

It is not entirely a bad thing, however, to approach Johnson without the accumulated preconceptions of the past. As scholars have been trying to indicate for years, the old popular image of Johnson as a crusty and reactionary eccentric is itself a myth. Even the usage 'Doctor' can be misleading in focusing exclusively on the authoritative Establishment figure of Johnson's later years, and it is often forgotten that the degree is an honorary one and that Johnson himself only used it on one recorded occasion.

Certainly the interest in Johnson the great English 'character' has often detracted from his true stature as a writer. With proud professionalism throughout a long career he writes on a huge range of subjects in a wide variety of genres. He is a major poet, despite the relatively small amount of verse that he produced. He is an important scholar of the English language and one of the greatest literary critics who has ever lived. Above all, he is a great moral writer, one who still speaks to us today in his remarkable combination of dignity and tough-mindedness, ethical generalization and practicality.

Yet there is no need to deny the fascination and greatness of Johnson's personality or to fall into the kind of critical purism that refuses to see that a sense of that personality illuminates the writings and helps them to come alive. With this in mind I begin the study that follows with an account of Johnson's biography combined with a brief chronological survey of his main writings. I move on to consider his intellectual, religious, political and literary background. The latter in particular requires fuller treatment than might sometimes be necessary in an introductory book of this kind because Johnson is so deeply and extensively involved in the literary life of his time as a professional writer and critic. Johnson's writing is demanding, if highly rewarding, for the modern reader, and so I offer in Part Two a close examination of some representative passages. The main focus of the reference section that follows is on brief biographies of people important to Johnson's intellectual, literary and personal life. It will be understood, of course, that space has permitted only a relatively small selection from the large number of candidates that could have been included under these categories.

Part One
The Writer in his Setting

Chronology

1735	*Voyage to Abyssinia* published. Marries Elizabeth Jervis (widow of Harry Porter).	
1736	Opens Edial Hall school. Begins *Irene*.	Butler, *Analogy of Religion*.
1737	Goes to London in March with David Garrick.	
1738	Writes for *Gentleman's Magazine; London*.	
1739	Writes anti-Walpole pamphlets and 'Life of Boerhaave'.	Hume, *Treatise of Human Nature*.
1740		Richardson, *Pamela*.
1741	Parliamentary debates in *Gentleman's Magazine*.	
1742		Walpole resigns.
1744	*An Account of the Life of Mr Richard Savage*.	Pope dies.
1745	Proposals for Shakespeare edition	Jacobite rebellion. Swift dies.
1746	Signs contract for *Dictionary*.	Collins, *Odes*. Joseph Warton, *Odes*.
1747		Richardson, *Clarissa*. Thomas Warton, *Pleasures of Melancholy*.
1748		Hume, *Philosophical Essays concerning the Human Understanding*.
1749	*The Vanity of Human Wishes; Irene* performed.	Fielding, *Tom Jones*.
1750	Begins *Rambler* essays.	
1752	Wife Tetty dies.	Gregorian calendar adopted in Britain.
1753	Writes for the *Adventurer*.	
1755	*A Dictionary of the English Language* published.	

3

1756	Edits *Literary Magazine.* Proposals for subscription edition of Shakespeare.	Seven Years War. Joseph Warton, *Essay on Pope.*
1758	Begins the *Idler.*	
1759	Mother dies. Writes *The Prince of Abyssinia (Rasselas).*	Voltaire, *Candide.* George III reigns. Macpherson, *Ossian.* Sterne, *Tristram Shandy.*
1760		
1762	Awarded pension by government.	Rousseau, *Emile, Du Contrat Social.*
1763	Meets Boswell.	Seven Years War ends.
1765	Shakespeare edition published. Meets Thrales. Awarded Honorary LL.D, Trinity College, Dublin.	Percy, *Reliques.*
1766	Helps Robert Chambers with Vinerian law lectures.	Goldsmith, *Vicar of Wakefield.*
1768		Gray, *Poems.*
1769		Wilkes expelled from Commons and re-elected. Shakespeare Jubilee at Stratford. Reynold, *Discourses.*
1770	Political pamphlet *The False Alarm.*	
1771	*Thoughts on the late Transactions Respecting Falkland's Islands.*	Mackenzie, *Man of Feeling.*
1773	Tour of Scotland and the Hebrides with Boswell.	Monboddo, *Origin and Progress of Languages.*
1774	Political pamphlet *The Patriot.*	Goldsmith dies. Thomas Warton, *History of English Poetry.*

4

1775	*A Journey to the Western Islands of Scotland* published. *Taxation No Tyranny.* Honorary DCL, Oxford.	
1776		Declaration of American Independence. Gibbon, *Decline and Fall of the Roman Empire.* Adam Smith, *Wealth of Nations.*
1777	Agreement with booksellers to write *Lives of the Most Eminent English Poets.* Campaigns without success to save Rev. Dr Dodd from hanging.	Chatterton, 'Rowley' *Poems.*
1778		Rousseau and Voltaire die.
1779	First four volumes of *Lives of the Poets.*	Treaty of Versailles ends American war.
1781	Death of Henry Thrale. Last six volumes of *Lives of the Poets.*	
1782	Poem 'On the Death of Dr Robert Levet'.	
1783	Stroke and recovery.	
1784	Remarriage of Hester Thrale. Johnson dies 13 December. Buried Westminster Abbey 20 December.	
1787		Hawkins, *Life of Johnson.*
1789		French Revolution.
1791		Boswell, *Life of Johnson.*

1 Samuel Johnson, the man and his life

Johnson's life has always fascinated people, and there were major biographies such as Sir John Hawkins's before the appearance of Boswell's great work. Boswell, himself, it has come to be understood, has his own limiting perspective, and writes as someone who knew Johnson only for the last twenty-one years of the latter's life. But Boswell is not to be blamed for the selective quarrying of his work later to produce the potent archetype of Johnson as crusty old Tory and eccentric. Macaulay, the most influential of the Victorian writers on Johnson, wrote, for example:

> The old philosopher is still among us, in the brown coat with the metal buttons and the shirt which ought to be at wash, blinking, puffing, rolling his head, drumming with his fingers, tearing his meat like a tiger, and swallowing his tea in oceans.

This turns picturesque details into something that *patronizes* Johnson, a thing that none of us can afford to do.

Yet the popular distortions and the over-emphasis on Johnson as a 'character' rather than as great writer do not, of course, mean that it is unrewarding to study the facts of his biography as such. Johnson's life is genuinely a fascinating and moving one to the highest degree. Knowledge of it is also, as pointed out in the introduction, indispensable to the full understanding of his work, though not always in the direct ways that might be supposed. In the end, however, the life and the works come to seem almost indivisible, and this despite the fact that Johnson often aspires to a deliberate, impersonal objectivity in his published writings. For his own personal experience and emotions always lie *behind* what he writes, and the movement towards objectivity is itself, as we shall see, part of a strenuous moral struggle, the same moral struggle, carried out with the same honesty and courage, as his life reveals.

'To struggle with difficulties': Johnson's character and early life

Samuel Johnson was born in the small midlands town of Lichfield near Birmingham on 18 September 1709 (using, as throughout this book, the New Style dating of the Gregorian calendar adopted in 1752). The town was dominated architecturally and socially by its cathedral. The fact that this had suffered damage from the Puritan Parliamentarian forces during the Civil War of the preceding century may well have contributed to a specially fervent tradition of loyalty to the established Church of England among some of the inhabitants of Lichfield, not least its most famous son, Johnson.

Two kinds of family influence blended in Johnson's background. Sarah, his mother, was from respected gentry stock with Anglican clerical connections; Michael, his father, was of much humbler origins, and it was of this side of the family that Johnson was later to say with a touch of inverted snobbery that he 'could hardly tell who was his grandfather'. Michael, however, prospered for a period and, as a prominent local bookseller, was Sheriff of Lichfield at the time of his son's birth. He was a large-boned, gaunt man with a tendency to melancholy, which his son always believed himself to have inherited.

Michael at fifty-two and Sarah at forty were considerably above the average age to have their first child. The birth was a difficult one and the baby's life feared for. To reassure the anxious mother, it was later recalled, the male midwife cried out, 'Here's a brave boy!' By 'brave' he meant, no doubt, no more than 'fine', but we cannot help thinking of the infant's struggles for life too, and the words have come to seem prophetic.

For Johnson's whole life was to be one of courageous achievement against what seemed enormous obstacles. 'Few examples are more moving, and offer more encouragement to human nature', writes Johnson's great modern biographer, Walter Jackson Bate, 'than that of Johnson, with almost all the odds against him ... strenuously trying to surmount them.' Johnson himself wrote nobly that:

> To struggle with difficulties, and to conquer them, is the highest human felicity; the next is to strive and deserve to conquer: but he whose life has passed without a contest, and who can boast neither success nor merit, can survey himself only as a useless filler of existence; and if he is content with his own character, must owe his satisfaction only to insensibility.
>
> (*Adventurer* 111)

Lichfield in 1785, showing the house where Johnson was born. Engraved from a drawing by E. Stringer.

To begin with there were the very obvious physical problems. An aunt once tactlessly said in Johnson's hearing when he was a child that 'she would not have picked up such a poor creature in the street'. Apart from all the side-effects of the difficult birth he very soon contracted from the wet-nurse to whom he was put out to breast-feed the terrible disease of scrofula, a tuberculosis of the lymph glands, which scarred his face and made him deaf in one ear and virtually blind in one eye (hence the characteristic screwed-up appearance of this eye in portraits of him reading). In an attempt to purify the infection a wound was kept open and running in his arm and not allowed to heal until he was six. For the rest of his life, he once said, there was scarcely a day in which he felt completely well.

Yet, despite his various ailments, Johnson had fortunately inherited an ox-like strength of constitution from his sturdy midlands stock (one uncle was a wrestler for a time at a London fair). He often said that he found his physical disabilities only a minor inconvenience in comparison with the psychological sufferings he had to undergo. As is well known, he was prone to depression and a series of compulsions, obsessions and anxieties. He had a terrible fear of death and damnation, and the feeling that he might go mad was so strong that in later years he left a padlock for his intimate friend Mrs Thrale to restrain him with should the worst actually happen. There was in fact no danger of madness at all for one with so strong an ego as Johnson, but since his mind, as we shall see, was the whole basis of his compensation for his other disabilities and of his attempts to gain control and make his way in the world, his own mental stability naturally enough became a focal point for all his anxieties.

How much weight is to be attached in all this to his mother's early strictures about hell fire, which he mentions in a fragment of autobiography, it is difficult to say. The pressure of parental expectations and demands on a late-born eldest son was itself considerable, and these demands were clearly both internalized and fiercely resisted at the same time. The first recorded example of his notorious use of wit as a weapon was against his mother. When she called him 'an impudent puppy' one day he is said to have replied, 'Ay, but what do they call a puppy's mother?'. Yet there was also great guilt about this anger against his parents. In later life, for example, he once made himself stand in the rain for an hour at Lichfield market as an act of penance for a youthful refusal to help his father with the bookstall there.

A revealing story about the infant Johnson shows how early

his characteristic aggressive determination and resentful self-sufficiency manifests itself. Dame Oliver, the teacher of the infant school the boy attended, grew concerned for his safety one day when he had to go home alone. She followed him at a discreet distance and saw him peering down intently and crossing the street on all fours. As Boswell continues the story: 'He happened to turn about and perceive her. Feeling her careful attention as an insult to his manliness, he ran back to her in a rage and beat her, as well as his strength would permit.'

After his time at this infant school Johnson started at the age of seven at Lichfield Grammar School, which numbered several famous men among its former pupils. Very soon his compensatory competitiveness and determination found their appropriate outlet in his studies. He read voraciously both at school and in his father's shop, violently indeed rather than with systematic application, as was always to be the case ('Sir, who reads books *through?*' he was to say later in a famous comment). But his speed, his memory and soon his learning were remarkable. The vast energy and intellectual curiosity obviously combined to powerful effect with the desire for achievement and even domination. He recalled later that 'They never thought to praise me by comparing me with anyone; they never said, Johnson is as good a scholar as such a one; but such a one is as good a scholar as Johnson.' So much did his abilities impress and overawe the other boys that a group of them often came in the morning to carry him in triumph on their backs to the classroom.

The young Johnson's competitive and ambitious spirit, his awareness of being a boy of more than usual gifts, was itself unfortunately to turn into a source of terrible frustration as a new layer of problems began to manifest themselves. His father had begun to engage in a tannery as well as the bookshop and had financially over-extended himself. Before long the family was in considerable financial distress. Samuel knew well that the traditional avenues of the law, the church and the universities would all be closed to him without money. As he put it later in the most powerful line of his poem *London*, packed with all the weight of his own bitter experience: 'SLOW RISES WORTH, BY POVERTY DEPRESS'D.'

After leaving school Johnson spent some time working – but more time reading – in his father's bookshop. Then – miraculously it must have seemed at the time – a small legacy left to his mother made it possible for him to go up to Oxford as an undergraduate at the age of nineteen. The famous story of how he went skating on Christ Church meadow soon after his arrival at the university instead of attending meetings with his tutor need not perhaps be taken too seriously. Johnson is unlikely to have wanted to waste his new opportunities, and he certainly worked at his books, if with characteristic irregularity. Yet he said himself in retrospect: 'I was mad and violent. It was bitterness that they mistook for pride. I was miserably poor, and I thought to fight my way by my literature and my wit; so I disregarded all power and authority.'

The money his mother had received soon ran out and his hopes of obtaining more from other sources were disappointed. His clothes became shabby and the condition of his shoes was so bad that a charitable member of the college left a better pair by his door. Johnson, typically, took it as a slur and responded by throwing them down the stairs. Within thirteen months of his first arrival he had to give up his university career and return to Lichfield.

The 'first great crisis': Johnson's psychological conflicts

Understandably the departure from Oxford precipitated one of the worst crises of Johnson's life. Despite his enormous gifts, his academic hopes had been blighted and his future seemed bleak. Even the bookshop held few prospects of a living for him as his father's difficulties increased. The natural disappointment and discouragement that anyone would feel in such a situation was compounded in his case by the complex mechanisms of his psyche. Frustrated of their usual external expression in achievement, his aggression and guilt turned inwards. His depression grew, and he began to exhibit all the symptoms of what we now know to be the clinical form. He became increasingly powerless before a terrible apathy and self-condemnation, staring listlessly on occasions at the town clock, he later related, without being consciously able even to register what time it was. Fearful about his own state he forced himself to make violent efforts, walking to Birmingham and back, for example, a distance of thirty-two miles. But the reaction back again into torpor afterwards was, as might be expected, only the more extreme.

These problems came upon Johnson with peculiar intensity because he had not yet learned the coping mechanisms he later developed. Yet such pressures were to continue to plague him in one form or another for his whole life, and he suffered something approximating to a nervous breakdown again in his early sixties. His rigorous religious dedication was unfortunately to make these problems worse in some respects. He had been brought up in the firm disciplines of traditional Anglicanism, which in their own way were quite as demanding as Puritanism. With fierce independence he had rejected it all at an unusually early age. At Oxford, however, he had been deeply impressed by the remarkable spiritual writer William Law's most rigorist book, *A Serious Call to a Devout and Holy Life* (1728), a work that was also to make a great impact on the Wesley brothers, the founders of Methodism. It was some years before his convictions took their final settled form, but 'Religion,' as Boswell said, was certainly to become 'the predominant object of [Johnson's] thoughts'. His Christianity, naturally enough, entangled itself in his own psychological patterns. He came to focus with obsessive attention on the unremitting demands of charity and virtue, the strenuous duties and regulations of the Christian life. He suffered greatly from what he called by the traditional name of 'scruples': exaggerated ideas of imperfection and of his own sinfulness, an over-elaborate sense of spiritual responsibility, and fears of being condemned. Clearly such impulses, which were to grow stronger as his religious commitment deepened, greatly exacerbated his self-disgust at his own, in fact largely involuntary, apathy and lassitude.

Yet Johnson's religion also widened his perspective, gave his sufferings meaning and taught him to hope. If his mighty efforts made his problems worse in some ways by creating a greater degree of unconscious resistance, they are also, of course, a sign of heroic optimism. The amazing thing is that Johnson never gave up. It is both humorous and awe-inspiring, for example, to read his determinations against sloth in his *Prayers and Meditations*, his constantly renewed resolutions year after year until he is an old man. A full fifty years after this first great crisis, for example, we read:

> Good Friday, 1775: When I look back upon resolutions of improvement and amendments, which have year after year been made and broken ... why do I yet try to resolve again? I try because Reformation is necessary and despair is criminal .... As my life has from my earliest years been wasted in a morning bed my purpose is from Easter day to rise early, not later than eight.

Equally characteristic is the way that Johnson composed in Latin for a local doctor as full and objective an account of his own first major depression as he could. He was horrified when the doctor, impressed with its clarity, showed it to others, but, as Bate points out,

13

the struggle to rise above what threatened to overwhelm him by trying to isolate and describe it, hold it at arm's length, – to pluck its teeth, so to speak, by seeing it intellectually for what it was, and at the same time to avoid self-absorption and subjective rationalization – is, in a sense, the real story of Johnson's personal achievement.

(*The Achievement of Samuel Johnson*, 1955, rpt 1961, p. 11)

The student of Johnson soon comes to understand that, as this incident illustrates, the roots of these severe neuroses were tangled up in very complicated ways with his profound sanity and wisdom. Boswell captures Johnson's whole predicament in a magnificent image that portrays him not only as a great sufferer but also as a great epic hero of moral struggle and the life of the mind:

His mind resembled the vast amphitheatre, the Colisaeum at Rome. In this centre stood his judgement, which like a mighty gladiator, combated those apprehensions that, like the wild beasts of the *Arena*, were all around in cells, ready to be let out upon him. After a conflict, he drives them back into their dens; but not killing them, they were still assailing him.

(Hill and Powell (eds), 1934–64, II, 106)

At least a brief respite from the inactivity of the first major crisis came with Johnson's employment for several months as a teacher at the grammar school in Market Bosworth, Leicestershire. But despite his intellectual brilliance and commanding personality Johnson's eccentricities were hardly conducive to success in such a role and there were also problems with a domineering patron of the school. The situation grew intolerable, and one of his old friends, Edmund Hector, more and more worried about Johnson, now invited him for an extended stay in Birmingham.

Hector lived in the house of Thomas Warren, a printer and bookseller, who published the *Birmingham Journal*, and it may have been in his mind from the start to encourage his friend to write for it. This at any rate is what happened, and Hector and Warren also suggested that Johnson work on a task that he had himself mentioned before as being of interest, a translation from the French of a book by a Portuguese Jesuit, Lobo's *Voyage to Abyssinia*. Though he was fairly dilatory Johnson did succeed in completing the task, for which he received six guineas, and it is fascinating to see how early he has formed not only his distinctive style but also, as his preface shows, much of his view of life and literature. In this book, he says approvingly, unlike most travel books, the reader will find 'no romantic absurdities or incredible fictions'. Father Lobo's 'modest and unaffected narration' of different regions and nations will show instead 'what will always be discovered by a diligent and impartial inquirer, that wherever human nature is to be found, there is a mixture of vice and virtue, a contest of passion and reason'.

It was through Hector too that Johnson met the forty-six-year-old widow, Elizabeth Porter, whom he married in July 1735 when he himself was twenty-six. Of this marriage, with its potential for comedy and sentiment, it has been difficult for most commentators to speak soberly. Johnson's erstwhile pupil, the great Shakespearian actor David Garrick, described 'Tetty' as 'very fat, with a bosom of more than ordinary protuberance, with swelled cheeks of a florid red, produced by thick painting, and increased by the liberal use of cordials; flaring and fantastic in her dress, and affected both in her speech and her general behaviour'. He was to dine out later in London on his imitations of the incongruous pair's love-making. As she grew older Tetty undoubtedly became a trial to Johnson. She was virtually bed-ridden and perhaps addicted to opium, a common medicine in the period. She was also an enormous responsibility financially as her own money ran out. Yet Johnson mourned her very deeply after her death and was very grateful for the way she had accepted him despite the unprepossessing appearance he at first made. Lucy Porter, her daughter by the previous marriage, told Boswell

> he was then lean and lank, so that his immense structure of bones was hideously striking to the eye, and the scars of the scrofula were deeply visible. He also wore his hair [as distinct from a wig], which was straight and stiff, and separated behind; and he often had, seemingly, convulsive starts and odd gesticulations, which tended to excite at once surprise and ridicule.
>
> (I, 94)

Yet Tetty was prepared to overlook all this for the sake of Johnson's conversation, and she made the wonderful comment that 'This is the most sensible man that I ever saw in my life.'

With the sum of money his wife brought him Johnson founded a small school near Lichfield. Predictably it attracted few pupils and was not a success. By the following year Tetty's money was all spent, and Johnson decided that his only hope now was to leave her behind temporarily in Lichfield while he travelled to London with David Garrick in the hope of finding employment.

'Inspired hackwork': London and the new career

It is almost impossible for us to imagine now the great impact that London would have made on a man from the provinces possessed of so much appetite for life and intellectual curiosity as Johnson. Ever afterwards he was to be associated with the greatest enthusiasm for the capital. With six hundred and fifty to seven hundred thousand inhabitants London was two to three hundred times larger than Lichfield, and growing at such a rate that it would reach almost a million by the end of the century. Its nucleus was still the City of London itself, but it was rapidly spreading westwards in great developments of distinguished upper-class houses and squares and eastwards with industrial workshops and small working-class dwellings. It thus included enormous extremes of wealth and taste. Aristocratic families now spent more time in the capital and there was a virtually new class of highly prosperous financiers, bankers and the highest merchants. But, as J.H. Plumb has very well said in his classic study *England in the Eighteenth Century*, the eighteenth century was 'rough, coarse, brutal; a world for the muscular and the aggressive and the cunning. The thin veneer of elegance and classic form obscured but never hid either the crime and dissipation or the drab middle-class virtue and thrift. For the majority of England, life was hard and vile' (1959, p. 33). Aristocratic high-life, glittering sophistication and wealth coexisted in London with terrible poverty and what would seem to us completely unacceptable standards of hygiene. The streets were as yet largely unpaved, and there was a terrible stench from open sewers. At the lowest levels of all lay the life made familiar in the novels of Defoe and Smollett and in the works of Hogarth: the city of thieves, prostitutes and beggars; the terrible infant mortality in the slums and the gin-shops with their signs of 'drunk for a penny, dead-drunk for twopence'.

Johnson's Christian compassion, political instincts and psychological identification with the underdog meant that he had a great concern for social justice. He 'loved the poor', said Mrs Thrale, 'as I never yet saw any other man do, with an earnest desire to make them happy'. There are touching stories of his putting money in the hands of the beggar children who slept on the ashpits to keep warm. His own poem *London* includes vivid pictures of the dirt, dangers, corruptions, poverty and injustices of the city:

> Here malice, rapine, accident, conspire,
> And now a rabble rages, now a fire;
> Their ambush here relentless ruffians lay,
> And here the fell attorney prowls for prey;
> Here falling houses thunder on your head . . .

(ll. 13–17)

William Hogarth, Gin Lane

His many recorded comments in conversation, however, focus not on the poverty and dangers of London but on its great intellectual and cultural resources. 'The happiness of London', he announces, 'is not to be conceived but by those who have been in it. I will venture to say, there is more learning and science within the circumference of ten miles from where we now sit, than in all the rest of the kingdom' (*Life*, II, 75). For London was not only the centre of the government and the financial world, but also the focus of the arts, the sciences and fashion. In particular, it was at the heart of the great growth in middle-class culture that is one of the most marked features of eighteenth-century England. The development of trade and finance had created a new commercial prosperity, a consumer boom, increased leisure and a hunger for entertainment and self-improvement. London as a consequence was the centre of a new kind of literary industry. This period marks the real beginnings of the British press, and magazines and journals of all kinds proliferated. The sales of all kinds of literature increased, and some writers were finding it possible to earn a living. The great writers of a more conservative perspective such as Pope and Swift castigated the new literary profession under the pejorative name of 'Grub Street' (after the actual place where some of the new hack writers lived earlier in the century). Johnson's own reaction was a much more enthusiastic one, as we shall see, not least, of course, because the new industry was to prove his own lifeline.

'He that is tired of London', said Johnson, in a famous comment (now known to have been given its final form by Boswell), 'is tired of life, for there is in London all that life can afford.' Clearly it was the 'wonderful extent and variety' of London that most fascinated Johnson, as he said, adding that 'men of curious enquiry might see in it such modes of life as very few could ever imagine' (*Life*, III, 78; IV, 201). He was himself just such a man, and his long and wide-ranging career perhaps entitled him to speak on the subject more than anyone else who has ever lived in the capital. As his fame grew he was to dine with noblemen, converse with the King and belong to a club of the greatest politicians, writers, artists and intellectuals of the day. Yet, as Mrs Thrale said, his 'knowledge and esteem for what we call low or coarse life was indeed prodigious' as well. He was never to forget the poverty of his early years and his own time in Grub Street and he later shared his house, as we shall see, with several people who would vividly continue to remind him of all the lower extremities of London.

Johnson brought with him to the capital three acts of a blank verse tragedy called *Irene* which he had hopes for, but it was the new journalism rather than the more traditional literary modes that was to enable him to make what was at first a very precarious living. He applied himself soon after his arrival to the redoubtable Edward Cave, the proprietor of one of the most successful of the new journals, the *Gentleman's Magazine*, which was the first magazine in the modern sense of a digest of articles on various subjects from various sources. For the next few years he earned enough to live on by writing anonymous reviews, essays and brief biographies for Cave.

The process of identifying Johnson's work in the *Gentleman's Magazine* is still a matter that exercises bibliographers, since a large number of pieces can be attributed to him with some confidence and there are many others that he might well have written. What Walter Jackson Bate calls 'inspired hackwork' of this kind was to be part of Johnson's career for many years to come and even this early work is 'almost unparalleled in range and variety': 'There are lives of men eminent in literature, science and naval warfare; essays, prefaces and reviews that reveal knowledge of agriculture, trade, medicine, chemistry, classical scholarship, metaphysics, politics and even Chinese architecture' (*Achievement*, p. 14).

One of the most remarkable feats of the early career was Johnson's 'reporting' of the debates in the House of Commons. It was in fact illegal to report those debates at this time, so the magazine evaded the prohibition by employing Johnson, who only attended the gallery in the House in person once, to write up the speeches from abridged accounts as thinly veiled fictional debates in the senate of Swift's imaginary land Lilliputia. Many years later Johnson's versions were still regarded as genuine and some of the oratory attributed to famous politicians was so eloquent that it was reprinted in collected volumes of their speeches.

Early in his career of writing for Cave, Johnson also published perhaps the first of the handful of his greatest works and his first major poem, *London*, briefly quoted from above. This was an imitation of the Roman satirist Juvenal, best known for bitter realism and savage, eloquent denunciation. The point of this mode of imitation, of which Pope's *Imitations of Horace* are the greatest example, is the finding of apt parallels between the classical text and the modern world. Despite his own fondness for London, Johnson adopts the traditional convention of the moral superiority of rural life to condemn the corruptions of the metropolis, paralleling the vogue for Italian opera, for example, which conservative thinkers found decadent, with the gladiatorial games:

> With warbling eunuchs fill a licens'd stage,
> And lull to servitude a thoughtless age.   (ll. 59–60)

The evils of London are themselves in turn associated with the long rule of the Prime Minister, Sir Robert Walpole, accused of corruption by the opposition because of his manipulation of the patronage system:

> Here let those reign, whom pensions can incite
> To vote a patriot black, a courtier white;
> Explain their country's dear-bought rights away,
> And plead for pirates in the face of day;
> With slavish tenets taint our poison'd youth,
> And lend a lie the confidence of truth.   (ll. 51–6)

The poem is thus very much in the vein of Pope politically as well as stylistically, though with a characteristic Johnsonian combination of moral generalization and weightiness to it in places ('And lend a lie the confidence of truth'). Pope himself praised it highly, and it was very popular with the reading public at large.

For all the brilliance of Johnson's work throughout this period, however, he was certainly not an overnight success. The very opposite was in fact the case. These are, in Bate's words, 'years of trial and obscurity'. Though some of the more picturesque stories of his poverty at this time can perhaps be discounted it was to be fifteen years or so before Johnson was to gain much financial security and even in his fifties he was once arrested for debt. It was not until 1749 that he was to publish his first work with his own name on the title page and not until the *Rambler* essays and the publication of the *Dictionary* that he was to achieve fame.

It was during this period of obscurity that Johnson met the fiery and extravagant minor celebrity Richard Savage, a poet who claimed to be the rejected illegitimate son of the Countess of Macclesfield. One of the most colourful scenes in the whole Johnsonian story is the picture of the two friends wandering the streets of London all night talking because they had nowhere else to go, though it now seems that it was the fascination of Savage's company rather than complete destitution that kept Johnson from his bed. After his friend's death Johnson was to write another of his earliest masterpieces, the *Life of Savage* (1744). This makes vivid reading in its own right: the story of a man of the highest ambition, some talent and considerable sense of self-worth and moral rectitude who nevertheless worked as a Grub Street hack, became the accused in a murder trial and:

lodged as much by accident as he dined and passed the night, sometimes in mean houses, which are set open at night to any casual wanderers, sometimes in cellars, among the riot and filth of the meanest and most profligate of the rabble; and sometimes, when he had no money to support even the expenses of these receptacles, walked about the streets till he was weary, and lay down in the summer upon a bulk ['A part of a building jutting out', Johnson, *Dictionary*], or in the winter with his associates in poverty, among the ashes of a glass-house.

'The biographical part of literature is what I love best,' Johnson once said, and the *Life of Savage* is also a work of the highest importance in the history of biography. Johnson's early lives for the *Gentleman's Magazine*, the life of the great Dutch physician Boerhaave, for example, are very dependent on other immediate sources and written in terms of the tradition established since Plutarch that presents biography as a moral exemplar for the reader. The *Life of Savage* is a new departure for Johnson as the story of a man who was his intimate acquaintance for a year, but that very circumstance has also encouraged him towards a new conception of the genre. His own strenuous regard for truth has led him to the view that the facts must not on any account be suppressed even if they are unpalatable. It is in the small details of life anyway that moral character is expressed, and we are only likely to be able to sympathize with and learn from the examples of those whose virtues and vices are not set on a plane too far above or below us.

As Donald Stauffer, the author of the most comprehensive account of eighteenth-century biography, says, what Johnson thus achieves is a reconciliation between the exemplary moral tradition of biography and the growing interest in individual psychology and the documentation of particular detail. It is not that he ever comes to a modern 'scientific' conception in which facts are collected *for their own sake*. But he shows moral lessons arising from the particular details of life and personality – and in no trite and predictable fashion. Savage is a warning to the reader – a man destroyed as much by his own follies as by unfortunate circumstances. Yet the cautionary tale is deepened and complicated by Johnson's sympathy and even identification with his subject's anti-authoritarianism and sense of injustice. He refuses those 'who have slumbered away their time on the down of plenty' the luxury of looking down on Savage, and comments 'nor will a wise man easily presume to say, "Had

I been in Savage's condition, I should have lived, or written, better than Savage".'

'Dictionary Johnson' and the decade of great moral writing

Interest in parliamentary debates declined after Walpole's resignation in 1742, and there are signs of a change in Johnson's career from this time on. Though he continued to write for Cave for a few more years he also embarked on a wider variety of projects, with the hope perhaps not only of making more money but also of using his scholarly gifts in a less ephemeral way. He had already started, for example, on a project of cataloguing and printing a selection from the great Harleian library of the Earl of Oxford, which contained many important manuscripts of early English literature. He also published *Miscellaneous Observations on the Tragedy of Macbeth* and made proposals for and even started work upon an edition of Shakespeare, though the project was not to materialize for another twenty years.

The most significant project both from the point of view of Johnson's own career and also from the widest intellectual and cultural perspective was, of course, the great *Dictionary of the English Language*. In 1746, now aged thirty-seven, he signed the contract with a group of London booksellers and, recognizing the importance of what was being undertaken, they paid him one thousand five hundred guineas in fee. The work took nine years rather than the three he had estimated, and much of the money went on paying the scribes he used as assistants. Yet, as Paul Fussell says, 'the earnings from the *Dictionary* were the first substantial return literature had given him' (*Samuel Johnson and the Life of Writing*, 1972, p. 24), and they meant a certain degree of security. If he did not actually have much money left on the completion of his task, his reputation and confidence were such from now on that he at least knew that he could always make a living as a writer.

If Johnson's is by no means as is sometimes thought the *first* English dictionary, it is certainly, as will be explained more fully later, the first to serve as in any sense a *standard*. Most earlier dictionaries had been mere lists of difficult words, though there were several previous eighteenth-century dictionaries that aimed at greater comprehensiveness and proper definitions. But Johnson far outdoes all his predecessors in the logical power of his definitions, in his sense of the different shades of meaning and in the way that he illustrates proper usage by a range of authoritative examples from the great English writers of the past.

These principles are illustrated by his manner of proceeding on his great task, which is more clearly understood by modern scholarship, though the immense labour involved seems almost inconceivable to us today. In the first stage he read through all the established writers he could lay his hands on to find words and suitable quotations to illustrate them. His assistants afterwards copied these out on to slips of paper and filed them alphabetically under the key-words. At a later stage Johnson arranged all the material and began to draft his definitions and etymologies. Consideration of the quotations on the slips often necessitated further sub-entries at this stage of the work. Finally the illustrative quotations were pasted in chronological order beneath the definitions on large sheets of paper and sent to the press.

The complete work contains definitions of over forty thousand words, illustrated by about a hundred and fourteen thousand quotations from the best writers of the preceding two hundred years. It is the tiny handful of humorous, whimsical or mischievous definitions, of course, that have stayed in peoples' minds: '*Oats*: a grain, which in England is commonly given to horses, but in Scotland supports the people'; '*Lexicographer*: a writer of dictionaries, a harmless drudge'. Naturally these add to the liveliness of the work and contribute to a certain characteristically Johnsonian sense of irony that hovers around the project. But they constitute only the minutest proportion of the total number of definitions, and must not be allowed to detract from the seriousness of Johnson's undertaking overall. As W.J. Bate says, not only is this the first English dictionary to do the task for which it was needed, but all later English dictionaries of any importance develop out of Johnson's work.

'I now begin to see Land, after having wandered . . . in the vast sea of words,' Johnson told a friend in the year of the publication of the *Dictionary* (1755). At the same time as working his way through all the complications of his great task Johnson had also succeeded in negotiating the enormous difficulties of establishing himself as a professional writer. His first work under his own name was *The Vanity of Human Wishes* in 1749. With the *Rambler* essays, which appeared between 1750 and 1752, he began to achieve a degree of fame, despite the fact that their circulation was at first small.

For all his conservatism in many respects, Johnson, as Alvin Kernan shows in *Printing, Technology, Letters & Samuel Johnson* (1987), is actually a new kind of writer altogether, the culture hero of an age of print with greatly expanded outlets of publication and a new literary marketplace. He said himself, with pardonable exaggeration, that 'No man but a blockhead ever wrote except for money!' and he always sprang to the defence of the booksellers as a new kind of patron. His magnificent letter to Lord Chesterfield (7 February 1755) is often taken to mark the symbolic end of the old system of court and aristocratic patronage. Chesterfield's response to Johnson's requests for assistance had proved inadequate, but he had finally written an article in praise of the *Dictionary* just before its publication. Johnson counters this by writing:

> Seven years, my lord, have now past since I waited in your outwards rooms or was repulsed from your door, during which time I have been pushing on my work through difficulties of which it is useless to complain, and have brought it at last to the verge of publication without one act of assistance, one word of encouragement, or one smile of favour. Such treatment I did not expect, for I never had a patron before . . . .
>
> Is not a patron, my Lord, one who looks with unconcern on a man struggling for life in the water, and, when he has reached ground, encumbers him with help? The notice which you have been pleased to take of my labours, had it been early, had been kind; but it has been delayed till I am indifferent and cannot enjoy it, till I am solitary and cannot impart it, till I am known and do not want it.
>
> I hope it is no very cynical asperity not to confess obligations where no benefit has been received, or to be unwilling that the public should consider me as owing that to a patron, which Providence has enabled me to do for myself.
>
> Having carried on my work thus far with so little obligation to any favourer of learning, I shall not be disappointed though I should conclude it, if less be possible, with less, for I have been long wakened from that dream of hope in which I once boasted myself with so much exultation, my lord,
>
> Your Lordship's most humble, most obedient servant,
>
> S. J.

This letter and, even more memorably, the end of the 'Preface' to the *Dictionary* tell the inner truth of Johnson's situation at this time. His wife Tetty had died in 1752. His *Prayers and Meditations* refer to her thereafter with poignant regularity. Despite all the problems of their relationship his bereavement left Johnson feeling without an anchor in the world and from now on he was perpetually lonely and constantly compelled to try to persuade people to sit up with him until the early hours of the morning. In 1746 he had begun to rent the house in Gough Square that is now open to the public, and the combination of his increasing loneliness and his compassionate nature led him gradually to fill it up with an ill-assorted variety of people who had nowhere else to go, including the blind poet Anna Williams, Robert Levet, an unqualified physician who worked among the poor, and 'Poor Poll', a reformed prostitute he had rescued.

Clearly Tetty is also in his mind as he finishes the 'Preface' to the *Dictionary*. After apologising for all the avoidable and inevitable defects of the work he says that he may

> surely be contented without the praise of perfection, which, if I could obtain, in this gloom of solitude, what would it avail me? I have protracted my work till most of those whom I wished to please have sunk into the grave, and success and miscarriage are empty sounds: I therefore dismiss it with frigid tranquillity, having little to fear or hope from censure or from praise.

Johnson is obviously assimilating his loneliness and his whole personal predicament to traditional moral themes here. In so doing he generalizes his sufferings, makes them more eloquently moving and seeks to find a meaning in them. The futility of the very attempt to fix something as inherently changeable as human language at all merges with the sad irony of his wife's death before she could begin to enjoy his new-found fame with him to make his undeniably great achievement in the *Dictionary* only another example of the 'Vanity of Human Wishes'.

These are the same themes that dominate the whole decade of Johnson's finest moral writing – a decade that overlaps in part with the work on the *Dictionary*. It is inaugurated with his best known poem, *The Vanity of Human Wishes* itself, published in 1749, six years before the *Dictionary* appeared. Despite its brevity this is a work of amazing comprehensiveness, and it would be sufficient in itself, according to T.S. Eliot, to establish Johnson's greatness as a poet. Like *London* it is an imitation of the classical satirist Juvenal. The main body of the poem consists of a description of the various desires and aspirations that human beings have avidly pursued: wealth, political and military power, academic reputation, length of life and beauty. With eloquence, deep sombreness and distinctive compassion Johnson demonstrates that none seems to bring satisfaction. 'Wav'ring man',

> . . . betray'd by vent'rous pride

> To tread the dreary paths without a guide,
> As treach'rous phantoms in the mist delude,
> Shuns fancied ills, or chases airy good.   (ll. 7–10)

Fate makes sure meanwhile that 'Each gift of nature, and each grace of art' is accompanied by its own inevitable punishment. Johnson ends by altering Juvenal's own rather cynical conclusion to indicate that we should seek instead the lasting good of God and eternity, the only aspiration that will not ultimately disappoint us.

It is here, everyone agrees, far more than in *London*, that Johnson finds his true voice as a poet. Yet his great distinction comes, paradoxically, from the very strenuousness with which he strives to iron out all that is merely personal or 'original'. Through imitating Juvenal and assimilating the Roman poet to the 'vanity of vanities all is vanity saith the preacher' of the Old Testament Book of Ecclesiastes, Johnson is subsuming his own private feelings in a far-reaching and ancient tradition of how blind and self-deceiving human beings are. Even in the great passage on the scholar's life, which in many ways approximates to Johnson's own experience and which he was unable to read in public without tears, the phrasing is as generalizing and impersonal as possible, so that it reads, as we shall see later, almost like allegory. Yet, at the same time, Johnson's generalizations never lose touch with experience, and he is not afraid of concrete detail where necessary. At the end of the beautifully generalized meditation on the evils of old age, for example, he startles the reader by the terrifying vividness of his reference to the senility of a famous general and a great writer:

> From Marlb'rough's eyes the streams of dotage flow
> And Swift expires a driv'ler and a show.   (ll. 317–18)

The Vanity of Human Wishes was followed by three series of periodical essays, the *Rambler*, the *Idler* and the *Adventurer*. This form – a series of reflections that initially appears once or twice a week – is unfamiliar today and often indigestible in bulk compared to the original circumstances of publication. Even in the *Rambler* the range of subjects Johnson covers is quite wide, however. There are short fictional narratives, for example, and fictionalized biographies of representative types such as 'Squire Bluster', who destroys his own life and the peace of the whole neighbourhood by his bad temper and legal disputes (142), or 'Suspirius' the 'human screech-owl', an alarmist who always expects the worst (59). There is literary criticism of considerable significance, such as Johnson's response to the relatively new form of the novel (4), his comments on biography (60), which are especially interesting in the context of his own practice, and several essays on Milton. There is also an especially moving and impressive group in which Johnson concentrates on the social ills of the day (a mode he was to develop more fully in the *Idler*). The eighteenth century was a great age of philanthropy and social concern. There were movements for the improvement of prisons, for the abolition of imprisonment for debt, for the foundation of orphanages and homes for reformed prostitutes and eventually for the abolition of the slave trade. Johnson himself played a very active role in person and through his writings. *Rambler* 114 is an argument against the use of capital punishment (extensive in the period) for crimes against property, and the portrait of 'Misella' the prostitute, for example (171, 172), is really a powerfully compassionate plea for rehabilitation.

As we might expect the largest number of essays are those that concern specific moral topics such as affectation, inconstancy, self-delusion and so on. The modern reader, of course, is not likely to approach the essays of one termed 'the great moralist' with any great enthusiasm. Even if the medicine does us good we expect it to taste unpleasant. But in reading Johnson, it has been aptly said, we read about ourselves. In compassionately pointing out our self-protecting attempts to deceive ourselves and others, he offers something much more helpful and hopeful than pep talks or condemnation. He always manages to differentiate himself from the traditional moralists of the past by his realism, honesty and truth to experience: 'For what is the advice that is commonly given? A few general maxims, enforced with vehemence, and inculcated with importunity, but failing for want of particular reference and immediate application' (*Rambler* 87). Johnson, on the contrary, is determined to bring morality down to earth. He has a strong anti-heroic sense (also apparent in his attitude to biography) that we must find our happiness and express our moral characters not in great events but in our daily affairs and domestic lives. He is strikingly practical at times. *Rambler* 108, for example, points out on the lines of a modern time-management book that we could achieve an enormous amount in the little gaps of time that every day holds:

> It is usual for those who are advised to the attainment of any new qualification, to look upon themselves as required to change the general course of their conduct, to dismiss

business, and exclude pleasure, and to devote their days and nights to a particular attention. But all common degrees of excellence are attainable at a lower price; he that should steadily and resolutely assign to any science or language those interstitial vacancies which intervene in the most crowded variety of diversion or employment, would find every day new irradiations of knowledge, and discover how much more is to be hoped from frequency and perseverance, than from violent efforts and sudden desires.

The nuggets of practical wisdom are always contained, however, within a much wider and more humane perspective, and in this respect the remarkable prose style cannot really be separated from the content. The long words (less frequent on closer examination than commonly supposed) and sonorous rhythms create a sense of dignity and eloquence but are also the vehicles of precise moral definition. Through the balanced syntax Johnson weighs one option against another, creating, in the end, a magisterial sense of authority. This is someone, we come to feel, who is approaching the modern world with the accumulated wisdom of the past, but is also taking nothing for granted. He has faced the truth about human life with realism and seriousness, yet he can still encourage us to act and to hope.

After the *Rambler* came the somewhat lighter and more accessible *Idler* and *Adventurer* essays, and these in turn were followed by what has remained Johnson's most popular work, the prose fiction *Rasselas* (1759). For a long time this was thought to have been written to defray the expenses of his mother's funeral, but it now seems that it was intended instead to pay for a trip down to Lichfield to visit her in her last illness (though she died before Johnson actually took the trip). The book tells the story of a young prince and his sister and friends who escape from a 'happy valley' where all their desires are satisfied but which they find boring. With all the world before them they embark on 'the choice of life', the search for the way of life that will bring them happiness.

The book is perhaps better regarded as a fictionalized moral parable, a longer version of the moral stories in the periodical essays, than as a novel in the full sense. Its moral wisdom, its sobering and yet encouraging effect led Boswell to say that he was not satisfied unless he re-read it at least once every year. What Boswell does not comment on, however, is the book's wit and compassion and the way it *involves* us in the experience and the characters' search, one trait at least that it does share with novels. The central protagonists are young, virtuous and wealthy. Their quest for happiness creates suspense, for it is in all our interests that they should succeed, and if they cannot then who can? Needless to say the book reaches the conclusion that there is no life of definitive happiness on earth, but it completes and crowns all Johnson's moral writings of the decade in the way that it combines piety and realism, compassion and humour, pessimism and hope. They are at least happier, it seems, in their search than they would have been if they had stayed in the happy valley. While affirming that the choice of eternity is the most important thing, Johnson still permits his characters to keep some of their earthly hopes as well. He recognizes that such hopes are inveterate anyway and impossible to quash completely and understands that they help to keep us active and striving.

All through this great period of Johnson's most productive and distinctive moral writing he was also producing prefaces and dedications for the works of his friends or those he regarded as worthy causes, as well as a large number of reviews. The profound and humane moral concern revealed in the great works touches almost everything Johnson writes, even the most occasional of pieces. One of the reviews for the *Literary Magazine*, his response to Soame Jenyns's superficial book *A Free Inquiry into the Nature and Origin of Evil*, has itself justly become a classic. But the range of subjects Johnson is prepared to speak on is also remarkable. There are prefaces to a *Dictionary of Trade and Commerce* and to a book of draughts, for example, and Johnson even went to the trouble of studying the subject of maritime navigation in order to help a destitute and aged Welsh physician, Zachariah Williams, with a preface to his book on determining longitude at sea.

The 'Great Cham of Literature'; Boswell and the Thrales

From the time of the *Rambler* essays people had begun to seek Johnson out. The young Bennet Langton, for example, later to be a close friend, came to London especially to call upon the 'decorous philosopher,' but was very surprised to see coming down

> from his bed-chamber, about noon . . . as newly risen, a huge uncouth figure, with a little dark wig which scarcely covered his head, and his clothes hanging loose about him. But his conversation was so rich, so animated, and so forcible . . . [that Langton] conceived for him that veneration and attachment which he ever preserved.
>
> (*Life*, I, 247)

The famous, apparently secure and authoritative Johnson of later years, the Johnson of Boswell and 'The Literary Club', the 'great Cham of literature', was almost imperceptibly developing out of the earlier Johnson whose image has been virtually obliterated from the popular mind: the wilder, impoverished hack writer of the 'years of trial and obscurity'. The *Dictionary* confirmed the process, and led to an honorary MA from Johnson's old university, Oxford. Later this was to be followed by two honorary doctorates. In 1762 Johnson's growing fame was crowned, rather startlingly, by the award of a government pension. He had, after all, in many ways been an opposition or at least anti-authoritarian figure. But the pension was, of course, for literary rather than political services rendered, and it was made clear that it had no strings attached to it. Johnson was to write later in the early 1770s four much criticized pamphlets in general support of government positions, but this was partly to help his friend Henry Thrale's political aspirations and partly because he had himself become convinced that the growing cry for liberty was by then an even greater danger than oppression.

In the same year as the award of the pension, when Johnson was fifty-three, he had his first, momentous meeting with James Boswell, who was then only twenty-two. Boswell, the mercurial, ambitious, rampantly promiscuous son of a Scottish laird, was to take Johnson on as a kind of father figure and moral mentor and to write the most detailed and greatest of the many memoirs and biographies of him. When Boswell, like so many ambitious Scotsmen after the Act of Union (1707), came to London, he had the intention in mind of meeting Johnson. Aware of the latter's well-known prejudices against the Scots he had nervously warned his host, the bookseller Tom Davies, not to mention his origins. Davies ignored him and told Johnson that Boswell was a Scotsman. In a panic the young man cried out, 'Sir, I do come from Scotland, but I cannot help it,' which led to the crushing reply, 'That, Sir, is what I find many of your countrymen cannot help.' But the friendship flourished all the same, and Boswell soon conceived the plan of writing his great *Life* and recording as much of Johnson's conversation as he could.

It has been customary in recent years for Johnson scholars to emphasize the ways in which Boswell's portrait is a partial one, and this is quite right. Boswell knew Johnson only in the last twenty-one years of the latter's life, as we have said. He has his own axes to grind too; but the fact remains that he displays enormous industry, devotion and talent himself and that he has managed to write what is perhaps the greatest biography in any

Boswell at twenty-five, by George Willison

language. Though he has permanently set a magnificent image of Johnson in the popular literary mind, there is no question, as will already have become apparent, of his *creating* Johnson. What he has actually done is to grasp a kind of Platonic essence of Johnson as a moral and cultural hero, and to mould the facts in that direction, omitting, sometimes deliberately and sometimes because he could not possibly have known them, other facts that could have been of equal significance in other hands. But *all* biography, of course, no matter how purportedly scientific, like all history, is bound to be selective in some such way, and Boswell's interpretation of Johnson is a cogent and coherent one that accords in essence with the facts, and he is surely a keen enough recorder of such facts in themselves to suit the most stringent of standards.

For all its other great merits, it is as a record of Johnson's conversation that the book has always been most popular. The remarkable discovery this century of Boswell's own voluminous papers and journals at Malahide Castle in Scotland has not only

31

served to demonstrate his own great gifts as a writer but has also shown the procedure he adopted of recording Johnson's conversation by writing it up every night while it was still fresh in his mind. Absolute verbatim accuracy can hardly be claimed in such circumstances, of course, and there are rare occasions when we can see Boswell trying to make Johnson more like 'Johnson' than he in fact was. One of the most amusing entries is when Boswell describes Johnson explaining to Garrick during the rehearsals for *Irene* that he would have to stop coming to see him behind the scenes because he found that 'the white breasts and silk stockings of his actresses excited his amorous propensities'. Here, it seems, is classic Johnson, highly sexed but scrupulously moral; decorously Latinate in phrasing. But Johnson in fact, despite his reputation of having swallowed his own dictionary and being full of 'hard words,' was never afraid of calling a spade a spade. What he actually said, it transpires, was that 'the white bubbies and silk stockings of your actresses excite my genitals'!

Yet there can be no doubt that Boswell's is a brilliantly authentic record of Johnson's conversation overall. As with the dictionary definitions, what the reader is most likely to remember are the famous expressions of rudeness and prejudice: the comment, for example, on hearing the noble scenery of Scotland praised, 'Sir, take it from me, the noblest prospect a Scotsman ever sees is the highroad to England'; or the remark after going to hear a sermon by a Quaker woman, 'A woman's preaching is like a dog standing on its hind legs. It is not done well, but we are surprised to find it done at all.' Johnson, clearly, is often talking for effect, or, as he put it, 'talking for victory', and there is a side to him that is deliberately contrary and contradictory. Yet, as Bate points out, even in the example of the woman preaching there is that remarkable power of imagery and analogy (in this case deliberately lowering) that is to be found in the prose. The majority of this conversation, furthermore, though often enlivened by wit, is on matters of the highest seriousness. On a typical day in Boswell's company soon after he first makes his acquaintance, for example, Johnson talks about the uselessness of benevolence based on instinct rather than principle; the arguments against Christian miracles put forward by the free-thinking Scots philosopher David Hume; the need to preserve a hierarchy of rank in society; and a critical book on the poetry of Alexander Pope. But he is at ease enough with his new friend to discuss his own personal tendency to melancholy as well and this is also the occasion on which he makes the marvellous comment about his preference for the company of young people: 'Sir, I love the young dogs of this age.'

On another representative occasion fourteen years later, with Johnson now aged sixty-nine, the conversation at a dinner party at the eminent lawyer William Scott's touches upon 'subordination of rank' again but also includes a discussion of fame, with especial relevance to David Garrick; the proper use of wealth; the great value of travel ('He talked with an uncommon animation of travelling into distant countries . . . . He expressed a particular enthusiasm with respect to visiting the wall of China . . .'); the merits of *Robinson Crusoe*; and Johnson's satisfaction at the part he had played in 1762 in exposing a well-known attempt to impose upon the public, the so-called 'Cock Lane Ghost', a fraudulent poltergeist.

On a fuller reading, then, it is the amazing range and copiousness of this conversation that impresses. There seems to be nothing that Johnson cannot grasp, nothing that he is not interested in and prepared to speak about. In the *Tour to the Hebrides* Boswell recounts how he explained one evening to the company 'the whole process of tanning, and . . . the nature of milk and the various operations upon it, as making whey, etc.'.

Even apart from Johnson himself Boswell's book has a remarkable cast of characters that includes almost all the other most famous men of the time. For Johnson numbered among his closest friends such men as Oliver Goldsmith, the author of *The Vicar of Wakefield* and famous plays and poems; the great painter Sir Joshua Reynolds; Edmund Burke, the politician and political writer; and, as we have seen, David Garrick, the best-known actor of the period. The famous 'Club', founded in 1764, came to include other luminaries such as Edward Gibbon the historian; Adam Smith the political economist; Charles James Fox the politician; R.B. Sheridan the dramatist; and Sir Joseph Banks the naturalist. It is doubtful, as Bate says, whether any similar group has ever 'had so distinguished a membership'. But it is acquaintance with Johnson, the mainstay of 'The Club', that brings them together and they clearly recognize his own considerable authority.

'The Club' is an exclusively male world. But Boswell also records Johnson's contacts with a variety of remarkable women, too numerous to do justice to here. For, despite his later reputation for sexism, Johnson was always keen to encourage women writers and prepared to recognize intellectual talent wherever it was to be found. In the years on the *Gentleman's Magazine*, for example, he met the formidable Elizabeth Carter, poet and self-taught translator of the classics. Later he made the acquaintance of other so-called 'Bluestockings' including the 'Queen of the Blues', the author and intellectual hostess Elizabeth Montagu. Of her (though their friendship was later to cool) he said, 'That lady exerts more mind than any person I ever met with; Sir, she displays such powers of ratiocination, such radiations of intellectual eminence as are amazing.'

Many others, including several of Johnson's women friends, felt compelled to record his conversation. But it is primarily Boswell's skill and diligence that have brought it about that, as Bate says, 'Forever, by millions of people, [Johnson] will be imagined as talking on any and every subject at taverns or at the Thrales'. What he said will be quoted time and again, from the richest collection of conversation in history; and books every year will be written, recalling the story of this period of his life' (*Samuel Johnson*, 1977, p. 500).

The brilliance and authority of this public Johnson is just as much a part of the total complex figure as the anxious obsessional inner man that is sometimes over-emphasized in modern studies. Yet there is no doubt that there was a darker side to Johnson's life in the early 1760s, despite the growing public acclaim – a side to some extent concealed both by and from Boswell. The financial security the pension brought made it harder for Johnson to force himself to write, and once again he fell deeply into what he saw as sloth and the consequent self-castigation and depression. This becomes the constant refrain in the 'Prayers and Meditations' of this time:

> My indolence, since my last reception of the Sacrament, has sunk into grosser sluggishness, and my dissipation spread into wilder negligence. My thoughts have been clouded with sensuality, and, except that from the beginning of this year I have in some measure forborn excess of Strong Drink, my appetites have predominated over my reason. A kind of strange oblivion has overspread me, so that I know not what has become of the last year, and perceive that incidents and intelligence pass over me without leaving any impression . . . .
> (21 April 1764)

His new proposals for a Shakespeare edition were welcomed in 1757, and he even took up subscriptions, but little work was actually done. He began to fear insanity intensely once more, and the danger of an actual breakdown became very real.

From this fate he was rescued by a new friendship that made the next twenty years much happier than they would otherwise have been. In the depth of his depression in 1764 he met Henry

Thrale, a wealthy brewer with cultural and political aspirations, and his vivacious, intellectual wife Hester. Within a short period the couple had, as it were, adopted Johnson, and he spent much of his time from now on in the apartment they set up for him in their large house at Streatham. He delighted in the comforts, good food and intellectual stimulation of this ready-made family (though it had problems of its own) and for most of the rest of his life it provided him with the emotional support he needed. He found in Hester Thrale above all the perfect confidante, and her own perceptive comments reveal that she knew him on a more intimate basis than Boswell did.

Slowly recovering health, Johnson was persuaded to complete his great Shakespeare edition (1765), with its noble preface and brilliant notes, which the distinguished scholar Edmund Malone was to say 'threw more light on Shakespeare than all its predecessors had done'. Johnson had once written, magnificently, that 'the only end of writing is to enable the readers better to enjoy life, or better to endure it' (*Review of a Free Inquiry*). What breathes forth from every page of this great edition is his sense of enjoyment of the vital characters Shakespeare creates and his admiration for the psychological and moral wisdom that he conveys:

> Other dramatists can only gain attention by hyperbolical or aggravated characters, by fabulous and unexampled excellence or depravity, as the writers of barbarous romances invigorated the reader by a giant and a dwarf; and he that should form his expectations of human affairs from the play or from the tale would be equally deceived. Shakespeare has no heroes; his scenes are occupied only by men, who act and speak as the reader thinks that he should himself have spoken or acted on the same occasion; even where the agency is supernatural, the dialogue is level with life . . . . This therefore is the praise of Shakespeare, that his drama is the mirror of life; that he who has mazed his imagination in following the phantoms which other writers raise up before him, may here be cured of his delirious ecstasies by reading human sentiments in human language, by scenes from which a hermit may estimate the transactions of the world, and a professor predict the progress of the passions.
>
> (*Yale Edition*, VII, 64–5)

Another aspect of Johnson's far-ranging intellectual achievement, his work on English law, has only been revealed in its full extent by twentieth-century scholarly investigation of this

35

period of his life. He had long been fascinated by the law, and Boswell had been in the habit of asking his opinion on knotty cases. But Johnson is also now understood to have made a much more systematic contribution in the 1760s when he helped his friend Robert Chambers, Vinerian Professor of Law at Oxford, who was suffering from a kind of writer's block, to prepare a major series of lectures he was contracted to give.

Johnson in the 1770s

The 1770s were a time of great political turbulence in Britain with the twin threats of the American struggle for independence and the controversies between the government and the charismatic and opportunistic radical John Wilkes, who was excluded from the House of Commons but re-elected several times by a volatile electorate. Johnson, in part encouraged by Henry Thrale, Member of Parliament for Southwark, wrote several pamphlets during this period in broad support of government positions, as has been mentioned, and it is the work of these years in particular that has contributed to his exaggerated reputation for conservatism. Ever since his initial acceptance of the pension, he had incurred continuous hostility in some quarters, and he felt himself to be an embattled figure in some respects. He was indignant about the American Revolution ('I can love all men *except* an American,' he said) and personally appalled by Wilkes, who had a reputation as a libertine as well as a radical. On one occasion Boswell wickedly engineered that they should sit together at a dinner party, and it is irresistible to quote at this point his account of what ensued:

> When we entered Mr. Dilly's drawing-room, he found himself in the midst of a company he did not know. I kept myself snug and silent, watching how he would conduct himself . . . .' And who is the gentleman in lace?' — 'Mr. Wilkes, Sir.' This information confounded him still more; he had some difficulty to restrain himself, and taking up a book, sat down upon a window-seat and read, or at least kept his eye upon it intently for some time, till he composed himself . . . . The cheering sound of 'Dinner is upon the table', dissolved his reverie, and we all sat down without any symptom of ill humour . . . . Mr. Wilkes placed himself next to Dr. Johnson, and behaved to him with so much attention and politeness, that he gained upon him insensibly. No man ate more heartily than Johnson, or loved better what was nice and delicate. Mr. Wilkes was very assiduous in helping him to some fine veal. 'Pray give me leave, Sir; — It is better here— A little of

the brown— Some fat, Sir— A little of the stuffing— Some gravy— Let me have the pleasure of giving you some butter— Allow me to recommend a squeeze of this orange;— or the lemon, perhaps, may have more zest.'— 'Sir, Sir, I am obliged to you, Sir,' cried Johnson, bowing, and turning his head to him with a look for some time of 'surly virtue', but, in a short while, of complacency.

(Life, III, 68–9)

Despite his involvement in political and literary controversies the new friendships and financial security Johnson enjoyed at this time made these years of 'Indian summer' for him on the whole. He could indulge his enthusiasm for travel, for example. All the inconveniences of travel (and we must remember eighteenth-century conditions as well as the fact that he was growing old) are as nothing, he once remarked, to the pleasure of it. He took trips with the Thrales to Wales and France, but his great courage, intellectual curiosity and zest come out most notably in his famous expedition to Scotland and the Hebrides with Boswell when he was sixty-three years old. For a man of this age suffering from bronchitis and rheumatism to embark on a three-month expedition of this kind was truly remarkable. It was to involve difficult trips on horseback through the wilder parts of the Highlands and dangerous voyages in small boats in the often stormy Hebrides. It is an adventure full of contrasts, the subject of marvellous anecdotes. In the accounts by Boswell and several others we see Johnson lost in prayer on the island of Iona where the Christian missionaries had prepared to convert Europe or lying peacefully in the boat during a terrible storm with a greyhound at his back to keep him warm. On another famous occasion, to the lasting astonishment of his hosts, he describes the recent discovery in Australia of the extraordinary animal called the *kangaroo* and to give an idea of what it was like,

> volunteered an imitation of the animal. The company stared
> . . . nothing could be more ludicrous than the appearance of
> a tall, heavy, grave-looking man, like Dr. Johnson, standing
> up to mimic the shape and motions of a kangaroo. He stood
> erect, put out his hands like feelers, and, gathering up the
> tails of his huge brown coat so as to resemble the pouch of the
> animal, made two or three vigorous bounds across the room!
> (Rev. Alexander Grant, *Tour to the Hebrides*, ed. F.A. Pottle
> and C.H. Bennet, 1936, footnote p. 98)

Boswell's published account, *A Journal of a Tour to the Hebrides*, is a highly entertaining travel book. Johnson's *A Journey to the*

Western Islands of Scotland is a much less immediately attractive work – sombre, factual, sounding much of the time like a treatise. Johnson has a strong sense of his responsibility to give a topographical, economic and social survey of a society that was very different to his own, and the work is full of his very keen interest, for example, in all the specific details of agriculture:

> The soil is then turned up by manual labour, with an instrument called a crooked spade, of a form and weight which to me appeared very incommodious, and would perhaps be soon improved in a country where workmen could be easily found and easily paid. It has a narrow blade of iron fixed to a long and heavy piece of wood, which must have, about a foot and a half above the iron, a knee or flexure with the angle downwards. When the farmer encounters a stone which is the great impediment of his operations, he drives the blade under it, and bringing the knee or angle to the ground, has in the long handle a very forcible lever.
>
> (IX, 79)

Although, as Johnson writes elsewhere in the *Journey*, 'these diminutive observations' may 'seem to take away something from the dignity of writing and therefore are never communicated but with hesitation, and a little fear of abasement and contempt', they, of course, reflect Johnson's realism and keen practicality, as well as his tremendous interest in how the Highlanders and the Hebridean islanders actually live. In this latter respect the work has quite properly been compared with modern cultural anthropology. Gradually, as we read on, all the circumstantial details about the difficulties of agriculture with such limited tools and the introduction of new conveniences through trade begin to trace out the real theme and organizing principle of the work: a careful juxtaposition of and adjudication between the advantages and disadvantages of old-fashioned and commercial societies.

At a deeper level, as Donald Greene very finely says, Johnson's fascination with the rigours of life on islands whose climate and soils seem scarcely able to support crops at all becomes 'an image of the sombre total situation of the human race. These few puny but amazing creatures continually battle against the overwhelming forces of nature; and, by dint of their intelligence and effort, they wrest from it the conditions for a life of some kind of decency' (*Samuel Johnson*, 1989, pp. 131–2). In the moving conclusion the pessimism of the work is once more

Reynold's last portrait of Johnson (1782–4)

tempered by admiration for human courage and resource-fulness. Johnson back in Edinburgh visits a school for the deaf and comments:

> It was pleasing to see one of the most desperate of human calamities capable of so much help: whatever enlarges hope, will exalt courage; after having seen the deaf taught arithmetic, who would be afraid to cultivate the Hebrides?   (164)

In 1777 there was another famous instance of Johnson's generosity and benevolence when he tried to help the unfortunate

Dr Dodd, a fashionable clergyman condemned to death for forgery. Johnson drafted petitions, wrote letters and even a sermon for Dodd to deliver in prison. In gratitude the condemned man addressed his benefactor as 'thou great and good heart'. Sadly all the efforts were to no avail and Dodd was duly hanged.

Johnson's last great literary project was the *Lives of the Poets*. A group of London booksellers approached him with the idea of writing brief prefaces to a collected edition of modern British poets. The work grew in Johnson's hands. Between the ages of sixty-eight and seventy-two he wrote fifty-two separate lives. Some, it is true, are very brief, but those of Milton or Pope, for example, develop into full, if incisive biographies and the word count as a whole, Paul Fussell reminds us, is equivalent to that of five modern novels. The series obviously contains much of Johnson's finest literary criticism, and it amounts in the end to a great survey of the poetry of his own period and the one that precedes.

As biography it is equally remarkable. He incorporates his own earlier *Life of Savage* and we can see from the comparison with the later work that his prose style in the biographical sections has become less formal and that he has moved even further in the direction of concrete realism and detail. No one who has read them can ever forget, for example, Johnson's fascinated yet compassionate accounts of Pope's morning preparations to conceal his infirmities or of the indignities of Swift's last years. Such details, however, are still assimilated, as would not be the case in modern biographies, to traditional moral schemes, the 'vanity of human wishes' in particular. The series thus becomes not only great literary criticism, not only great biography, but also, in the fine words of Walter Raleigh, 'a book of wisdom and experience, a treatise on the conduct of life, a commentary on human destiny'.

The final phase

Things were now to grow dark again for Johnson personally. In April 1781 Henry Thrale died, and Johnson looked 'for the last time upon the face that for fifteen years had never been turned upon me but with respect or benignity'. The Thrales's marriage had never been a happy one. Hester, released at last, was soon to grasp for happiness in a new marriage to an Italian singing master, Gabriel Piozzi. Johnson, shocked beyond measure, felt personally betrayed as well and was soon to be completely estranged from the woman who had been his chief emotional support for many years. His own loneliness increased unbearably, and his health grew steadily worse from this time on.

It is unnecessary to linger on the details of this last phase of Johnson's life. In June 1783 he suffered a stroke which deprived him temporarily of the powers of speech. He recovered, but his heart was failing and this led to extreme swellings in his body through dropsy, severe coughs and many other ailments. His fear of death, always acute, naturally intensified, but it also appears that he attained a new sense of spiritual consolation at this time. As always his brute courage and determination were especially remarkable. 'I will be conquered,' he said to a friend, 'I will not capitulate.' Even in the last week of his life, with a characteristic mixture of bravery, impatience and stubborn irritability, he despaired of the doctors and attempted to cure himself of the terrible swelling in his legs by stabbing himself in three places with a pair of scissors. It was to no avail, and he died on 13 December 1784.

Thinking of Johnson's death, a friend, the Member of Parliament William Gerard Hamilton, said: 'He has made a chasm which not only nothing can fill up, but which *nothing has a tendency to fill up.* – Johnson is dead. – Let us go to the next best: There is nobody; *no man can be said to put you in mind of Johnson.*' Yet Johnson's moral struggle for order, control, meaning is representative in the widest human sense. 'His soul was not different than that of another person,' said Mrs Thrale: it was simply 'greater'. Ending his own great biography, Walter Jackson Bate comments that Johnson gave those who knew him and those who read him and read about him 'the precious gift of hope': against enormous obstacles he had 'proved that it was possible to get through this strange adventure of life, and to do it in a way that is a tribute to human nature'.

2 The intellectual background

The weighty couplets of Johnson's greatest poetry, the magnificent eloquence of his prose create an incomparable sense of authority. He seems magisterial in his impersonality, the spokesman for a timeless moral truth. The poet, says Imlac in *Rasselas* chapter X, 'must divest himself of the prejudices of his age or country; he must consider right or wrong in their abstracted and invariable state; he must disregard present laws and opinions, and rise to general and transcendental truths, which will always be the same . . .'.

Several modern critical approaches – Marxist, feminist and those arising from the theories known as 'deconstruction' – have taught us to be suspicious of the framework of authority that a writer constructs. Such perspectives can hardly be central in an introductory survey of this kind, but they are certainly not irrelevant in the case of a writer as authoritative as Johnson. His aspiration to objective and general truth paradoxically arises not only out of struggles within his own individual psyche but also out of the particular historical, political and socio-economic circumstances of his time. Johnson's work, in other words, has an *ideological* dimension, and reflects the desire to find and to reassert principles of authority and stability in a period of bewildering change when traditional absolutes were being called into question.

Johnson, partly by temperament and social background and partly by hard-won conviction, has a firm allegiance to the Church of England and a pessimistic sense of what political change could achieve. Yet he lives through the main portion of a century famous for democracy, the secularization of thought, philosophical optimism and a new belief in progress, and dies only five years before the culmination of some of these processes in the French Revolution.

A well-known French historian of ideas went so far as to write in 1935:

> Never was there a greater contrast, never a more sudden transition than this! A hierarchical system ensured by authority; life firmly based on dogmatic principle – such were the things held dear by the people of the seventeenth century; but these

– controls, authority, dogmas and the like – were the very things that their immediate successors of the eighteenth held in cordial detestation. The former were upholders of Christianity; the latter were its foes. The former believed in the laws of God; the latter in the laws of Nature; the former lived contentedly enough in a world composed of unequal social grades; of the latter the one absorbing dream was Equality.

(Paul Hazard, *The European Mind (1689–1715)* trans. 1953, p. xv)

This is grossly exaggerated and over-simplified, of course, especially from the perspective of the British Isles. But the passage does capture the genuine drama of change and the sense of 'Enlightenment', even if these changes are best seen as the result of processes that had been going on for several centuries.

The ideal of the unity of Christendom had been shattered by the Protestant Reformation and the subsequent wars of religion. The sixteenth and seventeenth centuries saw remarkable scientific advances, but far more important as a cause of actual social change was the growth of trade and commerce. The voyages of discovery brought new goods to Europe, new profits and eventually, through colonization, new markets. The huge increase of trade required new forms of commercial organization, and joint-stock companies, banks and stock markets developed. Europe experienced what amounted to a great 'commercial revolution'. The new prosperity created a greater degree of social mobility and increased the numbers and the status of various urban groupings that might be considered middle class in modern terms. This was inevitably to have cultural and political consequences as well as economic ones.

England itself was in the forefront of many of these changes. It had experienced what were essentially its own wars of religion in the seventeenth century when a parliament that supported Protestantism rose up against and eventually beheaded a high Anglican king, Charles I. The restoration of that king's son, Charles II, by no means solved all the problems, but after his Catholic younger brother, James II, was driven from the throne in 1688, a new political and religious settlement became possible. England began to assume recognizably modern features as a prosperous parliamentary democracy in which religious toleration was granted to most groups. The philosophy of John Locke, in whose work many of these changes were explained and justified, was of enormous prestige on the continent, and the same was true of the work of the great Sir Isaac Newton and other British scientists. As the eighteenth century progressed the sense of political stability became more firmly established, and there was a marked growth into a commercial and consumer society. By the 1760s Britain was the possessor of a vast overseas empire that included India and the whole of North America, though America itself, of course, was to gain its independence before long.

All these changes – historical, political, economic, social, religious, philosophical, cultural – obviously work together, although it will be necessary to separate some of them out for the purposes of analysis. But what Johnson essentially has to confront is a great change in human consciousness, and the effects of this are still very much with us to this day. As we trace the various strands through and explore Johnson's own energetic responses to them we shall find that he is far from entirely negative despite his popular image as a reactionary. His magisterial style and deliberately depersonalized sense of authority can be examined sceptically as brilliant rhetorical strategies to help him achieve his ideological aims. But though it is helpful to keep the questions raised by these recent critical approaches in mind, most readers are still in the end likely to be impressed with the genuine weight of conviction and moral good sense Johnson conveys.

Christian humanism

Johnson has often been described as a 'Christian humanist'. The word 'humanism' today often carries self-consciously secular, even anti-religious connotations. In the history of ideas, however, it refers to a broadly optimistic view of human nature associated mainly with Greek tradition. This comes to blend with biblical and Christian ideas in a variety of ways, as we shall see.

The mainstream classical tradition is, on the whole, optimistic. It is a civic tradition that believes that human beings are by nature sociable, even political: made in such a way as to find fulfilment through living in harmony with their fellows in social life and in the life of the state. It emphasizes free will and privileges the reason as the greatest human faculty, not so much because of its capacity to understand the cosmos as for being the source of moral judgement and moral behaviour. Socrates in particular regards speculative science as a distraction from moral conduct. In the work of his great disciple Plato, reason has the potential to see beyond the whole world of change into the transcendent world of ideal moral truth. The Stoics of later antiquity are more ambivalent about political life, but they take the emphasis on reason as a divine spark in human beings even further by adopting a more negative view of the passions than their predecessors.

From the very earliest centuries Christianity has been much influenced by classical thought. The Christian religion goes far beyond classical optimism, of course, in its assertion of the supernatural destiny of human beings. Yet any version of classical 'humanism' that can properly be termed 'Christian' as well combines the high respect for 'Right Reason' (as this moral reason came to be called) and free will with a sense of the limitations on them as a consequence of the fall, original sin. Wide variations along the spectrum of optimism and pessimism can thus occur within this same basic tradition. Broadly speaking it was the less positive views of human life in this world that dominated the first half of the medieval period. These blend in well with the more pessimistic aspects of Plato's teaching: the idea that we live in a shadowy world of images compared to the transcendent world. In Boethius, for example, a writer of late antiquity who had a great influence on Johnson as well as on Chaucer, Platonic, Stoic and biblical ideas combine in a strong sense of the way that fallen man is blindly deceived by his own foolish wishes for secular things. This is the complex of ideas from which the 'Vanity of Human Wishes' tradition comes.

Yet the *possibility* of human freedom and the value of reason are not usually in themselves denied. From the twelfth century on, and especially in the great synthesis of St Thomas Aquinas (1225–1274) a more positive teaching, to which the title of 'Christian humanism' may properly be given, emerges. The Renaissance revival of learning itself increased optimism about the power of human reason to such a degree that some thinkers seem to lose any real Christian bearings altogether. But the majority of the main Renaissance thinkers retain the double perspective characteristic of Christian humanism in which human beings are both semi-divine in potential and yet poor, wretched fallen creatures, 'the glory, jest and riddle of the world' in Pope's famous words. 'Reason' remains ethical reason, and these writers continue to differentiate it from theoretical speculation, which they now associate with the arid ideas of medieval theologians. The content of Renaissance humanist ethics also usually retains strong Christian elements. The anti-militarist, anti-heroic emphasis of Erasmus, for example, which had such a strong influence on Johnson, reflects not only a movement away from an aristocratic ethos but also a deliberate appeal to the spirit of the gospel.

There can be no doubt of Johnson's own broad allegiance to this great tradition. He was himself, of course, deeply learned in the classics even by the standards of his own time. His own scholarly work clearly marks him as a late product of the Renaissance revival of learning. He was also a dedicated Christian layman. One of the central influences on his thought is Richard Hooker, the major Elizabethan apologist for Anglicanism against the Puritans, who drew many of his ideas from St Thomas Aquinas and who had the specific aim of reaffirming the place of reason and nature against the more radical Protestants.

Many pressures – intellectual, social, even economic – had conspired by Johnson's time and were continuing to conspire to alter and threaten the tradition of classical and Christian humanism and the moral absolutes to which it was wedded. The decline in that tradition and the increased knowledge of other types of societies through the voyages of discovery created a tendency to think of morality in less absolute terms. Johnson clearly wishes to reassert and reapply traditional moral and Christian criteria in the bewildering new world, but he does so in by no means a simplistic way. Though he condemns some changes out of hand, and may chose at times, especially in the later phases of his career, to present himself as entrenched against liberal opinion, he is basically confident that ancient wisdom can be assimilated with modern knowledge and conditions. 'Genius' in his view is a 'mind of large general powers' applied to particular studies, and he himself takes all knowledge, both ancient and modern, as his province. Despite his great learning it is above all 'what comes near to us, what we can turn to use' that he values. 'Human experience,' he says resoundingly, 'which is always contradicting theory, is the sole test of truth' (*Life*, I, 454). He always creates the impression that he is testing tradition and taking very little for granted, and he is thus able to bring the best of that tradition into a new alliance with the empirical and psychological emphasis of science and of late seventeenth- and eighteenth-century British philosophy.

Science, progress, Enlightenment

The work of the great astronomers, Copernicus, Galileo, Kepler and others in the sixteenth and seventeenth centuries obviously made an enormous impact on traditional ways of thought. As a recent historian of ideas says,

> the majority of even educated Europeans in 1600 still drew their world picture from the great medieval synthesis of Aristotle and the Bible. That picture centred the whole universe on the earth, as well as the whole life of the earth on man, its only rational inhabitant. The first intellectual

achievement of a new age was to make it unreasonable to hold such a view.

(J.M. Roberts, *The Triumph of the West*, 1985, p. 238)

Assisted by the new instruments, such as the telescope and the microscope, the observation of facts led to large general explanations whose validity could be tested. Galileo (as the story has it) had found that the swinging of the chandelier in the cathedral at Pisa and the motion of weights dropped from the leaning tower were both measurable and could be translated into mathematical formulae. The great Sir Isaac Newton was eventually to be able to apply the same processes to the very order of the planets around the sun. Working in combination with mathematics, the new empirical science seemed to make the whole realm of nature something that the mind of man could comprehend, compute and predict. The prestige of observation and experiment was gradually to displace the authority of classical science, and, it also, of course, made belief in the literal sense of the Bible problematic.

It would be a mistake, though, to believe that the new science inevitably worked against the interests of religion. On the continent, as we shall see, what could be considered the scientific movement in the broadest sense of 'Enlightenment' did come to be associated in a very general way with free thinking. But Newton himself and others among the major scientists were personally devout. In England, in particular, Newtonian science gave a great boost to the arguments for God as the great designer of the universe, and Christianity and the Bible were reinterpreted to fit the new emphases rather than being put at threat by them.

The existence of printing ensured a wide circulation for the new scientific ideas. Francis Bacon, an eminent lawyer and career-politician, Lord Chancellor of England in the early seventeenth century until his prosecution on corruption charges, was an essayist and moral philosopher who was also a keen amateur scientist. (His death was picturesquely supposed to have been hastened by a chill caught during experiments in freezing a chicken.) In several eloquent works written with a quasi-religious fervour he produces manifestos for empirical observation and experimental method in the sciences. He is remarkably forward looking above all in his Utopian sense of the great social benefits that science could bring to humanity: 'The true and lawful end of the sciences is that human life be enriched by new discoveries and powers.' Through science there would become possible 'a restitution and reinvigorating (in great part) of man to the sovereignty and power . . . which he had in his first creation'. Before this time it was common to believe that the world was in steady decline or dominated by great inevitable historical cycles or by the direct hand of God's providence. Bacon is one of the first thinkers to argue that enormous progress could be achieved by collaborative human effort.

As Bacon had hoped, Britain itself was to be very much in the vanguard of the advances in science. A group of London scientists was given a charter by Charles II in 1662 and became the Royal Society for the Improving of Natural Knowledge. The King took a genuine interest in the proceedings, and many famous men, including such distinguished literary figures as the Poet Laureate John Dryden, also belonged. Among other early achievements the society tested the laws about the behaviour of gases discovered by another member, the great chemist Robert Boyle.

Newton's success in apparently comprehending and explaining the rational method behind the whole universe through his theories of universal gravitation made him by far the most famous of the new scientists, and popular interest in his ideas was enormous. Pope praised him in a famous 'Enlightenment' couplet:

> Nature and Nature's Laws lay hid in Night:
> God said Let Newton be! and all was Light.

This sense of confidence in human science and reason combined well with the prosperity brought about by the new commerce and capitalism, and the enthusiastic belief in human progress was spread by the wider dissemination of books. The French writer Fontenelle, Perpetual Secretary of the French Academy of Sciences and 'perhaps the greatest popularizer of science in any day' in the words of Louis Bredvold in *The Brave New World of the Enlightenment* (1961, p. 40), wrote with astonishing assurance in 1702, for example, that Europe was about to see 'A century which will become more enlightened day by day, so that all previous centuries will be lost in darkness by comparison' (Preface, *History of the Renewal of the Royal Academy of Sciences*). Voltaire in the mid-century confirmed this, writing with equal confidence that the preceding age of Louis XIV could not only stand comparison with other 'happy ages when the arts were brought to perfection and . . . are an example to posterity' but that it was in fact superior to any of them in that 'rational philosophy only came to light in this period; and . . . a general revolution took place in our arts, minds and customs . . .' (*The Age of Louis XIV*).

48

Michael Rysbrack, Monument to Newton

The image of 'Enlightenment' is taken up in modern usage to describe this whole new sense of confidence in human powers, science and reason. In France and other continental countries the movement to promulgate it often came into conflict with the powerful interests of the Roman Catholic Church, which had considerable control over education. In that sense, as we have noted, 'Enlightenment' carries secularist and even anti-religious associations, though this is hardly the case in England and by no means inevitable elsewhere.

As Voltaire makes clear, the new cult of progress had other far-reaching cultural implications. One of the most interesting of them from the point of view of literary students is the debate between the 'ancients' and 'moderns' to which Voltaire's comment is itself a contribution. This began as a purely literary debate in seventeenth-century France about the relative merits of classical and modern literature, but the prestige of the new science obviously underlay the claims of the 'moderns' (not the modern writers as such but their supporters, the 'modern' party; as 'ancients' means not the classics but the supporters of the ancients party).

Jonathan Swift's *Battle of the Books* (1697; published 1704) is one of the most specific English responses to the debate. He and Pope, as traditionalist writers much influenced by the classics, incline to the ancients' party. Despite Pope's praise of Newton they are suspicious of modern science not only for this reason but also because they see it as a speculative distraction from civic and moral duty. They follow here the Socratic tradition of the Renaissance humanists, who had condemned the idle theories of the medieval logicians and theologians. Swift and Pope transfer this traditional humanist satire on to the speculative and experimental scientists as well, whom they portray as engaged in trivial and uncoordinated activities: 'O! would the Sons of Men once think their Eyes/ And Reason giv'n them but to study *Flies*!' says Pope's Dullness (*The Dunciad*, IV, 453–4). Swift has wonderful satire on the experiments of the Royal Society in *Gulliver's Travels*, portraying scientists, for example, trying to make food by returning excrement to its original constituent parts.

Johnson himself is a much finer classical scholar than either Swift or Pope, and in many respects traditionalist in the same ways as they are. His personal tendency to depression and his strong sense of original sin and the fall make him sceptical about any Utopian claims, and he is naturally opposed to anti-religious continental forms of enlightenment. In a comment in the 'Life of Milton' on the passage in *Paradise Lost* where the angel

Raphael advises Adam not to worry about astronomy, Johnson, naturally enough, agrees with the angel (and the humanists) that moral conduct is the most important thing:

> Prudence and Justice are virtues and excellences of all times and of all places; we are perpetually moralists, but we are geometricians only by chance . . . . The innovators whom I oppose are turning off attention from life to nature. They seem to think that we are placed here to watch the growth of plants, or the motions of the stars. Socrates was rather of opinion that what we had to learn was, how to do good and avoid evil.
>
> (Hill (ed.), 1905, I, 99–100)

Yet what we actually find in Johnson's work is a real open-mindedness and balance about these matters, and ultimately a careful mediation between humanist values and the new science. When he asserts in the passage above that moral truth is far more important than scientific knowledge he does not mean to suggest that the latter is negligible. He makes the point clearly in a letter to Susannah Thrale on 25 March 1784 about a proposed visit to a famous astronomer:

> With Mr Herschel it will certainly be very right to cultivate an acquaintance, for he can show you in the sky what no man before him has ever seen, by some wonderful improvements which he has made in the telescope. What he has to show is indeed a long way off, and perhaps concerns us but little, but all truth is valuable and all knowledge is pleasing in its first effects, and may be subsequently useful . . . . Take therefore all opportunities of learning that offer themselves, however remote the matter may be from common life or common conversation. Look in Herschel's telescope; go into a chemist's laboratory; if you see a manufacturer at work, remark his operations.

As is well known, Johnson was himself fond of engaging in chemical experiments as a hobby, and he took a great interest throughout his life in various forms of technology. In one of his most significant early biographies he praises the great Dutch physician Doctor Boerhaave for his careful use of experimental method and the way he uses his scientific talents in the service of mankind:

> When he laid down his office of governor of the university in 1715, he made an oration upon the subject of *attaining to certainty in natural philosophy*; in which he declares himself in

51

the strongest terms, a favourer of experimental knowledge, and reflects with just severity upon those arrogant philosophers who are too easily disgusted with the slow methods of obtaining true notions by frequent experiments; and who, possessed with too high an opinion of their own abilities, rather choose to consult their own imaginations, than inquire into nature, and are better pleased with the delightful amusement of forming hypotheses, than the toilsome drudgery of amassing observations.

Johnson certainly does not accept all the Utopianism associated with the scientific movement and the cult of progress in his own time. It would be a foolish error to believe that science could *radically* transform our fundamental condition as fallen creatures. But the very fact of the fall is itself a good argument for the necessity of science: the 'calamities of life, like the necessities of nature, are calls to labour and exercises of diligence' (*Rambler* 32). Once we recognize our state we are called upon to do the best we can to improve it within the limits that are inevitably imposed and to try to help both ourselves and others. Science can be a powerful agent of this, as he emphasizes in his work on Boerhaave, and in this aim it has his complete support. No man admittedly can do much on his own:

> But he has no reason to repine though his abilities are small and his opportunities few. He that has improved the virtue or advanced the happiness of one fellow-creature, he that has ascertained a single moral proposition, or added one useful experiment to natural knowledge, may be contented with his own performance, and, with respect to mortals like himself, may demand, like Augustus, to be dismissed at his departure with applause.
>
> (*Idler* 88)

Johnson is thus prepared to recognize the ways that things *have* improved and can improve further. Despite his admiration for and frequent citation of the moral authority of the classics, he is in the last analysis a 'modern' not an 'ancient' in his readiness to recognize the wider dissemination of culture and knowledge in his own time: 'I am always angry when I hear ancient times praised at the expense of modern times. There is now a great deal more learning in the world than there was formerly; for it is universally diffused' (*Life*, IV, 217).

Johnson, as his frequent citations in the *Dictionary* show, greatly admired Bacon, Newton and Boyle. Like them, he is convinced that there is no incompatibility between science

and the Christian religion and, indeed, on the contrary finds
his faith strengthened by consideration of the universal order
science has revealed. Despite his pronounced hostility to the
more virulent continental forms of the movement we call the
'Enlightenment', he is in many respects, as has been shown
in an influential essay by Robert Shackleton (*Johnson, Boswell
and their Circle*, 1965), properly regarded as an 'Enlightenment'
figure himself, and this is by no means to the prejudice of his
Christian humanism.

New philosophy

The paradoxical double sense of human glory and wretchedness
characteristic of Christian humanism was bound to be disturbed
at the Reformation when radical Protestantism, in the desire to
highlight our *absolute* need for grace, emphasized the completeness of the fall. It was as a direct consequence of these controversies that the seventeenth century, in Johnson's words, saw
a 'contest about the original benevolence or malignity of man'
(*Preface to Shakespeare*, VII, 88). Whereas some thinkers, both
religious and secular, emphasized our total corruption, others
were in effect to deny the fall completely in an extreme stress
on the natural goodness of man.

Protestantism clearly had a more individualistic emphasis
than medieval Catholicism. The same cultural tendency to
individualism was encouraged by the social mobility that
capitalism and the growth of town life brought about. The new
science itself meanwhile inevitably had an impact on philosophy
and moral thought. The emphasis on observation, experiment
and measurement dented the authority of the general schemes
of the past, and in its own way privileged human experience.
New human sciences on the analogy of the natural sciences
began to be built up out of the data provided by individual
experience and by the study of human societies of very different
kinds. Scientific economics and psychology, sociology, anthropology – all of them have their real origins at this time.

Radical developments in science and philosophy and the
decline of Christian humanism especially affected the status
of traditional 'Right Reason'. 'Reason' in some quarters now
became an ambitious system-building rationalism, by analogy
with the speculative theorizing of mathematics and science.
In keeping with another side of the new science it could
equally well be presented as a much narrower and more purely
empirical faculty than had previously been the case. Loss of
confidence in the traditional *moral* function of reason is reflected

in the way that a small minority of thinkers argue that we are totally dominated by selfish passions. Others more optimistically come to see individual emotion, benevolence, sympathy or an innate moral sense as the proper motivating factors of human behaviour. Since Johnson's own 'moral philosophy' or, as I prefer to call it, 'moral psychology' is in part a response to these developments it will be helpful to survey the work of the leading figures briefly.

The famous seventeenth-century French philosopher Descartes used a method modelled on the proofs in geometry to scrutinize all traditional ideas with radical scepticism and to build up again an elaborate system on the sole foundation of the existence of the individual consciousness. This kind of continental rationalism, to be taken further in Spinoza and Liebnitz, must be sharply distinguished both from the humanist tradition of moral reason or 'Right Reason' and from more empirical developments in Britain, where Descartes's followers were in a small minority.

Descartes's English contemporary Thomas Hobbes, for example, is also influenced by mathematics and the desire to explain everything mechanically. He is a rationalist in his sceptical, critical use of reason, and his thought constitutes an even greater threat to traditional values. On the whole, though, he represents the more empirical side of the new science. He writes more as a psychologist than an abstract philosopher in focusing attention on the passions of the individual human psyche. Adopting an extreme, though secularized, version of the Protestant view of man's depravity and influenced by the disturbing political events of his time, Hobbes put forward a philosophy that was virtually the antithesis of classical/Christian humanism. Instead of emphasizing our naturally sociable nature as a 'political animal' he portrayed human beings as radically selfish, their life in the state of nature 'solitary, poor, nasty, brutish and short', and proposed as the only solution to anarchy an absolutist political power that would keep us under control. His writings caused an uproar, and there were many attempts to refute him. Anglican writers in particular opposed his bleak view of human nature by stressing human goodness, and this was useful ammunition against the Puritans at the same time. But Hobbes's thought remained a force to be reckoned with, a haunting presence to be argued against throughout the whole of the next century.

Much more central and congenial to the spirit of the new age of the later seventeenth century was John Locke, who stood on the opposite side to Hobbes politically and had to flee to

Holland on the failure of the campaign to keep James II from the throne. He returned only at the triumph of the Whigs in the 'Glorious Revolution' of 1688. His thinking can be found at the heart of almost all the main concerns of the period that follows, whether psychological, political, religious, aesthetic or philosophical as such. He argues consistently for the religious toleration of dissenters, for example, a crucial issue in bringing stability after the trauma of the civil wars. He is one of the most influential exponents of what he calls in another important work *The Reasonableness of Christianity* (1695), and his role in the political thought of the eighteenth century can hardly be exaggerated either, as we shall see.

Even in the technical field of philosophy as such, Locke's popularity and influence were soon to be immense. His *Essay concerning Human Understanding* (1690), despite a continued commitment to reason, highlights the association of ideas as the mainspring of mental activity, and the 'reason' he espouses in itself constitutes a definite narrowing down of the humanist tradition in that it is without any trace of the Platonic idea that reason has the capacity for grasping the transcendent. His famous view that the mind is a *tabula rasa* or blank sheet with no innate ideas in it can lead to an emphasis on education and environment that makes all moral values seem relative. His argument that human identity consists primarily in conscious-ness extended through time is even more threatening to traditional ideas of moral character.

Yet Locke's sceptical emphasis on the limitations of human knowledge has a distinctively complacent ring to it in the assertion that what we *can* know is sufficient 'for the con-veniences of life and the information of virtue'. He himself is always reasonable, polite, accommodating rather than con-frontational in tone. He adopts new empirical, psychological and quasi-scientific arguments, but often arrives at reassuringly conventional positions by different routes. Hobbes, for example, in his reductionist way, had made pleasure and the avoidance of pain the real motives behind all our actions. Locke takes it for granted that Hobbes is right in essence, but is careful to link pain and pleasure to obedience to the traditional moral law. His account of that moral law makes it sound sociable, even convenient, and he emphasizes how *reasonable* it is to obey God's will because it will bring us the reward of happiness in the afterlife, and the opposite will bring us punishment and misery.

It is accommodations such as these expressed in so reassuring a tone that make Locke so popular in the period. He has a

great influence on the theology of the time, and, along with
Newton, he is constantly cited and praised in Addison and
Steele's periodical the *Spectator,* which was read by the whole
élite and had as its avowed aim to bring 'Philosophy out of
closets and libraries, schools and colleges, to dwell in clubs and
assemblies, at tea-tables and in coffee-houses'.

Locke's former pupil, the Earl of Shaftesbury, also became
a highly fashionable philosopher in the period, though he was
a much less careful thinker than his teacher. He espouses
a sensitive, highly optimistic version of Platonism which it
is hard to avoid attributing in part to the privileges of his
aristocratic lifestyle. To be a philosopher, he explains, 'in a just
signification, is but to carry good-breeding a step higher. For
the accomplishment of breeding is to learn whatever is decent
in company or beautiful in arts; and the sum of philosophy is
to learn what is just in society and beautiful in Nature and the
order of the world.' This strong belief in the beautiful harmony
of nature anticipates and influences the romantic movement.

The marked 'cosmic optimism' that Shaftesbury displays here,
the view that all is for the best in the universe, corresponds to
a belief in the natural goodness of human beings. As reason
narrows down in significance and becomes more empirical it
is hard to see how it can fulfil its traditional moral functions to
the same extent, and Shaftesbury as a Platonist and an admirer
of the Stoics is unhappy with the way that Locke seems to
found morality on a rather calculating form of 'reason' that
has lost any *inherent* relation to the realm of transcendent
moral truth. He fills what he regards as the vacuum that
has been left by arguing for a natural, *intuitive* moral sense
in human beings. Understandably he does not find it easy to
define, but it appears to consist mainly in a virtuous feeling
of sympathy and benevolence. Properly considered this has the
capacity to produce virtuous behaviour entirely independent of
the concern with rewards of punishments in the afterlife and,
indeed, of belief in God at all.

It is Hobbes, though, not Locke who is mainly in Shaftesbury's
mind. The former's Anglican opponents had emphasized human
goodness to such an extent that they were in danger of under-
mining Christian orthodoxy. Shaftesbury feels even less con-
straints than his predecessors and is prepared to ignore the
idea of original sin altogether in a totally secular emphasis on
the natural goodness of human beings.

It was left to the great Anglican moralist Bishop Joseph Butler
in the mid-century to try to steer between the twin dangers
that Hobbes and Shaftesbury offered to traditional Christian

thought and in a sense to reconcile their influences. His careful mediation, though criticized by some as prudential, allows for both self-love and human benevolence in the total picture. Some people [i.e. Hobbes], he says, regard the whole of human life as 'one continued exercise of self-love'. Self-love is certainly important, but then so is benevolence, for the existence of which there is ample empirical evidence. Yet, properly considered, Butler goes on to say, benevolence itself is part of self-love, if in no cynical sense. For Providence has carefully arranged it so that 'Duty and interest [i.e. self-interest] are perfectly coincident for the most part in this world, but entirely and in every instance if we take in the future and the whole'. Butler attributes the central role in all this to 'Conscience', a faculty that clearly has much in common with traditional 'Right Reason'. In conceptualizing conscience as evaluating different alternatives and weighing probabilities, however, Butler also seems to have been influenced by more recent thought. There are analogies here and in the whole of this carefully realistic moral philosophy to Johnson's own thinking, especially in the way Butler succeeds in preserving Christian orthodoxy while also frankly appealing to the terminology and categories of his own time.

The rhapsodic secular enthusiasm of Shaftesbury, however, had a much wider appeal, especially in literary circles. Though his aristocratic élitism is very different in tone from the work of the French writer Rousseau in the middle of the century, it has recognizable affinities with it. Rousseau's belief in nature and in natural goodness is far more passionate and primitivist than Shaftesbury's. His thought has more radical political implications and his role in the growth of romanticism is much more dramatic. But the thinner aestheticism of Shaftesbury combines with the fervour of Rousseau in the cult of sentiment which had so many manifestations in the second half of the eighteenth century and which will be explored more fully later in this book. It is enough to note here that these are trends which Johnson was to devote the latter part of his career to opposing. He spoke of Rousseau with almost unparalleled severity as 'a bad man . . . one of the worst of men; a rascal who ought to be hunted out of society, as he has been . . .'. Johnson had, said Mrs Thrale, the deepest aversion to all that is commonly understood by the word 'romantic'.

At the opposite extreme of technical rigour from Shaftesbury and Rousseau is the work of the Scots philosopher David Hume, and it is both impossible and unnecessary to give a full account of his work here. He is very important as a writer on religion and on the ethics of commercial society, as we shall see, but the significant point in the present context is the way that his radical development of the sceptical empiricism of Locke further weakened the traditional status of reason as a moral authority. Indeed, Hume goes so far as to say that reason is both inevitably and properly the slave of the passions. It is through passions such as sympathy rather than through reason, or even through a fixed moral sense of the kind Shaftesbury believes in, that we achieve virtue. This is the way forward for moral philosophy in the second half of the eighteenth century. The contradiction to thousands of years of traditional humanist thought about the relative status of reason and passion could hardly be more vividly illustrated.

Johnson and reason

On one very well-known occasion Boswell asked Johnson about the 'idealist' philosophy of Bishop Berkeley, who held that material objects exist not in themselves but only in the mind that perceives them and ultimately in the mind of God:

> I observed, that though we are satisfied Berkeley's doctrine is not true, it is impossible to refute it. I never shall forget the alacrity with which Johnson answered, striking his foot with mighty force against a large stone, till he rebounded from it, 'I refute it *thus*'.
>
> (*Life*, 6 August 1763, I, 471)

Johnson was often termed a philosopher in the period, but what was meant by this was a teacher of wisdom, a *moral* philosopher, and even in that respect he does not make claims as a theorist. Yet it would be wrong to take his famous common-sense response to Berkeley as the symptom of anti-intellectual disdain. This was a time when the whole educated general public was interested in philosophy. Johnson's own conversation is laced with references to figures such as Hume and Rousseau, and he was very well aware of the implications and tenor of the new thinking and indeed devoted to opposing it in crucial respects. He was especially appalled by what seemed to him a growing complacency and false optimism, and thus hostile to the view that we should rely on our *feelings* or on some *innate* moral sense, since this seemed to him to deny the reality of the fall. We are all 'corrupt', he wrote emphatically, 'if corrupt to different degrees' (*Adventurer* 137). If we are *by nature* fallen, then that which comes naturally to us, our feelings or some innate moral sense, can hardly be the source of true morality. He can put, he says, no trust in that 'instinctive, that constitutional goodness which is not founded upon principle' (*Life*, I. 443–4).

Instead Johnson continues to affirm traditional 'Right Reason' as the basis for morality against the growing scepticism, subjectivity and relativism of the time. Clearly reflecting classical and Christian humanist thought, he says that however depraved our minds may be in practice they still derive from a 'celestial original' (*Rambler* 6) and describes reason in the most traditional terms as 'the great distinction of human nature, the faculty by which we approach to some degree of association with celestial intelligences' (*Rambler* 162).

But if Johnson's focus on traditional reason goes against the most significant thinking of his time, he has certainly been influenced by that thinking in the way he conceptualizes its operations. It is by no means clear that Johnson is relating reason to transcendent truths in any direct fashion. Like the 'conscience' to which Butler appeals, Johnson's 'reason' seems to work by reflection and by weighing probabilities. Some modern scholars have also suggested that Johnson sees 'reason' as compounding truth out of an aggregate of particular experiences by direct analogy with empirical processes in science, although this argument has not been universally accepted. What is beyond dispute, however, is that Johnson not only incorporates Baconian science into his general scheme but also, as we shall see, makes specific use in his treatment of reason of the new psychology he saw as originating with Hobbes.

Such thinking makes a useful ally with Christian tradition not only against ambitious continental rationalism but also against a more general complacency. For if Johnson believes in the centrality of reason, and certainly never denies its possibility, he is very much on the more pessimistic side of the classical/Christian humanist tradition, influenced by Protestant thought and by the experience of his own struggles. Though the human mind can achieve a great deal, we have to be constantly aware of the fallen corruption of our wills and our capacity for self-deceit. 'Not to have reason, and to have it useless and unemployed, is nearly the same,' he writes in *Rambler* 162, and *The Vanity of Human Wishes* demonstrates in practice 'How rarely reason guides the stubborn choice,/ Rules the bold hand or prompts the suppliant voice' (ll. 11–12). For Johnson, as for Swift, human reason is not something we can be complacent about but in itself a hard-won moral achievement, a difficult victory over subjectivity and illusion.

Johnson on the problem of evil

Only on one formal occasion, his review of Soame Jenyns's *A Free Inquiry into the Nature and Origin of Evil* (1757), did Johnson address philosophical problems systematically, and then solely in order to perform a demolition job on ideas that he finds offensive. But the fact that it was subject-matter of this kind that brought about such a response is itself highly significant. Jenyns's book relates to issues we have already mentioned such as the abuse of reason in theoretical speculation and false philosophical optimism, and Johnson's review has a special centrality in his thought.

The so-called 'problem of evil', the need to reconcile the goodness and power of God with the existence of evil in the world, obviously goes to the heart of Johnson's Christian faith and of his experience of life. The essential Christian answer is not a philosophical one at all in a sense, but depends on belief in the doctrine of the fall and on faith in God's providence, which is able to bring good out of evil. But there remains a very real problem, of course, not only for Christianity but for all systems that depend on belief in a good God or at least in the essential goodness of the universe. Christian writers had themselves engaged in speculative philosophical discussions of the issue, and Christian doctrine had become almost inextricably involved with classical philosophy, as we have seen. The Greek idea of the Great Chain of Being, the idea of a gradation of levels of being extending from God to inanimate matter, had appealed to Christian thinkers, especially in societies that were themselves hierarchical, and had proved useful in explaining why some kinds of relative imperfection were inevitable in the universe.

By the eighteenth century, however, much philosophy on this subject had become Christian in terminology alone, if that. The idea of the fall was minimized by many Christians as well as by non-believers and the concept of God's providence was often replaced with the scientific idea of a relatively autonomous nature or the classical idea of a beautiful cosmic harmony. A theology of providence still leaves room for an acknowledgement of the reality of evil, but a philosophy of cosmic optimism (as found in the Stoics, Shaftesbury, and Pope's *Essay on Man*) is more likely to say that evil is not really evil at all if seen from the proper perspective:

> All discord, harmony not understood;
> All partial evil, universal good:
> And, spite of pride, in erring reason's spite,

One truth is clear: Whatever is, is RIGHT.

(*Essay on Man*, I, 291–4)

It is not entirely clear why Soame Jenyns, a minor politician, dilettante writer and man-about-town, took it upon himself to write a treatise on such matters. The book is heavily dependent on the *Essay on Man*, Pope's brilliant but somewhat modish verse treatise quoted from above. Johnson is irritated by the arrogance, complacency and superficiality Jenyns (and to a lesser extent Pope) display, and he finds both works examples of the false use of 'reason' in speculative theorizing:

> When this author presumes to speak of the universe, I would advise him a little to distrust his own faculties, however large and comprehensive . . . . Surely a man who seems not completely master of his own opinions should have spoken more cautiously of omnipotence, nor have presumed to say what it could perform or what it could prevent.

Although cosmic optimist arguments of the kind Jenyns proposes often overlapped with ones used by Christian writers, Jenyns does not scruple to parade his own unorthodoxy. Johnson in response takes great care to differentiate speculative philosophical arguments from Christianity. He is not afraid, for example, despite his traditionalism in other respects, to point out that the Great Chain of Being must be logical nonsense because the gap between an infinite God and the 'next' level of being must itself be infinite and how can one measure the gap between the lowest level of existence and non-existence?

The real grounds of the argument between Johnson and those who think like Jenyns, however, is the question of the reality of evil. For it is only, Johnson believes, when we truly face the existence of evil that we experience our need of salvation from it, or, in more purely secular terms, can be encouraged to try to overcome it as best we can. The whole Baconian scientific enterprise, for example, depends on recognizing the inadequacies of our present condition and seeking means to improve it. Very penetratingly Johnson understands that Jenyns's views have ideological implications even in the area of social justice, for there is no need to try to improve the lot of the poor and ignorant if they do not really suffer evils at all. Johnson replies resoundingly:

> This author and Pope perhaps never saw the miseries which they imagine thus easy to be borne. The poor, indeed, are insensible of many little vexations, which sometimes embitter the possessions and pollute the enjoyments of the rich. They

are not pained by casual incivility, or mortified by the
mutilation of a compliment; but this happiness is like that
of a malefactor who ceases to feel the cords that bind him
when the pincers are tearing his flesh . . . .

And again:

To entail irreversible poverty upon generation after generation
only because the ancestor happened to be poor is in itself
cruel, if not unjust . . . . I am always afraid of determining on
the side of envy or cruelty. The privileges of education may
sometimes be improperly bestowed, but I shall always fear to
withhold them, lest I should be yielding to the suggestions
of pride, while I persuade myself that I am following the
maxims of policy; and under the appearance of salutary
restraints, should be indulging the lust of dominion, and
that malevolence which delights in seeing others depressed.

The 'Vanity of Human Wishes'

Johnson opposes cosmic optimism because the realities of evil
are at the heart of his faith and his experience. As we have
seen, cosmic optimist arguments, themselves ultimately from
non-Christian sources, were by now often espoused by self-
consciously secular thinkers and went together with an emphasis
on the natural goodness of human beings. If evil was not purely
an illusion then it was the result of ignorance or the corruptions
of an over-sophisticated society. This more general movement
in the moral thought of the period towards individualism and an
optimistic ethics of feeling seemed to deny our fallen nature and
condition, and Johnson sets himself deliberately to oppose such
tendencies. Though he does not in fact go as far as the radical
Protestant view of the complete depravity of man or Hobbes's
cynical secular version of the same position, he often speaks in
an extreme way in his urgent and exasperated desire to counter
the dangerous new complacency. Asked by Lady MacLeod, his
hostess in the Hebrides, whether man was not naturally good,
he shocked her by replying 'Madam, no more than is a wolf'.
  Inevitably, though, none of us finds it easy to face the realities
of our condition. We all seek to convince ourselves that we are
somehow above other people and an exception to the general
rules. It is worth keeping in mind the classical derivation of the
word 'idiot' as 'a solitary man' as well as Johnson's own fears of
madness when we hear him say so forcefully that 'every man in
his solitude is mad'. His rigorous definition of 'madness' here
is the inability to control wandering thoughts by reason or a

frequent 'recession from the realities of life to airy fictions', a 'habitual subjection of reason to fancy':

> Many have no happier moments than those that they pass in solitude, abandoned to their own imagination, which sometimes puts sceptres in their hands or mitres on their heads, shifts the scene of pleasure with endless variety, bids all the forms of beauty sparkle before them, and gluts them with every change of visionary luxury.
>
> (*Idler* 32)

Our modern approval of imagination is largely a result of the romantic movement. It is often forgotten that classical and Christian thinkers up to Johnson's time were just as likely to think of the imagination – the image-making faculty in the mind, the 'power of forming ideal pictures' as Johnson puts it in the *Dictionary* – as the source of delusion, sexual fantasy, and even mental disturbance. He defines *Imaginative*, for example, as 'Fantastick; full of imagination', and goes on to illustrate it by two very pejorative quotations, Bacon's comment that 'Witches are imaginative, and believe oft times they do that which they do not' and the theologian Jeremy Taylor's injunction 'Lay fetters and restraints upon the imaginative and fantastick part, because our fancy is usually pleased with the entertainment of shadows and gauds'. All this is compounded by his deep guilt about his own indulgence in day-dreaming, fantasy and supposed sloth.

What we need instead is to be brought down to earth, to be reminded of the shared, fundamental, bleakly objective truths of the human condition that we would all prefer to evade if we could:

> Yet hope not life from grief or danger free,
> Nor think the doom of man revers'd for thee.   (ll. 155–6)

This couplet from *The Vanity of Human Wishes* could stand as a central motto for Johnson's moral writing. 'Doom' here means literally 'judgement', but in the sense of our allotted fate or destiny, the fact that we are frail transient creatures destined to die. It is only in facing these realities that true hope lies.

It is for this reason that Johnson adopts the strategy of providing as wide, objective and dispassionate a view as possible in his poem. What he offers is a survey by a personified figure of 'observation' rather than by the man Johnson, whose individual perception, like everyone else's, he believed, was necessarily flawed:

> Let observation with extensive view
> Survey mankind, from China to Peru.

We should note that 'observation' is also an empirical word, implying a careful survey of the evidence. The impression he wishes to create is that he has explored human life in all its fullness and canvassed all the options. The generalizations he finally produces, he suggests, are drawn empirically from a wealth of experience and individual particulars, not super-imposed dogmatically:

> *Remark* each anxious toil, each eager strife,
> And *watch* the busy scenes of crowded life,
> *Then* say, how hope and fear, desire and hate
> O'erspread with snares the clouded maze of fate.
> . . .
>
> Such was the scorn that fill'd the sage's mind,
> Renew'd at every glance on human kind;
> How just that scorn ere yet thy voice declare,
> *Search* every state, and *canvass* ev'ry prayer.
>
> (ll. 3–6, 69–72; my italics)

What results is one of the greatest pictures in all literature of the deceitfulness and irrationality of the human mind. Traditionally throughout the centuries the 'vanity of human wishes' theme had been associated with the fall of great men or the calamitous changes of fortune that make reliance on worldly goods a mistake. Johnson has infused the ancient truths with his own compassion and psychological insight. He has *internalized* the whole theme, demonstrating that his protagonists bring about their own fates through the psychological self-destructiveness of their foolish desires and ambitions.

Johnson as moral psychologist

Ideas such as the 'vanity of human wishes' are not likely to have an immediate appeal for most modern readers. But Johnson rarely preaches at people. As his more inward approach to the theme suggests, he is not a prescriptive moralist, but a subtly analytic one, who studies the very roots of human motivation. He understands very clearly that something like a new science of human nature began in the seventeenth century, especially with Hobbes's work on motivation. Before Shakespeare's death, he explains,

> Speculation had not yet attempted to analyze the mind, to trace the passions to their sources, to unfold the seminal principles of vice and virtue, or sound the depths of the heart for the motives of action. All those enquiries, which

from that time that human nature became the fashionable study, have been made sometimes with nice discernment, but often with idle subtlety, were yet unattempted.

(Preface to Shakespeare, Yale edn, VII, 88)

At the very heart of Johnson's work is his own achievement as a moral psychologist, an achievement all the greater for the fact that it is enacted in the thesis and antithesis of the essays, in powerful literary language, in fictional structures that engage our imaginations (in the more positive sense) and appeal to the different parts of our complex psyches. Both in *The Vanity of Human Wishes* and in his other moral writings, the periodical essays in particular, he puts the best of the new psychology of his time at the service of traditional moral discourse, and sharpens both by all his mastery of rhetoric. Combining ancient wisdom and the Christian tradition of the examination of conscience with modern empirical psychology and his own enormous courage and honesty in facing the truth about himself, Johnson immensely deepens the traditional view of man as a blind self-deceiving creature. He follows the traditional humanist injunction of the necessity for self-knowledge, but he also recognizes how extremely difficult it is in practice to attain:

> as very few can search deep into their own minds without meeting what they wish to hide from themselves, scarcely any man persists in cultivating such disagreeable acquaintance, but draws the veil again between his eyes and his heart, leaves his passions and appetites as he found them, and advises others to look into themselves.
>
> *(Idler* 27)

What would really help us would be 'a taper, by which we are lighted through the labyrinth of complicated passions . . .' (*Rambler* 77). Accordingly, he sets out to analyse all the elaborate arts by which we seek to deceive not only others but ourselves, all the defences by which we try to protect our threatened egos. We tell ourselves, for example, that a single good act proves our virtue, or mistake our ready praise of morality for its practice (*Rambler* 28). Johnson understands not only our great expertise at 'the voluntary exclusion of unwelcome thoughts' (*Idler* 103) but also, it seems, the unconscious techniques that may sometimes be involved. Friendship is often poisoned, for example, he says, by 'a thousand secret and slight competitions, scarce known to the mind upon which they operate' (*Idler* 23) and there is not so much actual hypocrisy in the world as might be thought, because 'we do not so often endeavour or wish to impose upon others as on ourselves . . .' (*Idler* 27).

These are insights that have led Johnson to be claimed as an ancestor of Freudian views on unconscious repression and psychological defence mechanisms. Despite the apparent pessimism, as so often in Johnson, the ultimate effect is certainly not discouraging. It is the very recognition of the difficulty of the task that makes Johnson so challenging and even invigorating to the reader.

The ambivalence of hope

A further qualification to Johnson's pessimism and at the same time a further mark of his subtlety as a moral philosopher and psychologist is the humane ambivalence towards hope and even the imagination itself that sometimes comes to the fore. For all his commitment to reason, his view of our restless, desiring natures actually sounds like Hobbes at times. He writes, for example, that

> the gratification of one desire encourages another: and after all our labours, studies and enquiries, we are continually at the same distance from the completion of our schemes, have still some wish importunate to be satisfied, and some faculty restless and turbulent for want of its enjoyment.
>
> (*Rambler* 103)

Imagination, linked with hope in Johnson's thought, is the agent of this fundamental restlessness of our minds that prevents us from living in the present. It constantly deceives us, tying our hopes to specific temporal objects when we are not in possession of them, but turning away from them in dissatisfaction as soon as we do: 'The mind of man is never satisfied with the objects immediately before it, but is always breaking away from the present moment, and losing itself in schemes of future felicity' (*Rambler* 2). The ultimate solution for us is to come to recognize that there is only one truly 'rational' hope, only one 'of which we are certain that it cannot deceive us' (*Rambler* 203) and that is the hope of heaven, 'the reasonable hope of a happy futurity' (*Letters*, 3 July 1778).

As this implies, though, and as the end of *The Vanity of Human Wishes* especially reinforces, Johnson is no stoic:

> Where then shall Hope and Fear their objects find?
> Must dull Suspence corrupt the stagnant mind?
> Must helpless man, in ignorance sedate,
> Roll darkling down the torrent of his fate?

Must no dislike alarm, no wishes rise,
No cries attempt the mercies of the skies?
Enquirer, cease, petitions yet remain,
Which heav'n may hear . . .   (ll. 343–50)

We must still expect to 'hope and fear' rather than quashing these emotions as his classical source implies we should, but we have to transmute and convert them by turning them to their proper, eternal objects.

For 'hope and fear' are natural to our fallen human state, inevitable even. They are not simply things to be got rid of. The radical 'insufficiency of human enjoyments' is a general experience. We are so constituted that we *cannot* find security and satisfaction in the present, and precisely because we are not in heaven, we can never succeed in eradicating the imagination's tendency to envisage something better than we yet have. If this restless 'hunger of imagination' 'preys on life' and helps to prevent us being happy here, it is also in itself a remarkable sign that we are made for greater things, a *divine* discontent. Rasselas in the Happy Valley wonders why all other creatures are happy there but human beings are not, and he comes to the conclusion that we have some latent sense that will never be satisfied by the present, the senses and this world.

It is *Rasselas* perhaps that shows Johnson's thought in its fullest subtlety, realism and originality. In describing the mis-guided search for definitive happiness on earth, the 'choice of life', it canvasses all the apparent options to no avail, as we might expect. When the Princess comes to recognize that it is not the 'choice of life' that is important but 'the choice of eternity', she is meant to speak for us all. But Johnson, with characteristic realism, does not leave it there. What really differentiates him from most of his predecessors in similar traditions is that he understands that we cannot and should not expect to eliminate even secular, temporal hopes and fears in this life, misguided though they often are. In the remarkable 'Conclusion, in Which Nothing Is Concluded' he allows his characters to keep their innocent hopes for happiness on earth as well as in eternity, but shows their recognition at the same time that their desires are unlikely to be obtained. The acceptance of eternity *relativizes* our earthly hopes: stops us from eating our hearts out in the futile search for a perfect and permanent happiness that can never be ours on earth. In this sense it makes us more content with our lot as well as offering the genuine hope of something better. But the human hope of happiness – even earthly happiness –

is so 'strongly impressed', as another character puts it, that it is impossible to quash it. We shall never achieve such happiness in any definitive sense here, but provided we do not over-invest in our hopes and let them carry us away then they will help to keep us busy and active and even happy in a characteristically unstable way. 'Do not suffer like to stagnate,' says Imlac, 'it will grow muddy for want of motion.'

The point is made very clearly in a brilliant letter worth quoting in full. Johnson has been on a trip to visit one of his oldest friends, the farmer vicar Dr John Taylor, who combined his ambitions for church preferment with – in this instance at least – remarkably unsuccessful attempts to breed horses. The letter, addressed to Mrs Thrale's eldest daughter, begins with Johnson's characteristic honesty, realism and courage, and soon moves into a light-hearted and affectionate version of the 'Vanity-of-Human-Wishes' motif as it concerns Taylor. Yet this itself modulates towards the close into a different, more optimistic, if still very clear-sighted emphasis:

My dearest Love:

The day after tomorrow will carry me back to Lichfield, whence I purpose to find the way to London with all convenient speed. I have had a poor, sickly, comfortless journey, much gloom and little sunshine. But I hope to find you gay, and easy, and kind, and I will endeavour to copy you, for what can come of discontent and dolour? Let us keep ourselves easy and do what good we can to one another.

Dr Taylor says that he has a bigger Bull than he ever had, and the cow which he sold for an hundred and twenty guineas, has brought the purchaser a calf for which he asks a hundred pounds. The Dr has been unsuccessful in breeding horses, for he has had sixteen fillies without one colt, an accident beyond all computation of chances. Such is the uncertainty of life. He is, I believe, yet in hopes of the deanery.

> Thus on we sigh on from day to day
> And wish and wish the soul away.

He is however, happier than if he had no desire. To be without hope or fear, if it were possible would not be happiness: it is better that life should struggle with obstructions, than stagnate and putrefy. Never be without something to wish and something to do.

(28 November 1781)

Johnson's work creates a tough-minded synthesis of old and new, pessimism and optimism. He reaffirms ancient wisdom and moral absolutes against what seems to him a dangerous new complacency, subjectivity and relativism, but he makes use of the new psychology in so doing. He is thus able to mediate between a traditional moral discourse and the new empiricism, and this gives his work enormous centrality and authority in the new circumstances. He offers genuine hope to his readers, but one that seems to come out of a profound realism, and he never underestimates the difficulty of the human task.

3 Religion

It will have already become clear that Johnson's orthodox Christianity, his conviction of the reality of the fall of man and his belief in an afterlife are very important to his whole moral system. A full and sympathetic understanding of his work certainly requires some grasp of the religious beliefs that lie behind it. At the same time it is essential to recognize that Christian concepts have little *direct* presence in most of Johnson's work. He is a moralist not a devotional writer or theologian, and his wisdom and realism have always been just as readily appreciated by those who do not share his faith as by those who do.

It is easy to portray Johnson's religion melodramatically and to see him simply as the prey to neurotic guilts, fears and melancholy. Certainly, as noted earlier, his faith naturally enough entangled itself with his anxious and obsessive temperament, but it was also at the same time a source of hope, order and transcendence of that temperament to him, part of the strenuous process away from subjectivity that is at the heart of his moral achievement and his moral system. It was far from eccentric to take the Christian religion seriously in eighteenth-century England, and it is useful, therefore, to set Johnson's own commitment in the context of his time.

The historical background

In France and in other continental countries, as we have seen, the power of the Roman Catholic Church and its control over education often led supporters of the Enlightenment towards anti-clericalism and a deliberate rejection of traditional Christianity. Voltaire, for example, was a vocal enemy of the Church. In England the situation was very different, in part because of the influence of the British scientists themselves and in part because of a complex sequence of historical events in which religion had played a central role.

The sun-centred universe proposed by sixteenth- and seventeenth-century astronomy was clearly a threat to a completely literal reading of the Bible. The impressive achievements of this new science as a whole seemed to take nature from the *direct* hand of God, making it less mysterious and giving human beings a greater control over their own destiny. The consequence, though, at least in England, was not so much the increase of scepticism as reinterpretation and the encouragement of *rational* religion. Newton's theories in particular gave a great boost to the traditional arguments for the existence of God from the design of the created universe, and there was a whole school of Christian apologists known as the 'Physico-theologians', much admired and quoted by Johnson, who devoted themselves to making such links.

England had its own traumatic religious war in the seventeenth-century conflict between the radical Protestant Puritans and the High-Church court, supporters of the necessity for bishops and ritual, and seen as close to Roman Catholicism by their opponents. The Civil War was followed by the republican rule of Cromwell, and this was a time which Johnson, like other traditionalist supporters of the Church of England throughout the next century, always regarded with horror as an example of the link between an excess of individualistic religious freedom and disorder in the state. He writes that it is 'scarcely possible'

> to imagine the tumult of absurdity and clamour of contra-diction which perplexed doctrine, disordered practice, and disturbed both public and private quiet in that age, when subordination was broken, and awe was hissed away; when any unsettled innovator who could hatch a half-formed notion produced it to the publick; when every man might become a preacher, and almost every preacher could collect a congregation.
>
> ('Life of Butler', I, 214–5)

The bishops and the Church of England were re-established at the Restoration of Charles II in 1660. In 1662 Parliament reimposed the Anglican Book of Common Prayer on all churches and in 1664 declared other religious meetings illegal. Thousands of clergymen sympathetic to Puritanism resigned their livings and the prisons were filled with Protestant 'dissenters' who refused to obey the new laws.

After Charles II's Catholic brother, James, was forced off the throne in the bloodless revolution of 1688 and replaced by his own Protestant daughter Mary and her Dutch husband William of Orange, a fuller religious accommodation became possible. Some scrupulous High Anglican bishops and clergy refused to take the oath of allegiance to the new monarchs because of their previous oaths to James. Johnson admired these 'non-jurors', who continued as a small minority tradition through the next century. Much more significant, however, for the future of England was the improved position and greater toleration of dissenters under a new king who was himself a Lutheran. Despite the tensions that remained the consequence was a limited but in its own way genuine religious pluralism for the country.

A reaction against fanaticism and zeal had naturally enough followed the Restoration, and the 1688 Revolution increased the tendency to stress the very basic beliefs that united Protestants rather than more divisive specific doctrines and the inner light of individual inspiration. The influence and prestige of Newtonian science worked in similar directions, since the focus was on God the great designer of nature rather than as the God of biblical revelation as such.

In the last decades of the seventeenth century and the earlier part of the new period, a handful of free-thinking intellectuals, the so-called 'deists', took such liberalism to the extreme of denying the need for revelation at all. Sometimes there was an overlap between such thinking and a fashionable aristocratic scepticism and libertinism, as in the case of the Tory politician Lord Bolingbroke, a friend of Pope. (Johnson amusingly illustrated *irony* in the *Dictionary* by the example 'Bolingbroke is an holy man'.) But Pope's own *Essay on Man*, though influenced by Bolingbroke and not concerned with revelation as such, presents itself, or tries to present itself, as quite compatible with Christianity. In general the number of deists and free-thinkers remains small and their influence is much exaggerated in conventional accounts of the period. Bishop Butler produced a powerful rebuttal in his *Analogy* (1736), where he showed that arguments from nature were just as much a matter of 'faith' as arguments from revelation.

The main point was that there was no need for the widespread sense of enlightenment and progress in eighteenth-century Britain to lead to hostility to traditional religion as it did on the continent. Though there were then, as now, several major parties within the Church of England, neither the Low-Church nor the High-Church groupings had reached anything like the full-grown form that they would attain in the nineteenth century, and the Church as a whole had come to promulgate a rational religion of decent conduct and fairly broad doctrine, orthodox enough in its own terms, but none too specific or detailed.

Mainstream Anglicanism of this kind is very easy to criticize, but it would be quite wrong to suggest that the period as a whole was one of laxity and worldliness. Lancelot Blackburne, the notorious Archbishop of York, never performed a single confirmation in his diocese, but at the opposite extreme we find the tireless labours of Thomas Wilson, Bishop of Sodor and Man. Historians of religion in recent years have felt more inclined to stress the very genuine piety and learning within the ranks of the eighteenth-century Church, and Johnson's personal dedication as a layman has its own story to tell.

By the latter half of the century the deist threat as such had completely receded, but intellectual opponents of Christianity of much greater stature had emerged in the Scots philosopher David Hume and the great historian Edward Gibbon. The latter seemed to imply in his major work that Christianity was responsible for the decline of the Roman Empire. Hume was especially notorious for his sceptical *Essay on Miracles* (in *Philosophical Essays concerning the Human Understanding*, 1748), an attack on the idea of believing in testimony. Many attempts were made to refute Hume, and Johnson himself comments revealingly that all Hume's objections to Christian miracles had already occurred to him before he read the philosopher. In fact though, the infamy which Hume brought upon his own head seems to confirm the view that the influence of such thinking was relatively small in eighteenth-century Britain. Johnson inveighs at times, like all moralists, on the 'licentiousness and levity' (*Rambler* 208) of the age. There is no doubt that he felt himself a deliberate public apologist for Christianity, like G.K. Chesterton and C.S. Lewis this century, and there would have been no need for such a function in an earlier period. At the same time he often says that there is very little real 'infidelity' about (*Life*, II, 359).

At the opposite extreme to Hume and Gibbon as a reaction to mainstream eighteenth-century orthodoxy was 'Methodism', the religious revival led by the Wesley brothers. This reassertion of the necessity of 'born-again' 'enthusiastic' Christianity always had its greatest successes among the poor and it was forced later to separate itself from the national Church, against the intentions of its founders. In a famous phrase that captures all the continued conservative fear of religious 'enthusiasm' Bishop Butler said to John Wesley that it was 'a very horrid thing' to lay claim to the individual inspiration of the Holy Spirit. Johnson had respect for John Wesley, but also shares the common tendency to speak disparagingly at times of 'Methodists' and 'Methodism'.

Johnson's Anglicanism

The intense personal sincerity of Johnson's religion is apparent in the accounts of his life and in his own marvellous *Prayers and Meditations*:

> Almighty God, heavenly Father, who desirest not the death of a sinner, look down with mercy upon me depraved with vain imaginations, and entangled in long habits of Sin. Grant me that grace without which I can neither will nor do what is acceptable to thee. Pardon my sins, remove the impediments that hinder my obedience. Enable me to shake off Sloth, and to redeem the time mispent in idleness and Sin by a diligent application of the days yet remaining to the duties which thy Providence shall allot me. O God grant me thy Holy Spirit that I may repent and amend my life, grant me contrition, grant me resolution for the sake of Jesus Christ, to whose covenant I now implore admission, of the benefits of whose death I implore participation; for his sake have mercy on me O God; for his sake, O God, pardon and receive me. Amen.
>
> (Easter Eve 1757)

His urgent sense of death and judgement has an earlier, seventeenth-century tone to it, and his strong emphasis on human imperfection, the fall and the need for salvation has quite properly been called Augustinian (after the theology of St Augustine of Hippo [354–430]) and may even seem close to that of the more extreme Protestants:

> With respect to original sin, the enquiry is not necessary; for whatever is the cause of human corruption, men are evidently and confessedly so corrupt, that all the laws of heaven and earth are insufficient to restrain them from crimes.
>
> (*Life*, IV, 123–4)

Yet we should note that what we see here, as in Cardinal Newman's famous passage on the signs of a great 'aboriginal calamity' in the human race, is an empirical appeal to the evidence of human behaviour rather than a doctrinal assertion of total depravity. Johnson does not deny reason and our capacity for virtue as radical Calvinists might. The pessimism of such passages works to heighten awareness of the need for rigorous discipline and self-examination, but they are intended to urge us in those directions rather than to imply their complete impossibility without grace.

If anything Johnson's form of personal piety and especially his strong devotion to the institution of the Church seems more likely to have come from a High-Church tradition than an Evangelical one, and there has been interesting further evidence recently of such sympathies in his revisions for the fourth edition of the *Dictionary*. But his religious thinking as a whole reflects the rational Anglican tradition of the time, itself, it is important to repeat, perfectly compatible both with Christian orthodoxy and strong personal devotion. In the first Vinerian lecture there is the significant statement that 'the will of God cannot be known but by revelation or the light of reason'. Johnson refers elsewhere to 'the great and unchangeable rules of revelation and reason' (*Sermon* XIV, Par. 30). In specific contexts, as in his passionate prayer above, Johnson stresses our need for grace and the impossibility of the kind of self-control the Stoics preached, but his published writings by and large imply, it has been said:

> that the Christian revelation was given not to annihilate pagan morality but to complete it by adding to it the doctrine of immortality and of future rewards and punishments. These doctrines gave ultimate sanction to morality, but they did not destroy its rational foundations . . . .
> (Jean H. Hagstrum, *Samuel Johnson's Literary Criticism*, 1952, p. 69)

Johnson admires and is greatly influenced by Richard Hooker, the Elizabethan spokesman for the 'middle way' of Anglicanism against the Puritans and himself the most famous advocate of the role of reason as well as pure revelation. (It is worth noting that Hooker also advocates tradition, a high-church emphasis.) Recent scholarship has shown that many of the specifics of Johnson's thinking also derive from the Anglican theology and controversy of the Restoration and the eighteenth century, in which he was very widely read. Such theologians, influenced by Locke, often re-interpret 'reason' in more pragmatic ways than Hooker and they are more prudential in their attitudes to morality. Johnson seems to reflect the same tendencies. Like Bishop Butler, the most central Anglican moral theologian of the period, whose work has already been discussed, he is not afraid, for example, to appeal to self-interest and self-love and to the idea of reward and punishment in the afterlife in his arguments for Christianity.

Though he has a personal interest in the technicalities of theology and doctrine, Johnson essentially espouses a Christianity of broad basic beliefs. He has great respect for some Protestant divines who are not of his communion, and is even prepared to speak sympathetically at times of Roman

Catholic doctrines. But he has a staunch, Tory devotion to the temporal interests of the Church of England, and he always argues firmly for the importance of the national Church as a source of order in the state. He springs to the defence of that Church when he feels its privileges are under threat, and in this respect he is adamant that dissenters must not be allowed any more freedom than they already possess.

For Johnson the whole secret of happiness, peace and order lies in religion. His Christian fervour and his sense of the fall deepen his perspective on every subject on which he speaks and writes, and his belief in an afterlife also obviously has crucial implications. Yet his real and central concern is always very evidently with how we should live *now*, and it is this urgency that has kept his work relevant for believers and non-believers alike.

4 Politics

The birth of 'modern' Britain

The great events of the seventeenth-century Civil War, the execution of Charles I and the republican rule of Cromwell, were to continue to reverberate for a long time to come. As noted before, the Restoration of Charles II by no means solved all the problems of the years of conflict, and questions of religion and the power of the crown continued to dominate events. In the Exclusion Bill crisis of 1679–80 the attempt was made to prevent the future king James II from inheriting the throne. Later James's zealous efforts on behalf of Catholicism led to his exile and replacement by his Protestant daughter Mary and her Dutch consort William. The so-called 'Jacobites' (after the Latin *Jacobus*, James), however, continued to support the claims of James's Catholic son, James Edward, the 'Old Pretender'.

William and Mary were followed in turn on the throne by Anne, younger daughter of James II and a Protestant like her sister, but she had no male heir, and there was renewed controversy about what to do at her death. In the event, religion dictated the choice again, and George I of Hanover, a Lutheran, was chosen king in 1714, despite the fact that there were others with a closer claim to the throne. The Jacobite threat did not simply go away, however. In 1715 there was a serious Jacobite invasion and another in 1745, led this time by the famous and glamorous 'Young Pretender', Bonnie Prince Charlie.

Yet the departure of James II in 1688, the so-called 'Glorious Revolution', heralded a more recognizably modern political system for Britain. It was unmistakably affirmed in the Revolution Settlement that power was to lie with the monarch *in parliament*. This is the famous British 'balanced constitution', the envy of continental liberals: a system in which there is a separation between the power than makes laws and the executive power and in which no one element is supposed to predominate.

Thomas Hobbes in the seventeenth century, reflecting the earlier fear of anarchy and civil war, had proposed as the only solution to political conflict submission to an absolute power, a *Leviathan*. But it was the thought of his Whig antagonist Locke that had carried the day. Although Locke was not writing with the 1688 Revolution in mind, his *Two Treatises of Government* were soon taken as providing its theoretical justification and the underpinning of the settlement. Locke's explanation of the origins of government in a social contract entered upon for the defence of property and his praise for the mixed constitution set the terms for all the significant political discussion of the next century. As a modern commentator says, 'Locke's reasonable arguments that the subject is the source of political power, that the laws should protect his interests and that society is a rational, humane thing were the perfect corollary to 1688 and blew like a refreshing wind at home and abroad' (A.R. Humphreys, *The Augustan World,* 1964, p. 102).

Parliament itself, of course, was elected at this time not by universal suffrage but by owners of property above a certain level. There is no doubt, though, that the period saw a genuine expansion of the political nation, a much greater involvement in the political process by a wider section of the community. Propaganda and polemic in the civil wars had given a great boost to print, and newspapers and periodicals flourished. The English began to be famous throughout Europe as a nation fascinated by politics, and debate was fostered by the popular new institution of the coffee-house as well as by the press. The widening of political awareness and involvement was to continue steadily throughout the next century, and in the eyes of some historians it is the most significant political development of the whole period.

The new party politics reflects both the continuation of the old conflicts and this expansion of the political élite. It was a direct legacy of the polarization in the Exclusion Bill crisis of 1679–80 in which the so-called 'Tories' were those who supported Charles and James, the 'Whigs' were those who supported the exclusion. 'Party' conflict continues in the eighteenth century, but it is much clearer and more intense in some decades of the century than in others and the two sides must not be thought of as identical to modern party labels or to a modern system of government and opposition. As J.A. Sharpe explains, eighteenth-century political 'parties' were

> not as coherent or disciplined as their modern equivalents. Both 'Whig' and 'Tory' comprehended different groupings and alliances, and these tended to shift their positions or alter their alignments in response to various stimuli, whether over political principle or personal faction politics.
>
> (*Early Modern England,* Edward Arnold, 1987, p. 339)

A London coffee-house, c. 1705

The Tories were associated with loyalty to the institutional Church of England and many of them had Jacobite sympathies. As the latter point might suggest, they were more of an anti-establishment interest group, however, than a political party in any full sense. Different Whig factions were in office for most of the century, and other Whig factions always formed the most effective oppositions to the government too. Yet the whole conceptualization in terms of 'Tory' and 'Whig' is significant in itself, and goes deep in the period.

Prospects for stability and the containment of the Jacobite threat were increased when Britain became 'Great Britain' with the Act of Union between England and Scotland in 1707. The last supposedly 'Tory' administration for many decades collapsed with the death of Queen Anne in 1714 and her replacement by the Hanoverian George I. Securing the Hanoverian dynasty was at the heart of the strategy of Sir Robert Walpole, who had power equivalent to a modern Prime Minister as First Lord of the Treasury for twenty-one years from 1721. His peaceful foreign policy consolidated national prosperity and stability, though his clever manipulation of patronage led to charges of corruption from a furious opposition that included such great writers as Swift and Pope.

It was popular clamour for a trade war with Spain that finally brought Walpole down in 1742. To the great disappointment of the opposition little was to change and the Walpole tradition was continued for more than a decade by Henry Pelham and his brother the Duke of Newcastle. But as D.J. Greene says, the struggle between isolationism, 'the desire for self-sufficiency and the stability that goes with it' and the attractions of world power and a great empire is to be the central theme of British history for several centuries. That struggle reached its real climax in the mid-eighteenth century. Disputes about territory in North America finally set off a great war for empire between Great Britain and France, the Seven Years War of 1755–63.

Defeats and mismanagement in the early stages of the war led to the collapse of the government. Against the wishes of George II, William Pitt the elder (later to become the Earl of Chatham), a keen expansionist and imperialist who had long campaigned for such a war, became Prime Minister. Under his administration the war effort was successfully renewed and hostilities conducted with great brilliance. Both India and Canada were gained for the Empire, and despite the enormous setbacks that were to follow the cause of imperial expansion had become unstoppable.

The new reign of George III, which began in 1760, seemed

at first to promise much. The King was young, idealistic and conscientious and, unlike his grandfather and great-grandfather George I and George II, proud to consider himself British. Carefully formed in his political opinions by his tutor Lord Bute, he was committed to the idea of a non-partisan, generous-spirited government, and for much of his reign he had the support of the public at large. The bewildering alliances and changes of government for the first ten years indicated the difficulty of the task, however, and George's more extreme political opponents were successful for a time in creating the impression that the King was actually trying to overthrow the constitution.

A major focal point for opposition was the turbulent career of John Wilkes, a charismatic opportunist who was barred from the House of Commons for writing virulent polemic against the King and an obscene parody of Pope's *Essay on Man*. He was nevertheless re-elected three times by an indignant electorate, only to be excluded again on each occasion. The affair caused enormous outcry, and not only among middle-class radicals. There were popular riots on behalf of 'Wilkes and liberty' and genuine fears for public order resulted.

Rumblings had meanwhile been going on for some time in the thirteen American colonies against British taxation. After inept handling of the controversy from the British side, this broke out into open war with the Declaration of Independence of 1776. A series of reverses and the entry of other European powers into the war eventually brought about the resignation of Lord North, Prime Minister throughout most of this disastrous period. In 1783 the British government bowed to the inevitable and accepted American secession.

Johnson's political writings

The three main phases of Johnson's career as a writer on politics coincide neatly with the three main phases of eighteenth-century political history with which the student needs to be familiar: the administration of Walpole, the Seven Years War with France, and the reign of George III with its twin problems of domestic disaffection and the struggle for American Independence. It is fascinating to trace Johnson's own tough-minded responses to these great events. He first came to London at a time when popular opposition to the 'corruptions' of Walpole were at their height and the balance of the constitution was held to be at threat through the power of the 'First Minister'. Almost every major writer was attacking him specifically or in general. Richard Savage, whom Johnson soon befriended, was by now violently anti-Walpole, and it was natural for Johnson to be drawn into this current of opinion. In two early political pamphlets in 1739, *Marmor Norfolciense* and *A Compleat Vindication of the Licensers of the Stage*, he adopts a conventional Swiftian combination of irony and righteous indignation. In *London*, too, there is the same perspective, though its more valuable and characteristically Johnsonian core does not depend on any purely topical approach to corruption and injustice.

The next phase is one of more specific involvement as a political journalist through Johnson's appointment as editor of the *Literary Magazine*. He appeals unequivocally to the new public opinion, which is in a sense the base on which his very profession depends, and announces in the resounding first sentence of 'Observation on the Present State of Affairs' (1756) that 'The time is now come in which every Englishman expects to be informed of the national affairs, and in which he has a right to have that expectation gratified'. Despite his own earlier opposition to Walpole he is highly suspicious of Pitt and the arguments for imperialist expansion. Although he reluctantly concedes the necessity by now of a war to defend British interests, he speaks of it in an extremely dispassionate way and with a bald realism about the realities of colonialism and commercial power:

> The general subject of the present war is sufficiently known. It is allowed on both sides, that hostilities began in America, and that the French and English quarrelled about the boundaries of their settlements, about grounds and rivers to which, I am afraid, neither can show any other right than that of power, and which neither can occupy but by usurpation, and the dispossession of the natural lords and original inhabitants. Such is the contest that no honest man can heartily wish success to either party.
>
> ('Observations on the Present State of Affairs', X, 186)

Johnson's later pamphlets in broad support of the ministry at a time of crisis during the reign of George III have remained his best-known works on political topics. Though his pension was not for political services, he was bound to feel grateful for it, and he supported many of the King's aims. He was also influenced in these late pamphlets by his friendship with Henry Thrale, and *The Patriot* (1774), which ironically castigates the opposition's claim to the title, is specifically connected with the latter's campaign for election to parliament that year. *Thoughts on the Late Transactions Respecting Falkland's Islands* (1771) concerns the very technical details of a dispute that time made relevant again to recent history, but as usual in Johnson the rigorous detail is combined with elevated moral generalization. There are eloquent paragraphs on the horrors of war and his imagination catches fire as always at the thought of humanity's noble capacity for struggling with difficulties:

> There is nothing which human courage will not undertake, and little that human patience will not endure. The garrison lived upon Falkland's Island, shrinking from the blast, and shuddering at the billows.
>
> (X, 358)

The most notorious of the pamphlets, both at the time and in terms of Johnson's later reputation, are the two that confront the central issues of the period, the Wilkes controversy and the conflict over American independence. He wrote *The False Alarm* (1770) in support of the House of Commons's right as the representatives of the whole electorate to overrule the wishes of one particular constituency and exclude Wilkes. His sincere belief in popular sovereignty in parliament is clearly combined with a determination that the popular voice should not hold sway *outside* parliament, and this overlaps with a characteristic eighteenth-century fear of the mob.

Taxation No Tyranny responds to the American claims with similar arguments about the sovereignty of the British parliament, even over those who are not directly represented in it. As in the Wilkes pamphlet Johnson seeks to portray the apparent appeal for 'liberty' as a 'false alarm', a piece of hypocrisy and propaganda or at best paranoia. 'How is it', he asks in a famously deflating rhetorical question, 'that we hear the loudest yelps for liberty among the drivers of negroes?'

It is these late pamphlets combined with a series of picturesque anecdotes that have created the picture of Johnson the old reactionary Tory. Recent scholarship, beginning with D.J. Greene's major study *The Politics of Samuel Johnson*, has produced a much more complex picture. In reaction against previous over-simplifications Greene has an understandable tendency to maximize Johnson's radicalism. The truth is that Johnson's ideas often *are* quite traditional, but in their context they also become a weapon against what he presents as a privileged Whig Establishment. The contemporary reader would certainly be well advised to forget most of the modern associations of the word 'Tory' and even, as we have noted, the idea of an organized party in the modern sense at all.

One defining characteristic of the Tory interest in the eighteenth century is a firm loyalty to the Church of England and a desire to reaffirm its major role in the state. Here, as we have seen, Johnson eminently qualifies. The question of Jacobitism is much more complicated, both because the degree of Tory identification with Jacobitism is itself a controversial issue for modern historians and because Johnson's own personal attitudes remain uncertain. Sympathy for the exiled House of Stuart could exist in varying degrees of intensity and commitment and was likely to be concealed anyway by its very nature as a subversive creed. Boswell, as a Scot, was inclined to make much of the subject, but his own more dispassionate summary is that Johnson 'no doubt had an early attachment to the House of Stuart; but his zeal cooled as his reason strengthened'. What weight we attach to that 'no doubt' is the question. It is worth noting that D.J. Greene has reasserted recently that 'There is no evidence that Johnson was ever a Jacobite' (*The Politics of Samuel Johnson* 2nd edn. 1990, p. XXXVII). But if Johnson did have such sympathies they probably amounted to no more than a certain traditionalist nostalgia and another means of expressing dissatisfaction with a new, centralized Establishment.

One of Johnson's most endearing and enduring traits was his love of the poor. Bewilderingly to the modern reader he presents this too as a 'Tory' emphasis. Because we are fallen, corrupt, vulnerable creatures we need social order and authorities over us to respect and obey, but the corollary to this is that 'each particular relation gives rise to a particular scheme of duties' (Sermon 1), and the rich and the strong have the clear responsibility of caring for those below them on the social scale.

The kind of 'subordination' that this implies may sound suspiciously like a feudal system. Elsewhere, though, Johnson says firmly that he approves of the potential for social mobility in a commercial society. It is simply, he believes, that a system of 'subordination' is the best realistic chance that the majority of people, especially the poor, have of achieving a limited degree of social justice. When he was informed that the radical, Mrs Macaulay, wondered how he 'could reconcile his political principles with his moral; his notions of inequality and subordination with wishing well to the happiness of mankind', he replied: 'Why Sir, I reconcile my principles very well, because mankind are happier in a state of inequality and subordination' (*Life*, II, 219).

The point is that the cure for human evils is 'not radical but palliative'. Utopian attempts to bring about perfect peace and justice on earth can never succeed. 'I perceive, Sir,' said Boswell, 'that you laugh at most schemes of political improvement.' 'Sir,' replied Johnson, 'most schemes of political improvement are very laughable things' (*Life*, II, 102). We should strive to limit evil and injustice as best we can, but we cannot expect to remove them completely from this fallen world. 'All institutions are defective by their very nature' (*Sermon* XXIV), and what governments and political activity can actually achieve is very limited: 'How small of all that human hearts endure/That part which laws or kings can cause or cure.' (Lines written by Johnson for Goldsmith's poem, *The Traveller*.)

We also have to remember Johnson's genuine identification with the underdog. He came to London as a poor provincial himself, and Toryism, itself the party of the 'outs' and the underdogs at this time, was the natural vehicle for these sentiments. It is very much an *oppositional* creed against the status quo that finds expression in the pamphlets against Walpole and again in the suspicion of centralization and imperialism in the Seven Years War. Only in the last phase of his career can Johnson by any stretch of the imagination be said to be writing as a pro-Establishment figure. Even then he obviously likes to think of himself as fighting something of a rearguard action against a growing liberal consensus.

It would be unrealistic, perhaps, to expect total consistency in such a long career of political writing. But Johnson has obviously managed to convince himself that some of his earlier aspirations can best be fulfilled now by support for George III. We need to understand also that these late pamphlets do not involve a rejection of the balanced constitution and the significant, if limited, widening of the political base of the nation, but a feeling that the balance has now shifted too much towards the people – both in terms of the self-consciously 'popular' voice in parliament and, even worse, through the *extra*-parliamentary agitation of what Johnson regards as 'the mob'.

If Johnson's politics are far subtler than the stereotype would suggest this does not mean, of course, as J.P. Hardy points out, that we can see him as a 'political ancestor of those who agitated for the Reform Bill of 1832' or as a modern democrat (Introduction, *The Political Writings of Dr Johnson: A Selection*, 1968). Although there are parts of Johnson's political theories that may make a very real appeal today (and not only on the right), he is a man very much bound by his time.

Yet his political pamphlets will continue to be read for their robust mixture of topical detail and elevated generalization, their very characteristic combination of a hard-headed sense of the realities of power with a strenuous refusal to allow the political realm to escape moral judgement.

5 Commerce

Johnson's personal search for moral truth and stability and his desire to speak with moral authority in his work is obviously related to the needs of a time when various traditional social and political norms were called into question. The period of 'transformation' that Johnson lived through, was, in the words of a recent historian Paul Langford, 'social, cultural, religious, economic' as well as political. For several centuries urbanization and the growth of capitalism and commerce had been altering the social order of Europe. Though British political life saw no traumatic structural change in the period, the whole ethos of politics did alter, and, as has been increasingly recognized by modern scholars, Britain was in the forefront of commercial transformation in particular. Johnson himself writes in the preface to Richard Rolt's *Dictionary of Trade and Commerce* (1756): 'It may be properly observed that there was never, from the earliest ages, a time in which trade so much engaged the attention of mankind, or commercial gain was sought with such general emulation.' We still live in the type of society that first established itself in Johnson's period, and his thoughtful response to it has lost none of its relevance.

The Age of Commerce

The politicization of a wider section of the community described in the preceding sections went together with and was in part a consequence of this steady process of commercialization. The wars that William of Orange brought England into with Louis XIV of France necessitated the raising of large amounts of credit to pay for them. New organs for investment were required, and the Bank of England was founded in 1694. What amounted to a 'financial revolution' occurred, and the effects of this combined with an increase in foreign trade. Signs of a consumer boom began to appear as prosperity spread. Early in the next century Joseph Addison, editor of the most central and representative periodical the *Spectator*, comments wonderingly:

> Our rooms are filled with pyramids of China, and adorned with the workmanship of Japan. Our morning's draught comes to us from the remotest corners of the earth. We

repair our bodies by the drugs of America, and repose ourselves under Indian canopies. My friend Sir Andrew calls the vineyards of France our gardens; the Spice-Islands our hot-beds; the Persians our silk-weavers, and the Chinese our potters.

(No. 69)

London became a great commercial capital, the most flexible city in social terms (with the exception of Amsterdam) in the whole of Europe. A country-based aristocracy lived and spent money freely there for part of the year and they mixed, naturally enough, with bankers, the greater merchants, prominent intellectuals and professional men. The clubs which proliferated to an astonishing degree are, as has recently been said, 'the expression of a dynamic, increasingly urban society in which the traditional structures of corporate and communal life were either absent or inappropriate for the full range of contemporary conditions and aspirations' (Langford, *A Polite and Commercial People,* 1989, p. 100). Another commentator describes the situation that pertained in Johnson's own circle, for example, where

apart from the worlds of learning, literature and publishing, which were intrinsically his own as a writer and intellectual, there was a Moscovy merchant, John Rylands; Joseph Banks, explorer, President of the Royal society, adviser to excise authorities, admiralty and industry; Topham Beauclerk, son of a duke; Richard Clark, one attorney among several and Lord Mayor of London. Boswell's brother . . . was a merchant based in Valencia; Garrick's brother was a wine merchant; Adam Smith, sanest of economic philosophers, was a customs commissioner. There was Robert Adam, architect and entrepreneur in building. . . .

(Peter Mathias, *The Transformation of England,*
Methuen, 1979, p. 297)

The new sociability, prosperity and culture were by no means confined to the higher echelons. Voltaire, on a visit to England, thought the common people he saw at Greenwich were the nobility because of their fashionable dress. This so-called 'genteel mania' was the despair of conservative commentators, but many of the symptoms were only superficial. It would certainly be a mistake to think that the traditional upper classes – the aristocracy and the wealthier gentry – were displaced from the seats of power. It is important to remember that there was no one clearly identifiable middle class in the period, but rather a set of interest groups of very different incomes, education and culture, who might be considered 'middle rank' at the time. What cannot be denied, though, is that there was a marked increase in the wealth, status and aspirations not only of the great merchants and high financiers (the so-called 'moneyed men'), but also of many of the middling rural gentry, of the professional men and of that growing urban élite that has been aptly termed the 'pseudo-gentry'. Gradually these groupings were beginning to merge together into a broader mass of the polite, propertied and politically aware.

The process was facilitated by a vast improvement in transportation and communications. Between 1762 and 1774 as many as four hundred and fifty-two acts were passed for the construction and repair of roads. This was mainly a consequence of the needs of trade, but it combined with the new prosperity, intellectual curiosity and leisure to create a great enthusiasm for travel. Johnson himself, despite his image as purely a London man, was an adventurous and enthusiastic traveller, as we have seen, who began to travel as soon as he could afford it and continued well into his old age.

As provincial isolation broke down, a sturdy 'middle rank' commercial culture seemed to take over the country. This expressed itself in the increasing number of newspapers and journals, in the improvements in municipal building and in cultural opportunities both in London and the provincial towns, and in the growing cult of shopping in the period, which has received the attention of recent scholars.

The intellectual response

Traditional modes of moral discourse did not find it easy, however, to accommodate themselves to the conditions of a commercial society. Medieval Catholicism had condemned the taking of interest for loans as usury, and Christians had always condemned acquisitiveness, luxury and 'the pride of life'. For classical moralists, too, luxury was an evil, and an influential tradition of classical historiography saw the fall of the Roman republic into the decadence of the Empire as the consequence of luxury and avarice. Through Renaissance thinkers this had itself fed through into the eighteenth century in the ideas of 'civic humanism', which presented the virtue and independence of the landed gentry as the only insurance against the corruption of the state, and like most of these theories regards change as the road to decadence. Commercialization replaced the apparent stability of landed status with constant change and the virtuous disinterest of the landed gentleman with a bewilderingly complex specialization of labour that made it hard for anyone to be sufficiently detached to understand the whole complex mechanism of society.

After the successful conclusion of the Seven Years War commercial confidence grew even greater, but there were also conservative fears about over-expansion and the effects on the British people. John Brown's *Estimate of the Manners and Principles of the Times* (1757), for example, was published at a time of discouragement in the war, and it became a best seller. Similar condemnations of luxury, avarice and social climbing appear in the works of the novelist Tobias Smollett. Matthew Bramble, to a considerable degree Smollett's own spokesman, writes, for example, in *Humphrey Clinker* (1771):

> The tide of luxury has swept all the inhabitants from the open country – The poorest 'squire as well as the richest peer, must have his house in town, and make a figure with an extraordinary number of domestics. The plough-boys, cow-herds, and lower hinds, are debauched and seduced by the appearance of those coxcombs in livery, when they make their summer excursions. They desert their dirt and drudgery, and swarm up to London, in hopes of getting into service, where they can live luxuriously and wear fine clothes, without being obliged to work; for idleness is natural to man – Great numbers of these, being disappointed in their expectations, become thieves and sharpers; and London being an immense wilderness, in which there is neither watch nor ward of any signification, nor any order or police, affords them lurking-places as well as prey.
>
> (29 May)

Yet intellectuals obviously had to try to come to terms with the new commercial society, and there were attempts to revise the criteria. The most striking and uncomfortable work of such a kind appeared earlier in the century with Bernard Mandeville's *The Fable of the Bees* (1714), which Johnson knew well. The personal motives behind Mandeville's work are still debated to this day, but, combining a vivid version of Hobbes's cynical views on human selfishness with cosmic optimism in a paradoxical way, he tries to show that such vices as luxury and greed, far from being the downfall of a society, were in fact essential to a prosperous commercial state: 'private vices' indeed are 'public benefits'.

The great Scots philosopher David Hume defends commercial society in a much more idealistic fashion. Far from being full of vice, Hume argues, commercial, even luxurious societies are in fact the most refined, the happiest and the most virtuous ones:

> They must feel an increase of humanity, from the very habit of convening together, and contributing to each other's pleasures and entertainment. Thus, industry, knowledge and humanity are linked together, by an indissoluble chain, and are found, from experience as well as reason, to be peculiar to the more polished, and, what are commonly denominated, the more luxurious ages.
>
> ('Of Refinement in the Arts')

Also, like Hume, a product of the Scottish Enlightenment were the writings of a group of thinkers that included Adam Ferguson, Lord Kames and the famous economist Adam Smith. The application of scientific method to new areas of human life, a new historiography, a new knowledge of primitive societies through the successes of the explorers – all these played their part in this body of work, which some specialists regard as the origins of modern sociology. Perhaps the most important factor, though, is reflection on the differences between modern commercial society and other kinds of social organization and the implicit need, in some instances, to provide a justification for the new forms. Smith's famous *Wealth of Nations* (1776) says definitively that the commercial system 'is the modern system, and is best understood in our country and in our own times'. His own work is a massive contribution to that understanding and the classic argument for free market economics, though he is not without his own moral qualms and ambivalences.

Johnson and commercial society

To discuss Johnson in such company may at first sight seem strange. As we might expect, his traditional Christian beliefs, classical ideas and (in some respects) conservative politics certainly inclined him to be suspicious of many of these new developments. In 'Further Thoughts on Agriculture' (*The Visiter*, March 1756) he argues that agriculture not trade can be the only stable basis for a healthy economy. Elsewhere he invokes the traditional fear that 'commerce depraves manners' and summarizes Roman history in terms of a growth in luxury that leads inevitably towards corruption: 'The Romans, like others, as soon as they grew rich, grew corrupt, and, in their corruption, sold the lives and freedoms of themselves, and one another' (Review of Thomas Blackwell's *Memoirs of the Court of Augustus*, Works, 1756). The same danger, he suggests, is present in Britain through the expansion of the empire, for 'we continue every day to show by new proofs, that no people can be great who have ceased to be virtuous' ('An Introduction to the Political State of Great Britain', 1756).

Yet Johnson had himself profited by and was in some senses an index of the flourishing of middle-rank commercial society and culture, especially, of course, in his pride at being a professional writer and his praise of the booksellers and the public as 'good masters'. He was robustly down to earth and practical by nature in many respects, convinced that you learned more from life than from books, realistically aware of the importance of money and an active member of the Society for the Encouragement of Arts, Commerce and Manufactures. He was very keen to get involved in the details of the Thrales's vast brewery business and was able to write on and discuss the inventions and innovations of the bustling trade and industrial world of his time, including such technical matters as coining, tanning and malting. He was anxious to try to continue to apply traditional moral criteria to all the bewildering but exhilarating social changes of his time, yet he was sufficiently influenced by Mandeville to recognize that the old moral condemnations of luxury did not tell the whole story. He said to George Steevens and Boswell in 1776, for example:

> Now the truth is that luxury produces much good. Take the luxury of building in London. Does it not produce real advantage in the conveniency and elegance of accommodation, and this all from the exertion of industry? . . . A man gives half a guinea for a dish of green peas. How much gardening does this occasion? How many labourers must the competition to have such things early in the market, keep in employment?

> *(Life,* III, 55–6)

'You cannot spend in luxury', he said elsewhere, 'without doing good to the poor. Nay, you do more good to them by spending it in luxury than by giving it: for by spending it in luxury you make them exert industry, whereas by giving it you keep them idle' *(Life,* II, 222).

Most significantly of all, perhaps, Johnson opts in the last analysis for the ethos of commercialism in respect of social mobility. Certainly that ethos may destroy the traditional bonds of protection in earlier societies, and so an unbridled market economy can only be dangerous and heartless. On the other hand:

> To entail irreversible poverty upon generation after generation only because the ancestor happened to be poor, is in itself

Thomas Rowlandson, Johnson and Boswell Walking up the High Street *in Edinburgh*

cruel, if not unjust, and is wholly contrary to the maxims of a commercial nation, which always suppose and promote a rotation of property, and offer every individual a chance of mending his condition by his diligence.

(Review of Soame Jenyns's *Free Inquiry*)

Johnson's *A Journey to the Western Islands of Scotland* has been compared by some commentators to modern social anthropology, and it certainly shows a profound grasp of the origins of particular kinds of social organization and the way that they work as a whole system. Through all the circumstantial details about the difficulties of agriculture on such barren soil and the gradual introduction of new conveniences through trade the real theme and organizing principle seems gradually to emerge. The special fascination of Highlands culture for Johnson is the way that the primitive feudal system on which it depended had been destroyed by punitive military measures and the introduction of commercialism, and the work is a moving register of his complex ambivalences about commercial society. Johnson sees clearly that good things have gone, but refuses to indulge in romantic nostalgia:

> Such is the system of insular subordination, which, having little variety, cannot afford much delight in the view, nor long detain the mind in contemplation. The inhabitants were for a long time perhaps not unhappy; but their content was a muddy mixture of pride and ignorance, an indifference for pleasures which they did not know, a blind veneration for their chiefs, and a strong conviction of their own importance.
>
> (IX, 89)

At the same time the loss of the islanders' sturdy military independence is bound to make Johnson wonder whether there are not dangers when a 'great nation' becomes 'totally commercial . . . whether amidst the uncertainty of human affairs, too much attention to one mode of happiness may not endanger others? whether the pride of riches must not sometimes have recourse to the protection of courage?'(IX, 91).

If there are incidental contradictions and ambivalences in Johnson's attitudes to commercial society, there is also a deeper underlying consistency with his thought as a whole. Where it hurts the poor he is against it, but if it can improve their lot then it cannot be a bad thing. If trade, commerce and even luxury can add to the innocent happiness and pleasure of life then they are to be welcomed, and they have, like the political world, a degree of autonomy, though they are not to be allowed to escape moral evaluation:

> . . . no motivation can sanctify the accumulation of wealth, but an ardent desire to make the most honourable and virtuous use of it, by contributing to the support of good government, the increase of arts and industry, the rewards of genius and the relief of wretchedness and want.
>
> (Dedication for J. Payne, *New Tables of Interest*, 1758)

Overall Johnson registers the complexity and the excitement of the new world, its increased moral dangers and yet the new opportunities for good that it offers. Whether fully consciously or not, he seems to offer himself in his writings and his influential conversation as a mediator and guide in the new conditions and to suggest (though with great wariness) that it is possible to gain the benefits of commercial society without losing touch completely with traditional moral bearings.

6 Johnson and the art of human happiness: a recapitulation

One central motif brings together all the main intellectual, religious, political and economic influences in the period so far discussed: the vastly increased expectation of happiness and fulfilment on earth. Movements in philosophy and culture were highlighting individual feeling and the realm of daily life rather than the transcendent. At the same time commercialization and the new prosperity, the increased democratization in politics and the partial secularization of thought were all working to make both the expectation and the actual experience of happiness on earth more widespread. In the American Declaration of Independence the 'right to the pursuit of happiness' is even enshrined as one of the fundamental rights of man.

Johnson's own tendency to depression in itself obviously made the claim that we can be happy on earth threatening to him. Caustic and competitive in conversation though he often was, he was rarely cruel, but on one occasion a man who had entered into debate with him on the subject of the possibility of happiness unwisely produced his sister-in-law as a clinching argument. Johnson looked at her for a moment and then said, 'If your sister-in-law is really the contented being she professes herself . . . her life gives the lie to every research of humanity; for she is happy without health, without beauty, without money and without understanding!' (Mrs Thrale [Piozzi], *Anecdotes*, Ed. S.C. Roberts, Cambridge University Press, 1925, p. 182).

As we have seen though, it would be quite wrong to think that Johnson's views on this subject were purely the result of his own subjective experiences. On the contrary it is an age-old wisdom that he is opposing to the secular complacencies of his time, and the point of it all is far from mere pessimism. There is nothing wrong with the hope for happiness as such. That desire, indeed, is the inevitable 'end [in the sense of aim] of all human actions', 'inseparable from a rational being' (*Sermon* XVIII). It is simply that we have been seeking it in the wrong place and the wrong way. By disabusing us of our false hopes and exaggerated expectations Johnson genuinely believes that he is increasing the sum total of happiness. It is only when we fully recognize and accept the realities of our human condition that we come to understand where true, eternal happiness is to be found.

But one of the most distinctive things about Johnson's moral teaching is his healthy regard for ordinary human happiness on earth as well. He is at pains to assert that 'Religion' itself is not an enemy of any 'enjoyment in which human nature may innocently delight' (*Adventurer* 131). He himself, of course, had his own very energetic desires for happiness and pleasure. He found much to enjoy in food, companionship and travel, and the idea of pleasure is strikingly central to his literary criticism. Other things being equal, he is in favour of anything that increases that happiness and pleasure, including commerce and material luxury (though he recognizes dangers too). But it is only when we give up the feverish search for definitive happiness on earth that we have any chance of the more limited happiness that might be available to us. It is only when we see that the cure for human ills is not 'radical' that we cease wasting our time looking for panaceas and Utopias and begin to take practical steps. The recognition of the frailties and limitations of our fallen state is the basis for a true political order that may – at the very least – minimize unhappiness. That recognition is also, properly conceived, the foundation of the great Baconian scientific programme of doing what we can to remedy our deficiencies.

For we have big hopes and imaginations, but we are in other respects essentially 'little creatures', limited and contingent. We therefore have a special, paradoxical balance to strike. In accepting our limitations and freeing ourselves from excessive ambitions and exaggerated expectations we also come to learn the art of 'studying little things', as Johnson puts it, by which we make ourselves as happy as we can. At the same time we do not have to repress our more unrealistic projects for happiness completely. Provided that we do not let them run away with us, our hopes will keep us active and involved, even if they can never be fully realized.

Johnson sets himself with sombre realism against what he saw as the exaggerated expectations of his time. Far from being gloomy tracts, however, his writings combine hope with great practicality and constitute their own treatise on the art of human happiness.

7   The literary background

Some grasp of the main features of the late seventeenth- and eighteenth-century literary scene is essential for a full understanding of Johnson's achievement as a writer and critic. For Johnson was a man of letters in the widest sense, involved in that literary scene in a whole variety of ways. He was extremely well-read and extremely responsive to literature. His own life and career brought him into personal contact and friendship with a very large circle of writers. He also provides in his more formal literary history a wide-ranging overview of the literature of his own century and the century that precedes.

Johnson, it has often been said, is the last major writer in English whose work embodies the main literary tenets of the Renaissance. Yet he lives through a great literary revolution. He has to come to terms with new literary kinds that relate to the vast intellectual and cultural changes already traced in this study. Despite his traditionalism in other respects his own position also reflects in a very central way a major change in the whole socio-economic basis of literature, a change which he, perhaps to our surprise, wholeheartedly welcomes.

The Renaissance and 'neo-classicism'

Our sense of English literary history has been so influenced by the prestige of Shakespeare that we are apt to forget that his status was ever in question and that the Renaissance literary scene was dominated by the court and by classicism. Ben Jonson, with his court role as Poet Laureate for a time, his great interest in classical criticism and his plays that follow the classical 'rules', is in fact a far more representative figure than Shakespeare. In the sixteenth and seventeenth centuries the court was the cultural centre of England, and most serious writers were involved with it in one way or another. With the exception of a very small number of successful playwrights, patronage from the court and the aristocracy was essential for writers (Dryden wrote of 'Poets who must live by courts or starve'). No other financial system for the support of literature really existed, for, with very rare exceptions indeed, the reading public was simply not large enough to make it possible to gain a living by the sale of literary works.

The literary intelligentsia associated with the court in this period was naturally enough dominated by the ideals of the revived classicism of the Renaissance. The special intensification of interest in classical literature with the revival of learning led to a proliferation of literary criticism throughout Europe. The greatest classical critic, Aristotle, had enormous prestige, but it was the codification of ideas on literature by the Roman poet Horace that had the most influence. It was Horace, for example, who had most clearly formulated the idea of literature as combining moral instruction and delight. Although, like Aristotle, he constantly uses the criterion of the imitation of nature, *mimesis*, that concept is narrowed down and linked with the social ideals of his audience through the idea of decorum, the suggestion that the poet must follow fitting (and thus *socially* acceptable) norms in what he describes.

The belief in the high moral and civic purposes of literature, the idea of the imitation of nature and the traditional sense of the literary kinds or genres may all seem very alien to modern preconceptions, but they dominated literature for thousands of years, and all great poets up to the end of the eighteenth century took them for granted. The 'neoclassicism' (as it has been customary to call it) of the seventeenth century is not a terrible aberration but an attempt to make these ideas more systematic. But literary criticism does not take place in a cultural vacuum, of course, and the fact that it was the France of this time that saw the special development of these ideas is itself significant. The movement was linked not only with national pride, political absolutism and the desire to impose cultural authority, but also with the philosophical rationalism of Descartes and with the idea of an analogy between literary criticism and the discourses of theology and law. In that sense criticism and the question of literary judgement reflect the crisis of authority in the period. The growth of a professional secular intelligentsia is itself a major mark of the Enlightenment, according to Roy Porter, and it is clear that the intellectual's theorizing and specialization has an important part to play in all this. The growth of criticism throughout this period also relates, obviously, to the rise of a literary profession and to the new leisure, prosperity and desire for culture and pleasure.

The main ideas of French neo-classicism were appealingly codified on the analogy of Horace in Boileau's *Art Poétique*, and discussed in influential treatises with the main focus on tragic drama in the works of such critics as Bohours, Rapin and Dacier. For a long period scholars, especially in Britain, were inclined to present a hostile caricature of this tradition as being bound by a narrow idea of direct imitation of classical texts and a very rigid sense of 'the rules' for the different genres. The spirit of French absolutism was contrasted to the growing liberty of British literature, which was eventually to culminate in the romantic movement. Johnson himself was attributed very different roles in all this depending on the particular sympathies of the literary historian concerned. In some accounts he was the last bastion of an alien neo-classicism and in others the sturdy defender of British liberty against the rules.

In understandable reaction against these over-simplifications some scholars have suggested that the whole existence of neo-classicism is questionable and the word itself a misnomer. Others have argued that it has no relevance in England, at least after the work of Thomas Rhymer in the late seventeenth century. A more carefully conceived and more useful approach is that set forth in an influential essay by R.S. Crane, 'English Neo-classical Criticism: An Outline Sketch' (*Critics and Criticism*, 1952), where he explains that neo-classicism is not a rigid orthodoxy in which every critic believes the same thing but a cluster of organizing terms which set the agenda for critical discussion. These were in themselves flexible and capable of varying emphases. The idea of imitation of nature itself, for example, raised questions about whether that imitation was to be direct or selective and whether general, ideal or particular nature was intended. This could be related to the imitation of classical models without slavish reliance on classical authority through the view that the classical writers had themselves followed nature in such a definitive way that, as Pope put it, 'To copy *Nature* is to copy *them*' (*Essay on Criticism*, l. 140). Although there were, of course, mechanical and authoritarian critics in this tradition, neo-classicism essentially consisted of holding in balance such principles as judgement and imagination, propriety and freedom, imitation and originality and the general and the particular. The greatest neo-classical poets and critics always understood that genius, imagination and inspiration were more important than any theories or classical precedents and could create a 'grace beyond the reach of art', and this was strengthened by the influence of Longinus, a critic of late antiquity, and the tradition of the sublime that resulted from his rediscovery.

On the whole, though, it is special pleading to refuse to accept that there was a general movement in the period, even in England, towards an ordered art of clarity, moral truth and technical correctness. These ideals, as Johnson registers in the

99

Lives of the Poets, took later seventeenth-century English poetry towards a new public and social emphasis and away from the abstruse wit and the private focus on love and religion in the 'metaphysicals' such as John Donne and George Herbert.

French influence on the English Restoration was considerable because of the King's own period of exile in France, but more important were the analogous developments here in the sciences and in philosophy and the general hope for a time of peace and stability after the Civil War. Essentially, English writers took what they required from France, but used it for their own ends. John Dryden, the last and by no means the least of a line of great English court poets, is a boldly ambitious writer, but there is no doubt of his allegiance to what might be termed neo-classical ideas. He is perhaps the first great literary critic in English, and his essays expound such principles with great flexibility and eloquence. He is without question the most important single influence on Johnson's own literary criticism.

In a broader reflection of the same ideals, it was in his work, and still more in Pope's, according to Johnson, that the 'refinement' and improvement of English verse that had begun earlier in the seventeenth century with Edmund Waller and Sir John Denham, was to reach its peak. Dryden's and Pope's amazingly artful and varied rhyming couplet – called the 'heroic' couplet because the dignity of its ten-syllable line made it appropriate for translations of the classical epic – was to be the model of Johnson's own major poems.

Another major aspect of this 'improvement', according to Johnson, lies in the development of 'poetic diction', a controversial matter on which it will be necessary to say more later. In neo-classical theory the higher forms of poetry such as epic and tragedy naturally required a certain elevation of style. There was also a sense in which poetry itself was a higher form than prose and had to justify its status by emphasizing its difference from the normal language of everyday life. It was to Dryden, in Johnson's view, with his close study of Virgil in his translations, that we owed the proper establishment of such a diction, for there was before his time:

> no poetical diction: no system of words at once refined from the grossness of domestic use and free from the harshness of terms appropriated to particular arts. Words too familiar or too remote defeat the purpose of a poet. From those sounds which we hear on small or on coarse occasions, we do not easily receive strong impressions or delightful images; and

words to which we are nearly strangers, whenever they occur, draw that attention on themselves which they should transmit to things.

Those happy combination of words which distinguish poetry from prose had been rarely attempted; we had few elegances or flowers of speech: the roses had not yet been plucked from the bramble or different colours had not been joined to enliven one another.

('Life of Dryden', I, 420)

It is worth noting at this point, though, that Dryden's work is far from 'poetic diction' in its decadence in the middle and later eighteenth century. Such diction, as he and Johnson understand it, is not question of pure decoration but of literary and social decorum, of using the appropriate words for appropriate occasions, and though we have a very different sense of such matters the principle itself is not necessarily faulty. Dryden uses 'low' diction where necessary in his satires, for example, and Johnson himself accepts this readily. When Boswell complained to him that a certain phrase in Pope was too low, Johnson replied, 'Sir, it is intended to be low: it is satire. The expression is debased to debase the character' (*Hebrides, Life*, V, 83).

The new age

Dryden, Poet Laureate and propagandist for Charles II and James II, was to fall with his master James in the 'Glorious Revolution' of 1688. The establishment of a limited, constitutional monarchy signalled, as we have seen, a shift in power from the court to a new political élite. After 1688 the process accelerated through the financial and commercial changes already sketched, with the result that what amounted to a new political nation emerged.

Naturally enough the implications of all this were also considerable for literature. The demands of controversy in the Civil War had helped to create a new readership and new organs of publication. Newspapers and periodicals proliferated after the Restoration, and the widening of the élite also increased the market for other kinds of literature. The increase in sales made it possible for a literary profession of a new kind to develop, though it was at first very precarious. But from the last decade or so of the seventeenth century poets and other writers such as translators and compilers were encouraged to try to make a living from their literary talents, a harsh milieu that was often called 'Grub Street' from the name of the actual street in which many of these writers lived. Better writers such as

John Gay were also able to make substantial rewards from their work at times, and gradually throughout the eighteenth century the selling of literary works and a system that was at least a shadowy forerunner of the modern publishing industry came to replace aristocratic and court patronage as the primary mode of disseminating literature.

Addison and Steele, in the most influential literary works of the entire eighteenth century, the periodicals the *Tatler* and the *Spectator*, saw it as their role to form the manners and tastes of this new, wider élite, which had by now come to include a number of the upper merchants, the more fashionable of the country gentry and many of the increasingly prosperous and respected professional men. The evidence suggests that they achieved great success. Johnson writes of Addison:

> That general knowledge which now circulates in common talk was in his time rarely to be found. Men not professing learning were not ashamed of ignorance; and in the female world any acquaintance with books was distinguished only to be censured. His purpose was to infuse literary curiosity by gentle and unsuspected conveyance into the gay, the idle, and the wealthy; he therefore presented knowledge in the most alluring form, not lofty and austere, but accessible and familiar. When he showed them their defects, he showed them likewise that they might be easily supplied. His attempt succeeded; enquiry was awakened, and comprehension expanded. An emulation of intellectual elegance was excited, and from his time to our own life has been gradually exalted, and conversation purified and enlarged.   (II, 14–16)

Addison's essays on *Paradise Lost* and on the pleasure of the imagination had especial importance in this context, and they have been said to be the first literary and aesthetic criticism addressed to the audience rather than to other artists. Johnson's own periodical essays, which also include literary criticism, were clearly taking off from an already established tradition, though they are very different in style from their predecessors.

Also appealing to a new audience and, again, significantly, in prose like the periodical essay was the other virtually new genre, the novel. Later, of course, this was far to outstrip the periodical essay in lasting importance and to become the major literary form of the succeeding centuries. There had been prose fictions before, but this really is the period that marks *The Rise of the Novel*, in the words of the title of a famous book by Ian Watt. Only half emerging from journalism in the works of its first famous practitioner, Daniel Defoe, author of *Robinson Crusoe* and *Moll Flanders*, the mode soon attained maturity with the works of Samuel Richardson (*Pamela, Clarissa*) and Henry Fielding (*Joseph Andrews, Tom Jones*) in the 1740s.

In *Rambler* No. 4 Johnson gives his own, thoughtful, troubled and ambivalent reaction to the rise of the novel genre, which itself raises in his mind important but perhaps insoluble questions about the way literature imitates nature and the relationship between that and the writer's moral responsibility. The power of the new mode seems to lie in the fact that it is more 'realistic' than romance, and this gives it greater moral force too because we are more likely to identify with its characters. On the other hand, if the world be 'promiscuously described' (i.e. with complete directness) then why do we need literature at all instead of going directly to life? There is a greater moral danger here as well as a greater opportunity, for few people would be likely to take romance for reality, but the new mode creates precisely that possibility. At the back of Johnson's mind there seems to lie the example of Fielding, who had attempted to give a more neo-classical dignity and objectivity to the mode, but whose *Tom Jones* describes with attractive realism the exploits of a sexually uninhibited, spontaneous hero. Johnson once said to a woman of his acquaintance, 'I am shocked to hear you quote from so corrupt a work'. Yet he is far from condemning novels out of hand. He finds much to admire in the psychological and moral inwardness of Richardson's long-drawn out accounts of spiritual temptation and testing (though he said that if you read him 'for the story you would hang yourself!').

Despite his own traditionalism and the growing status of prose Pope was able, by force of genius and will, to dominate the literature of the first few decades of the eighteenth century. He was, it has been said, 'a court poet without a court', one who looked back to the old tradition of the poet as court mentor and recipient of patronage, but who was disaffected by politics and his Catholic religion from the court of the Hanoverians and the ministry of Walpole. For him poetry continues to be a great public art and his inspiration is often classical. In his great mock-epic *The Dunciad* he scorns all the manifestations of the new literary commercialism and Grub Street. Yet his own fortune was made by selling his translations of Homer on the subscription method to the wealthy and educated – a kind of half-way house between the old aristocratic patronage and the new marketplace.

More in keeping with the spirit of the new age was James Thomson, whose most famous poem *The Seasons* celebrated in expansive blank verse an optimistic vision of British society linked with a new attention to the description of external nature. A narrow conception of eighteenth-century literature once led critics to see Thomson as a 'pre-romantic', but he was, after all, a friend of Pope, and his own focus remains a social one, for all his interest in the exotic and remote. Yet there obviously are elements here that point in new directions as well.

Sentiment

During the administration of Walpole government patronage for poetry had declined, and after his fall there was less interest in political matters for a time anyway. The increasing centrality of prose and the marked separation from the political world after Pope and Thomson led to a certain marginalizing of poetry. A new generation of poets in the 1740s took a new direction, developing the Shaftesburian sentiment and the interest in nature and the sublime in Thomson without his positive social vision. In what John Sitter calls this 'poetry of loneliness', epitomized in the work of the Warton brothers, William Collins and Thomas Gray, sentiment, melancholy, subjectivity and fancy are cultivated for their own sake.

> Beneath yon ruin'd abbey's moss-grown piles
> Oft let me sit, at twilight hour of eve,
> Where through some western window the pale moon
> Pours her long-levell'd rule of streaming light;
> While sullen sacred silence reigns around,
> Save the lone screech-owl's note, who builds his bower
> Amid the mouldering caverns dark and damp
> . . . But when the world
> Is clad in Midnight's raven-coloured robe,
> Mid hollow charnel let me watch the flame
> Of taper dim, shedding a livid glare
> O'er the wan heaps; while airy voices talk
> Along the glimmering walls; or ghostly shape
> At distance seen, invites with beckoning hand
> (T. Warton, 'The Pleasures of Melancholy')

For such poets, keen to revive lyric poetry, Greek influence takes over from the Roman satirists. Milton's minor poems are also a major influence, as for Warton in the quoted poem, and there is a growing cult of primitivism and an attraction to non-classical literature such as Welsh poetry, ballads and medieval poetry.

As has often been remarked, where suitable ancient poetry

was not to be found some poets were prepared to provide it for themselves, and these new interests led directly to Thomas Chatterton's remarkable attempts to pass off his own medieval imitations as genuine and to James Macpherson's famous 'Ossian', purported translations from a Gaelic bard. Johnson himself played an important role in the latter controversy. Macpherson's fragments and epics, written in poetic English prose, had great appeal, not only to the Scots but to Europeans of the burgeoning romantic movement, who longed for the primitive power of more 'natural' societies in line with the thinking of Rousseau. Napoleon himself was a great admirer of 'Ossian'. But Johnson always refused to accept that these poems were true translations from a primitive source. Time and again he challenged Macpherson to produce his manuscript sources, and responded to a subsequent threatening letter from the irate Scotsman by providing himself with a cudgel and writing to him the famous words 'I will not desist from detecting what I think a cheat, from any fear of the menaces of a ruffian'.

The invention of the sensational Gothic novel – a tale of terror set in mysterious medieval castles – and the revived interest in and imitation of 'Gothic' (medieval) architecture both obviously reflect similar trends to those described above. Horace Walpole has a central role here with his novel *The Castle of Otranto* (1764) and the building of his pseudo-castle, Strawberry Hill. But all these tendencies and fads, so variegated in some ways, are part of a wider movement that reflects the philosophical tendency towards a privileging of individual emotion in the period, the movement known variously as sentimentalism or the cult of sensibility. The word 'sentimental' was on everybody's lips from the 1740s onwards and it came to represent this powerful and new emphasis on emotional sensitivity as an index of moral fibre and benevolence, as in Lawrence Sterne's *The Sentimental Journal* (1768), where it is bound up with considerable irony, and Henry Mackenzie's *The Man of Feeling* (1771).

As we might expect, Johnson, a sufferer from melancholy himself and very genuinely afraid of death, has little patience with the artificial cultivation of these emotions in verse. His own major poems, imitations of a Roman poet in the older mode of the heroic couplet, concern the moral life and human society. They are, as we have seen, at the very opposite pole from subjectivity. In a wider sense, though far from untouched himself by the new concerns, Johnson was, of course, hostile to most of the manifestations of 'sentiment' and to the very preconceptions that lay behind them.

The 'Age of Print'

The late eighteenth century is a great age of prose, print and scholarship. Johnson himself praised the increase of knowledge in his own age, commenting, for example, that

> The mass of every people must be barbarous where there is no printing and consequently knowledge is not generally diffused. Knowledge is diffused among our people by the newspapers.
>
> (*Life*, II, 170)

A solid reading public had grown up, eager not only for entertainment but also for knowledge, self-improvement and instruction, and the literary profession was by now firmly established. The scholarly interests of the Renaissance flowered out now into a much wider audience, and the new reading public had a great appetite for history, biography and literary history and for reference books of all kinds, of which Johnson's own *Dictionary* is only the most outstanding example. The first national encyclopaedia, the *Cyclopaedia* by Ephraim Chambers, appeared as early as 1728. The *Biographia Britannica*, which served as the first Dictionary of National Biography, was published in six volumes from 1747 to 1766. Works both by and on Johnson aptly illustrate the great interest in biography in the period, and works of history such as those by David Hume, William Robertson on Scotland and, of course, Gibbon on the Roman Empire achieved extraordinary sales.

Literary criticism, scholarship and history also flourished. Editorial work on Shakespeare took off in the period, as we shall see, and there was a growing interest in early British literature of all kinds. Thomas Warton's *History of English Poetry* (1774–81) is the first full literary history. In 1765 Thomas Percy published his great collection of English and Scottish ballads, the *Reliques of Ancient English Poetry*. Such works as Bishop Hurd's *Letters on Chivalry and Romance* (1762) meanwhile demonstrated how illuminating it could be to study the historical conditions at the time an author was writing.

All this publication in prose obviously represents the public world against the increasingly private world of poetry, a bourgeois and business-like interest in solid fact, but things are also more complex than that. Some of the new prose overlaps with the poetry of the time, as is very obvious with the Gothic novel. Individual sentiment is increasingly privileged, and everyone, whether qualified or not, it seems, now rushes to the press, as Johnson himself complained, so that there appears to be an 'epidemical conspiracy for the destruction of paper'. Johnson's essay on this new 'itch' of writing (*Adventurer* 115) is itself a plea for the restoration of standards – in part the reaction of a professional against the amateurs, in part of a traditionalist against the new self-expression.

The new scholarship itself has close links with the literary experimentation of the time. Not only the literary 'forgers' such as Macpherson and Chatterton but also poets such as Gray and Collins imitate 'primitive' poetry and find the fantasy of themselves as primitive poets exciting. Percy's collection of ballads led to a mass of imitations, and has obvious links even with Wordsworth's and Coleridge's *Lyrical Ballads* of 1798.

In a broader sense literary scholarship could both reflect and lead to a new kind of critical relativism. It would be foolish to condemn (say) early Welsh bardic verse by the rigorous rules of neo-classicism. But some wanted to go further still. The literary cult of primitivism, influenced by Rousseau's thinking, becomes more extreme, and Hugh Blair, for example, in his *Dissertation on the Poems of Ossian* (1763) writes that these earlier societies are much more favourable to imagination and poetry than more civilized conditions.

The role of Johnson

Johnson may be traditionalist with regard to many of the manifestations of 'sentiment' in his period, but he is not at all conservative in his response to the new conditions of authorship. Poetry, after all, is only a very small part of his own immense output, and this in itself reflects the growing domination of prose. Unlike his humanist predecessors Pope and Swift it is clear that he did not regard himself as a court writer who had been alienated by the hopeless corruption of the court. His famous letter to Lord Chesterfield has often been taken as marking the deathblow to the old system of aristocratic patronage (though this is an over-simplification in some respects). His own work is produced almost entirely in accordance with the demands of the market and for money. He publishes when he is commissioned to do so and as the market for a work appears or when he can convince the booksellers that he can make one. 'No man but a blockhead ever wrote except for money', he proclaims in a famous comment. Despite the difficulties of his own early career he always regarded the new system as vastly superior to the old, and spoke of the booksellers as 'generous, liberal minded men' whose enterprise 'raised the price of literature'.

Recognizing certain dangers in the new circumstances, Johnson still has no doubt at all that the opportunities of the new system far outweigh the disadvantages. As Alvin Kernan has shown in *Printing, Letters, Technology & Samuel Johnson,* Johnson is really the 'culture hero' of the new 'age of print'. He constructs 'a new role for himself as the writer who can earn his living by writing for the marketplace and still assert his authorial dignity and social importance'. He is able to carry the old standards forward in conditions in which they were in danger of being swamped. At the same time he is able to take advantage of those very conditions to widen access to the standards of the past by appealing to a new audience that is no longer defined as a *social* élite but as an intellectual one – those who think reasonably and morally.

It is possible, he demonstrates, in other words, to be a commercial success without compromising to the market's domination by fashion. In the last number of the *Rambler* he says justly that he has

> seen the meteors of fashion rise and fall, without any attempt to add a moment to their duration. I have never complied with temporary curiosity, nor enabled my readers to discuss the topick of the day. . . .

Instead he has attempted to improve the taste of his readers by his care for the language: 'I have laboured to refine our language to grammatical purity, and to clear it from colloquial barbarisms, licentious idioms and irregular combinations.' But his 'principal design' has been 'to inculcate wisdom or piety', for, as he writes elsewhere, this can be the only ultimate way to rise above the ephemerality of the market:

> He that lays out his labours upon temporary subjects, easily finds readers, and quickly loses them; for what should make the book valued when its subject is no more?

But:

> He that writes upon general principles, or delivers universal truths, may hope to be often read, because his book will be equally useful at all times and in every country.

> > (*Idler* 59)

Johnson's own achievements – the *Dictionary*, the edition of Shakespeare, the *Lives of the Poets* – are, of course, at the heart of the new scholarship and literary history of his time. An earlier scholarly activity, his catalogue of the great Harleian library and his eight volume selection of pamphlets from the library, *The Harleian Miscellany*, reveals his very genuine interest in and knowledge of the earlier literature of England. He was a friend of both Warton brothers and of Bishop Percy. He speaks respectfully of them and they acknowledge his help. But Johnson the great literary scholar does not, of course, approve of the ends to which that scholarship was sometimes put in the period: the encouragement of individual 'sentiment' for its own sake, relativism, even primitivism. Admiring Percy's great collection and encouraging its publication, he still mocks the modern ballad imitators, including those of his friend the editor, with a spontaneous parody:

> I put my hat upon my head
> And walk'd into the Strand,
> And there I met another man
> Whose hat was in his hand.   (VI, 269)

As we have seen, he soon perceives the fraudulent elements in 'Ossian' to the great disgust of its admirers, and he dislikes the more extravagant poems of Gray.

Keen though Johnson is to set Shakespeare and other early writers in their historical context, he holds to the neo-classical tenet that human beings are always fundamentally the same, whatever their social circumstances, and that moral truth is by its very nature unchangeable. Although he clearly recognises that literary standards are not in themselves absolute, he believes that many of them in the last analysis rest on the same foundation of moral truth. As the next sections will show, Johnson's literary criticism thus reveals the same search as his moral writings for lasting principles that rise above the fashions of the day and the whims of purely individual taste.

Johnson the critic

For very rough-and-ready purposes of classification Johnson's literary criticism can be divided into three categories: miscellaneous essays; the work in the edition of Shakespeare; and the *Lives of the Poets*. In effect, though, his formal criticism spans most of his long writing career, and he produces important work throughout, not to mention his many fascinating spoken comments on literature. He wrote once in a noble phrase there has been occasion to quote before that the only real reason for writing literature was 'to enable the reader better to enjoy life, or better to endure it' (Review of *A Free Inquiry*). One of the central points of his criticism is his sense that if literature is not interesting and entertaining then, whatever its other merits, it is nothing, for 'Works of imagination excel by their allurement and delight, their power of attracting and detaining the attention' ('Life of Dryden', I, 454). His own literary criticism, fortunately, passes with triumph the same test it sets. It must be among the least boring criticism ever written. We are constantly aware in reading it of the energetic responses of a powerful mind and heart, someone who enjoys literature with great gusto and has a wholesome appetite for the truth and reality he finds there.

Johnson, of course, brings enormous qualifications to the task of criticism: the breadth of his reading and learning; his vast knowledge of the English language and the shades of meaning of words; his powerful imagination and capacity for emotional identification. As a boy reading in his father's shop he stumbled across a volume of Shakespeare's plays and found his attention caught by *Hamlet*. After reading a little of the ghost's appearance he was so frightened that he had to rush upstairs in order to 'see people about him (*Johnsonian Miscellanies*, ed. G.B. Hill, Clarendon Press, 1897, I, 158–9). Reading *Lear* later, he was so upset by the death of Cordelia that he was not able to read the scene again until he had to edit it.

The forcefulness of Johnson's response to literature contributes to the forcefulness of expression in his criticism, and this sometimes, of course, amounts to the rudeness and stubbornness for which he is famous. Asked which of the two poets Smart or Derrick was superior he announced that there was no point in determining the precedence 'between a louse or a flea'. There are well-known 'howlers', which themselves, if the truth be known, contribute in some small way to most readers' enjoyment of this criticism: the claim that 'nothing odd will last; *Tristram Shandy* did not last' or the attack on Milton's *Lycidas* for insincerity in using pastoral. For these misjudgements are themselves at least felt and expressed with the same kind of vigour that is always characteristic of his literary responses. They are another facet of a disarming, indeed startling honesty, as in the occasional, winningly deliberate confession of being slapdash that can hardly fail to gain our sympathy when it appears in the midst of an otherwise magisterial assessment: [Thomson's] '*Liberty*, when it first appeared, I tried to read, and soon desisted. I have never tried again, and therefore will not hazard either praise or censure.'

At the same time, for all his strongly independent temperament and judgements, Johnson alludes frequently to the discourses of other critics and is careful, most particularly in the *Preface to Shakespeare*, to set his remarks in the context of received opinion. Living through an age that was a watershed in the history of criticism he both claims to be and genuinely is a representative as well as a powerfully individual figure as a critic.

'Neo-classicism' was itself a much more flexible system than might at first appear, but the emphases within it had already begun to shift, as we have seen. The criticism of Addison early in the century is significantly more psychological and subjective than before, and this was to be the way forward. Ideas such as originality and the need for imagination began to receive much more attention from the mid-century on. The Renaissance revival of learning had encouraged a new historical study of the classics, but, paradoxically, this would eventually undermine classicism by showing how different the classical world was from our own. Interest in earlier British literature also grew enormously. The new historical and textual scholarship led ultimately to relativism and historicism, the idea that each culture has its own radically different values and standards.

Johnson himself, as his notorious reaction to *Lycidas* shows, is at some distance from the full range of Renaissance conceptions, and much more interested in vigorous emotional truth than in the demands of genre. His own criticism powerfully displays the new interest in the reader's psychological responses. These elements in his work, certainly, are in the spirit of the new criticism that was to come into its own in the early nineteenth century. Yet the terms in which he discusses the issues are usually set by neo-classicism and there seems no point in denying that he is, in the broadest sense, a neo-classical critic. He has a stronger commitment to pleasure in literature, for example, as noted above, than most of his predecessors, but his criteria still remain within the rhetorical pleasure/instruction principle first enunciated by Horace. He writes as one profoundly committed to the idea of imitation and to the need for moral truth in literature. As is characteristic of his whole intellectual enterprise, he is able to combine some of the new empirical interests with a broadly traditionalist framework. He uses the concept of the association of ideas, for example, but he seeks always to *generalize* from the psychological data rather than accepting subjectivity. His commitment to historical and literary scholarship differentiates him from Swift and Pope, but his firm allegiance to the classical tenet that human beings are always and everywhere the same in essence prevents him from falling into the historicism and relativism that was becoming prevalent. Essentially, as W.J. Bate says, he is able to carry forward the best of the human centrality of the classical tradition by bringing out its deepest *psychological* truth and purging it of over-rigid rules and prescriptions.

The status of Shakespeare

Shakespeare's ignorance or neglect of the rules had created a stumbling block for traditional kinds of criticism. There were many in the seventeenth century who preferred the work of the more correct and classical Ben Jonson, and Charles Gildon castigated Shakespeare in this respect as late as 1723. In particular, Shakespeare was condemned, especially by French critics, for not following the three so-called 'unities' of drama. According to this influential theory (which had only shaky classical precedents), it was essential for a playwright to preserve unity of action by ensuring that there was one, clear main plot, unity of place by making that action all take place in one location and unity of time by not letting the plot act out events that took longer than twenty-four hours (*three* hours in the most rigid formulation). Shakespeare, of course, had used elaborate subplots, shifted scenes as he wished and introduced a gap of sixteen years, for example, in the middle of *A Winter's Tale*. He was also attacked for failing to keep to strict social decorum in his characterization and for mingling the genres of tragedy and comedy.

A growing number of commentators, however, were able to recognize Shakespeare's genius and to understand, as Pope put it, that condemning Shakespeare by neo-classical rules was like 'trying a man by the Laws of one Country, who acted under those of another'. This initial defence strategy gradually shifted its ground as the century progressed. From presenting Shakespeare and, to a lesser extent, other English writers such as Spenser as writers in a 'Gothic' mode with its own entirely different specifications to neo-classicism, it became more usual to celebrate their imagination and native energy as superior to art produced in terms of the rules. It was quite possible to make this assertion while remaining within the broad categories of neo-classicism, for that tradition itself realized the primacy of genius and inspiration. A certain ambivalence sometimes remained, however, as Johnson's own phrasing of the question indicates:

> Shakespeare engaged in dramatic poetry with the world open before him: the rules of the ancients were yet known to few; the public judgment was unformed; he had no example of such fame as might force him upon imitation, nor critics of such authority as might restrain his extravagance.
>
> (*Preface to Shakespeare*, VIII, 69)

The implication here that being forced into 'imitation' is a limiting thing is contradicted by the fact that it can hardly be good to have

Peter Scheemakers, Monument to Shakespeare

an 'unformed' public judgement, and the word 'extravagance' also implies negative criticism of Shakespeare's wildness.

In many circles these reservations were breaking down completely, however. The eighteenth century saw an enormous expansion in the prestige of Shakespeare and a greater enthusiasm for his work. A variety of factors were involved here clearly, not least simple national pride, for 'the chief glory of every people arises from its authors', as Johnson puts it. After the 1688 Revolution the parallel between British poetic and political 'liberty' and French absolutism became an irresistible one, and Shakespeare also fitted in well with the growing interest in original genius and imagination. The prestige of Johnson's friend, the great actor David Garrick, became very considerable and attending Shakespeare's plays was becoming a fashionable part of the growing leisure and culture industry. The Shakespeare festival at Stratford in 1769, which Garrick helped organize, was a symptom of what has been aptly termed the new 'bardolatry', though Johnson himself would have nothing to do with the proceedings. As Nicolas Till has written of Mozart, Shakespeare was beginning to be seen as a 'semi-divine' artist figure. Garrick described a visit to Stratford like a religious pilgrimage:

> All who have a heart to feel, and a mind to admire the truth of nature and splendour of genius, will rush thither to behold it, as a pilgrim would to the shrine of some loved saint; will deem it holy ground, and dwell with sweet though pensive rapture on the natal habitation of our poet.
>
> (F.E. Halliday, *The Cult of Shakespeare*,
> Duckworth, 1957, pp. 67–8)

From the 1770s onwards a stream of literary criticism appeared that anticipated romantic and Victorian attitudes of describing Shakespeare's characters as if they were real people and praising him for his invention of a completely new world of the imagination.

Shakespearian scholarship also proliferated. A recent book studying the history of eighteenth-century editorial practice was called *The Birth of Shakespeare Studies* (Arthur Sherbo, Colleagues Press, 1986), and this is no over-statement of what occurred. The Renaissance interest in the classics had led to a new concern for obtaining an accurate text, the beginnings of a new science of textual criticism through the careful comparison of one manuscript against another, and, where necessary, the emendation of a mistake in the apparent text to bring it closer to what the original author is likely to have intended. But Shakespeare's text, though printed rather than copied by hand on manuscript, was also, it came to be understood, highly problematic, since he is unlikely to have seen his works through the press and many of the existing versions are copies for and by actors.

Johnson's edition

Five other eighteenth-century editions preceded the appearance of Johnson's in 1765. He had presented his original proposals in 1745, but was put off by an argument about the copyright of Shakespeare. Other projects had then intervened. Even after

he issued subscriptions he had procrastinated. The satirist
Charles Churchill wrote rudely, 'He for subscribers baits his
hook,/And takes their cash – but where's the book?'. But Johnson
was certainly by far the best-qualified editor that had yet
appeared, and when the edition was finally published it was
clear that he was also the one with the best editorial policies. He
recognized the need for some emendation. In the description
of Falstaff's death in *Henry V*, for example, there is the famous
problem of the reading: 'His nose was as sharp as a pen
and a Table of greene fields' (II.iii.18). Johnson's predecessor,
Pope's enemy, Lewis Theobald, proposed an unusually inspired
emendation, thinking of Falstaff reverting to his country
childhood on his deathbed: 'and ababbled of green fields'.
On this occasion Johnson incorporates the new reading. But
he is the first editor to recognize that such changes should be
as infrequent as possible and that it was better humbly to accept
the original text unless it was clearly nonsense.

Johnson also had very sensible ideas about the necessary
principles for establishing the relative authority of the different
versions of Shakespeare's plays in existence (the 'quartos' and
'folios'). Unfortunately, according to the evidence provided by
modern scholars, he did not make sufficient use of what was
available to achieve all he set out to do. Yet, as a modern
commentator says, 'despite Johnson's failure to carry out what he
had proposed, the purchaser of his eight volumes of Shakespeare
still got the best and fullest edition of the plays so far published
in the eighteenth century' (H.R. Woudhuysen, *Samuel Johnson on
Shakespeare*, p. 26).

Johnson's notes make an enormous contribution here. He
often argues amusingly against the eccentric and arrogant
emendations of his predecessors and reveals his own, much
deeper knowledge of Elizabethan English acquired in particular
through his work on the *Dictionary*. But the notes are far more
than merely textual and linguistic and amount, indeed, to a
fascinating commentary on the plays in which some have seen
the finest of all Johnson's practical criticism. As we might
expect Johnson's elucidations are especially powerful when
what Shakespeare says implies and leads Johnson into humane
and generalized reflection. On the Duke's lines in *Measure for
Measure*, for example, 'Thou hast nor youth nor age;/But as it
were an after dinner's sleep,/Dreaming on both' (III.i.32–35)
Johnson writes:

> This is exquisitely imagined. When we are young we busy
> ourselves in forming schemes for succeeding time, and miss

the gratifications that are before us; when we are old we amuse the languor of age with the recollection of youthful pleasures or performances; so our life, of which no part is filled with the business of the present time, resembles our dreams after dinner, when the events of the morning are mingled with the designs of the evening. (VIII, 193)

As already mentioned, the eighteenth century saw a new interest in character criticism. Maurice Morgann's book on Falstaff, for example, in 1777 was the first full-length study of an individual character, and there were already signs of a romantic tendency to treat these characters as real people with their own existence outside the world of the plays. As we might expect, Johnson's notes show great interest in individual psychology as well. But behind his whole treatment lies Aristotle's seminal insight that literature is *more* true than history because it is more representative. To speak of Shakespeare's characters as if they are completely real and completely individual is to fail to understand this. Johnson's focus instead is on the representative and hence (inevitably) moral truth of Shakespeare's presentation of character, though not usually in a narrowly didactic way that would divorce this from *imaginative* truth. He recognizes, for example, and heavily stresses that Falstaff is immoral, but is also able to see that the whole presentation transcends simple moral judgement:

But Falstaff unimitated, unimitable Falstaff, how shall I describe thee! Thou compound of sense and vice; of sense which may be admired but not esteemed, of vice which may be despised, but hardly detested. Falstaff is a character loaded with faults, and with those faults which naturally produce contempt. He is a thief, and a glutton, a coward, and a boaster, always ready to cheat the weak, and prey upon the poor; to terrify the timorous and insult the defenceless. At once obsequious and malignant, he satirises in their absence those whom he lives by flattering. He is familiar with the Prince only as an agent of vice, but of this familiarity he is so proud as not only to be supercilious and haughty with common men, but to think his interest of importance to the Duke of Lancaster. Yet the man thus corrupt, thus despicable, makes himself necessary to the prince that despises him, by the most pleasing of all qualities, perpetual gaiety, by an unfailing power of exciting laughter, which is the more freely indulged, as his wit is not of the splendid or ambitious kind, but consists in easy escapes and sallies of levity, which make sport but raise no envy. (VIII, 523).

116

At the same time there is certainly no romantic sentimental-ization here either, and it is a general moral dictum rather than the 'real' personality of Falstaff that he comes firmly back to at the end:

> The moral to be drawn from this representation is, that no man is more dangerous than he that with a will to corrupt, hath the power to please; and that neither wit nor honesty ought to think themselves safe with such a companion when they see Henry seduced by Falstaff.

The Preface to Shakespeare *and the idea of 'nature'*

Despite the brilliance and substantiality of the notes it is the *Preface* that has always been regarded as the most important part of Johnson's edition from a critical perspective. It is 'perhaps the most famous essay on Shakespeare ever to have been written' according to a modern authority (H.R. Woudhuysen). The great paradox of Johnson's individuality and impersonality is clearly apparent here, for Johnson in one sense is presenting not his own opinion on Shakespeare, but a summary and survey of received views, which is obviously what he regards as the proper way to proceed in the preface to a great edition. There is very little that is purely original in what Johnson says. Instead the *Preface* is a representative document in the history of criticism. With patriotic pride Johnson opposes French absolutism and makes use both of the new historical knowledge and the new empirical psychology. Yet the terms of his discussion are still set by neo-classicism and he continues to believe that general literary principles can be derived from experience. He stands back from the growing subjectivity of the criticism of his time and his citation of Shakespeare's faults puts him at odds with the bardolatry of his own and subsequent periods.

At the same time, the magisterial way in which Johnson weighs and evaluates traditional opinions, sometimes giving his nod in their favour and sometimes against, shows him assuming enormous authority, even if he tries to claim that that authority comes to him from 'the common reader'. Occasionally, as in his rejection of the three unities, he images himself as standing bravely against the weight of all the tradition that has gone before. The continuous vigour and power of his expression always reveals the depth of his own involvement, even when he is at his most conventional, and the whole work, especially his comments on the 'dull duty of an editor', is enlivened by frequent personal touches of self-depreciation, humour and irony.

Befitting his great sense of responsibility here the *Preface* is very carefully structured and argued. He begins with a tight-packed argument, rather inaccessible at first to the reader, about the esteem due to past literature. He says that the idea that the reputation of ancient writers is inflated is one that moderns are likely to put forward out of jealousy. Although age may sometimes add false lustre to literature, the fact that a work has been esteemed by many readers over a long stretch of time is the truest test of literary merit we are likely to be able to find. But Johnson neatly turns the arguments of the supporters of ancient learning to the defence of a writer of the modern era, Shakespeare, who has by now attained to the status of a classic himself.

At the heart of Shakespeare's greatness, says Johnson, in famous phrases, is the fact that he is 'above all writers, at least above all modern writers, the poet of nature; the poet that holds up to his readers a faithful mirror of manners and of life'. We could perhaps be forgiven a certain disappointment here. The word 'nature', after all, is a problematic one. It is, one might say, a 'sacred cow' for the period, a concept regarded with great reverence, but used, as many scholars have shown, in a variety of meanings, and often invoked as a final authority by completely antithetical thinkers. For Johnson here it is first and foremost a strong reassertion of the ancient tradition of *mimesis* or imitation. 'Nature' equals 'reality' here, and the poet's function is primarily to imitate that reality.

The 'nature' or reality that Johnson has in mind is *human* nature, not the external nature of scenery that the romantics were concerned with. What Shakespeare imitates is the permanent, bedrock reality of human nature through the ages. But behind this, certainly, there lies the whole wider universe, governed, as Christian humanist thought proclaims, by the orderly laws of God, and this sense of order was deepened for believers in Johnson's own time by Newtonian science.

For 'reality' is not to be described randomly or superficially, in what is popularly called today 'a slice of life', nor is nature a primitivist concept, nature 'naked, undisciplined, uninstructed', as he put it elsewhere. 'Nature' is really a norm, and the writer must have an eye to the representative essence of things: nature in the Aristotelian sense of the inner dynamism that makes a thing what it is. That kind of truth is to be distinguished in its selectiveness from simple realism, which would convey only a surface level.

118

To imitate nature in this way is, as we have seen, to be both representative and particular, for the poet discovers the norms 'nature' provides, it is important to note, not in some abstract, purely ideal way, but by examining particulars. This is always the case, we should remember, when Johnson uses phrases such as 'the grandeur of generality' in his criticism. Detail and individual particulars that do not touch our human sympathy and that have no representative quality can never amount to major literature, but it is equally possible to be 'general' in a pejorative sense, vague, unrealized. D.J. Greene explains helpfully that 'general' is more likely to mean 'widely recognizable' than 'abstract' in Johnson.

The concept of 'nature' obviously has crucial implications for 'imagination' too. Despite his reservations in his moral writings as such, Johnson sees imagination as essential to literature. There are even occasions when what might seem a romantic conception is present and a writer is praised for apparently going beyond imitation, most notably in the famous 'Prologue Spoken at the Opening of the Theatre in Drury Lane, 1747', where Shakespeare is said to have 'Exhausted worlds, and then imagined new'. But 'imagination' for Johnson primarily means the art of *realising* an image, making an imitation seem vivid and emotionally real. Even the most fertile 'invention' has to be built up out of pre-existing materials, and needs to retain probability, a certain emotional truth and link with what does exist.

The imitation of nature is also crucial to Johnson's sense of how Shakespeare discharges the poet's traditional function of combining moral instruction and pleasure. Every page of Johnson's account is filled with his own vast appetite for knowledge, truth and entertainment from literature. It is because he provides the kind of imitation he does that Shakespeare is at the deepest level both instructive and entertaining, for our minds are so constituted that:

> Nothing can please many, and please long, but just representations of general nature . . . The irregular combinations of fanciful invention may delight a-while, by that novelty of which the common satiety of life sends us all in quest; but the pleasures of sudden wonder are soon exhausted, and the mind can only repose on the stability of truth.   (VIII, 61–2)

As is so often the case in his work, the way Johnson uses the whole concept of 'nature' in his criticism thus synthesizes traditional Christian humanism with the new empirical thinking, and combines conventional terminology and a deeply-felt personal response.

119

Shakespeare's merits and 'faults'

Johnson goes on to draw out the implications of the central idea of Shakespeare as poet of 'nature' in terms of language and characterization in particular. He reflects the period's new interests in the way that he stresses Shakespeare's psychological truth and talks about the reader's responses, but he uses these criteria to bolster up rather than abolish the old principles and without losing himself in subjectivity. He can hardly fail to recognize certain elements in Shakespeare that work against his own careful contrast between 'barbarous' romances with a 'giant and a dwarf' and Shakespeare's own characterization. But he points out that even when the agents are supernatural and the plot improbable a real truth to life is always preserved:

> Other writers disguise the most natural passions and most frequent incidents; so that he who contemplates them in the book will not know them in the world: Shakespeare approximates the remote, and familiarizes the wonderful; the event which he represents will not happen, but, if it were possible, its effects would probably be such as he has assigned; and it may be said, that he has not only shown human nature as it acts in real exigences, but as it would be found in trials, to which it cannot be exposed.   (VIII, 64–5)

Such criteria, he recognizes, bring him into direct conflict with those who have condemned Shakespeare for failing to follow the narrow version of decorum that says that kings must always be royal and Roman senators always dignified and for mingling the genres of tragedy and comedy. His answer is in both cases the same: 'there is always an appeal open from criticism to nature', and Shakespeare has followed the truer decorum of imitating life itself. This defence of tragicomedy in particular, though Johnson has one or two relatively unimportant predecessors, is so definitive as to be the nearest thing to an actual innovation in the *Preface*.

Now, though, in a way that seems startling to a modern reader, Johnson goes on to consider Shakespeare's genuine 'faults'. In a notorious earlier essay he had complained of the use of the 'low' word 'knife' in *Macbeth*. In the *Preface* he makes it clear that Shakespeare's language still often infringes his ideas of poetic diction, though we have to recognize that Johnson's sense of these matters is by no means mechanical. If Shakespeare is sometimes, it seems, too 'low', at other times he offends decorum in precisely the opposite way: 'The equality of words to things is very often neglected, and trivial sentiments

120

and vulgar ideas disappoint the attention to which they are recommended by sonorous epithets and swelling figures.'

It is above all in Shakespeare's failure to provide moral instruction that we find neo-classical strictures coinciding with Johnson's own deepest feelings. Shakespeare's works, Johnson has already said, are inevitably a source of moral teaching in that they are so brilliant in imitation of fundamental human reality. Yet they have no specific *intention*, it seems, of instructing in that way and thus may verge on the danger Johnson sees in novels of simply conveying reality 'promiscuously'. They offend at times in particular in a way that Johnson obviously found threatening against the demands of 'poetic justice', the view that the innocent should not be destroyed in the end.

In castigating Shakespeare's faults, however, Johnson takes the opportunity of coming to his defence once again in the context of a *supposed* fault, his neglect of the three unities of action, space and time that French theorists and practitioners of the drama had insisted on. Here Johnson is less daring than he pretends, for he had more influential predecessors in this than on tragicomedy. Once again, though, it is vigour of his argument that strikes us. The unities were necessary, it was held, to produce the illusion of reality, for an audience might believe they were in Rome, for example, but hardly Rome and then Egypt and then Rome again as in *Antony and Cleopatra*. Nonsense, says Johnson, for the audience is never deceived in the first place!

> The truth is, that the spectators are always in their senses, and know, from the first act to the last, that the stage is only a stage, and that the players are only players . . . where is the absurdity of allowing that space to represent first Athens, and then Sicily, which was always known to be neither Sicily nor Athens, but a modern theatre? (VIII, 77)

This is hardly an adequate account of the special nature of dramatic 'illusion' (Coleridge was later to talk of 'that willing suspension of disbelief that constitutes dramatic faith'), but it is difficult not to sympathize with the main thrust of Johnson's argument and to admire his robust logic.

From his adjudications of praise and blame Johnson now passes to an examination of Shakespeare in terms of the Elizabethan age itself. In his rapid survey of conditions of authorship, learning, sources and so on he shows a full grasp of all that the new scholarship of the time had discovered, but he firmly refuses to move towards the relativist position that the different standards of different societies were of equal validity.

There is, it has been said, more than a 'touch of condescension' in the way Johnson speaks of the Elizabethans, and this at a time when influential figures were implying that eighteenth-century civilization was too sophisticated in comparison with the earlier periods to create the greatest kinds of art. Johnson, for all his knowledge of the past, has no doubt of the cultural superiority of his own time, and he is always careful to assert that morality and justice are absolutes 'independent on time or place'.

The final section discusses Johnson's principles as an editor and evaluates with a remarkable combination of respect and irony the work of his predecessors in this task. As so often in Johnson, the work in which he is engaged – like many human endeavours – seems to him both worthy and futile, and there are several funny passages in which he describes how the writer of notes should proceed, for example, by criticizing the stupidity of the previous editors and then producing the correct reading like a rabbit out of a hat. He says that the reader should ignore notes where possible, but recognizes that if notes are an evil they are a necessary evil at times:

> It has to be lamented, that such a writer should want a commentary; that his language should become obsolete, or his sentiments obscure. But it is vain to carry wishes beyond the condition of human things; that which must happen to all, has happened to Shakespeare, by accident and time . . . (VIII, 112)

Johnson's *Preface to Shakespeare* stands, as we have seen, at a crucial place in the history of criticism, but he is not at this time, perhaps, fully aware of it. There is a sense in which he is fighting the battles of the past. Reflecting the new enthusiasm of his time he is defending Shakespeare against a narrower neo-classicism. But the new movements are soon to make neo-classicism virtually redundant. It may seem odd to think of so robust a work as the *Preface* as sad, but there is a certain sadness for us in realizing how radically we are cut off from Johnson's confident assumptions about literature and about morality, assumptions under which most of the great works of the past have been written. One thing we learn from the *Preface* is how *differently we* read Shakespeare. But that is not all there is to it, of course. The *Preface* fulfilled a valuable function for its own time when narrower views still prevailed in some quarters. Its assertion of the humane centrality of literature also serves as a challenge to the romantic subjectivity that was to follow and perhaps even to our own scepticism.

The Lives of the Poets *as biographies*

If Johnson found the work on his great Shakespeare edition intensely difficult, the *Lives of the Poets* grew in his hands from the short prefaces to the works of the English poets he was at first requested to write. Yet the original purpose still has an impact on the final whole, and the collection is a very uneven one formally, ranging from the briefest lives of minor poets to book-length studies of Milton, Dryden and Pope. Johnson's zest for the work comes across, though, in the vivid detail, and the *Lives* have always been among Johnson's most popular and accessible works.

Although on rare occasions anecdotes seem to have been selected solely for picturesque effect, Johnson has especially by now mastered the art of drawing convincing moral truths from specific particulars, so that this work becomes the culmination of his whole attempt to reconcile morally exemplary and empirical, factual biography. A powerful example is the combination of horrifying detail and general 'vanity of human wishes' irony in the memorable description of Swift's last years:

> He grew more violent; and his mental powers declined, till (1741) it was found necessary that legal guardians should be appointed of his person and fortune. He now lost distinction. His madness was compounded of rage and fatuity. The last face that he knew was that of Mrs. Whiteway; and her he ceased to know in a little time. His meat was brought him cut into mouthfuls; but he would never touch it while the servant stayed, and at last, after it had stood perhaps an hour, would eat it walking; for he continued his old habit, and was on his feet ten hours a day.
>
> Next year (1742) he had an inflammation in his left eye, which swelled it to the size of an egg, with boils in other parts; he was kept long waking with the pain, and was not easily restrained by five attendants from tearing out his eye.
>
> The tumour at last subsided; and a short interval of reason ensuing, in which he knew his physician and his family, gave hopes of his recovery; but in a few days he sunk into lethargic stupidity, motionless, heedless, and speechless. But it is said, that, after a year of total silence, when his housekeeper, on the 30th of November, told him that the usual bonfires and illuminations were preparing to celebrate his birthday, he answered, 'It is all folly; they had better let it alone.' (III, 48–9)

One great advantage is that even the lives of very minor

figures can thus be generalized into splendid exemplifications of what has been termed the 'irony of literary careers' (Paul Fussell), yet without losing touch with particulars that may have their own grimly comic dimension. In describing the death of the minor poet and playwright Edmund Smith, for example, Johnson tells how he gains a patron, leisure and opportunity to write a great tragedy and resolves to go into the country to do so. Unfortunately a combination of drink and arrogance about his own amateur medical skills leads to his downfall, and the planned high heroic literary tragedy turns into the mock-heroic, factual one of his own end:

> Having formed his plan and collected materials, he declared a few months would complete his design; and, that he might pursue his work with less frequent avocations, he was, in June 1710, invited by Mr. George Ducket to his house at Gartham, in Wiltshire. Here he found such opportunities of indulgence as did not much forward his studies, and particularly some strong ale, too delicious to be resisted. He ate and drank till he found himself plethoric [swollen with fluids]: and then, resolving to ease himself by evacuation, he wrote to an apothecary in the neighbourhood a prescription of a purge so forcible, that the apothecary thought it his duty to delay it till he had given notice of its danger. Smith, not pleased with the contradiction of a shopman, and boastful of his own knowledge, treated the notice with rude contempt, and swallowed his own medicine, which, in July 1710, brought him to the grave. He was buried at Gartham.
>
> (II, 17–18)

The longer lives turn into something more: flexible, empirical critical biography in which life and art are suggestively linked and yet also firmly separated. A great poet's work may represent a noble transcendence both of the difficulties of the life and the petty vices of the personality, as Johnson's admiration for *Paradise Lost* – despite his dislike of Milton's politics – conveys. In the case of Dryden, on the other hand, the personal moral weaknesses that Johnson unblinkingly surveys prevent the poetry from being as great as it might otherwise have been. Yet there is no denying at the same time that the genius the poetry reveals quite outsoars any purely biographical strictures.

What we are finally left with once again therefore in Johnson's treatment of the greatest writers is a compassionate and wondering, almost contradictory, sense of how human greatness and littleness are combined. Despite our petty lives we can achieve magnificent things, but at the same time our weaknesses and vices may detract from or diminish our achievements. The sense of Pope's physical and moral weaknesses, for example, casts an obvious ironic light on his personal vanity. Yet we are also aware of the difficulties Pope had to transcend in order to produce his great works, and Johnson's most generous admiration for the latter shows us what frail human beings are still capable of achieving at their best.

The Lives *as criticism*

As literary criticism the *Lives*, of course, amount to a great panoramic survey of the poetry of Johnson's own time and the period preceding. The 'Life of Cowley', which begins the collection, is a marvellously acid biography, but there had been lives of Cowley before and what was really needed was literary criticism. Cowley's position at the end of an important literary movement created the need for a summary as the prelude to a study of the poetry of the modern age. No such definition and survey of the work of 'the metaphysicals' such as John Donne, George Herbert and others had been attempted before, and Johnson's is a classic account that has set the terms for all subsequent discussion. Though he is hardly likely to approve of the mode overall he gets to the heart of it with great perception and clearly finds it interesting and in some respects attractive:

> Yet great labour directed by great abilities is never wholly lost: if they frequently threw away their wit on false conceits, they likewise sometimes struck out unexpected truth: if their conceits were far-fetched, they were often worth the carriage. To write on their plan, it was at least necessary to read and think. No man could be born a metaphysical poet, nor assume the dignity of a writer by descriptions copied from descriptions, by imitations borrowed from imitations, by traditional imagery and hereditary similes, by readiness of rhyme and volubility of syllables.   (I, 21)

He understands that a particular conception of wit lies behind this mode, and provides his own analysis of the topic in one of his most remarkable theoretical discussions, in which he crosses swords with Pope as well as with the metaphysicals and suggests that the truest kind of wit is that which is 'both natural and new, that which though not obvious, is upon its first production, acknowledged to be just ... that which he that never found it wonders how he missed it'. These are criteria that are at the heart of his own criticism.

In the 'Life of Milton' we see another attempt at coming to terms with earlier literature whose preconceptions are, to a degree we might find surprising, alien to him. He is hostile naturally enough to Milton's political opinions and to the particular form of the Christian religion he adopted. But Milton also follows some Renaissance literary conventions that have ceased to have much meaning by Johnson's period. The most notorious consequence is Johnson's reaction to 'Lycidas'. In condemning the poem for insincerity he fails to understand that it is not a personal elegy for Edward King anyway and that the pastoral mode he so savagely attacks is chosen by Milton precisely in that it generalizes the significance of King's death and relates him to a whole tradition. Johnson also dislikes the Renaissance habit of mind that finds elements of Christian truth in classical mythology, once again failing to see that the whole movement of the poem is from such pagan fiction to Christian truth. Even here, of course, Johnson's phrasing is so forceful that he has been cited ever since in 'Lycidas' criticism, and the misreading at least has the virtue of concentrating attention on what Milton *was* trying to achieve.

Johnson's prejudices and the very real reservations he feels do not, however, prevent him from appreciating the greatness of *Paradise Lost*, and his praise of the poem, culled below from different sections of the 'Life', is perhaps the noblest that has ever been written. He says that the thoughts 'called forth' in it:

> are such as could only be produced by an imagination in the highest degree fervid and active, to which materials were supplied by incessant study and unlimited curiosity. The heat of Milton's mind may be said to sublimate his learning, to throw off into his work the spirit of science, unmingled with its grosser parts. ... The characteristic quality of his poem is sublimity. He sometimes descends to the elegant, but his element is the great. He can occasionally invest himself with grace; but his natural port is gigantick loftiness. He can please when pleasure is required; but it is his peculiar power to astonish. ... He seems to have been well acquainted with his own genius, and to know what it was the Nature had bestowed upon him more bountifully than upon others; the power of displaying the vast, illuminating the splendid, enforcing the awful, darkening the gloomy, and aggravating the dreadful. ... Whatever be his subject,

he never fails to fill the imagination. . . . In Milton every line breathes sanctity of thought and purity of manners. . . . His great works were performed under discountenance, and in blindness, but difficulties vanished at his touch; he was born for whatever is arduous; and his work is not the greatest of heroic poems, only because it is not the first.

Naturally enough, he finds the work of Dryden and Pope easier to deal with, and these great lives constitute the real heart of the collection. He accepts without reservation the view that their poetry in the heroic couplet completed the definitive 'improvement' on the irregularities of the earlier seventeenth century. 'By perusing the works of Dryden', he writes of Pope, 'he discovered the most perfect fabric of English verse, and habituated himself to that only which he found the best. . . .' More importantly Johnson finds in them the epitome of what poetry for him was at its most valuable – a social and moral art, where representative human truth is presented with all the glories of imagination and wit, both 'natural and new'.

As with all the best neo-classical criticism inspiration, imagination, even originality are praised here, provided that they serve to express and *realize* rather than to evade that human centrality that is covered by the term 'nature'. Pope certainly had 'Imagination', Johnson says, that quality 'which strongly impresses on the writer's mind, and enables him to convey to the reader, the various forms of nature, incidents of life and energies of passion', but this is perfectly combined with 'Judgement' which 'selects from life or nature what the present purpose requires, and by separating the essence of things from its concomitants, often makes the representation more powerful than the reality' (III, 247). In the *Rape of the Lock* 'are exhibited, in a very high degree, the two most engaging powers of an author. New things are made familiar, and familiar things are made new.'

These criteria are flexible enough to allow Johnson to appreciate a much wider range of literature than we might at first expect. Not only does he recognize the greatness of the blank verse sublimity of *Paradise Lost*, as we have seen, but he is also prepared to praise Thomson's *The Seasons*. Despite his preference for the heroic couplet he recognizes that this 'is one of the works in which blank verse seems properly used. Thomson's wide expansion of general views, and his enumeration of circumstantial varieties, would have been obstructed and embarrassed by the frequent intersections of the sense, which are the necessary effects of rhyme.' Thomson's 'sublimity', like Milton's, is proper to his subject, 'the whole magnificence of Nature', and his originality praiseworthy in that it is a new view of something that still remains 'natural':

> he looks round on Nature and on life with the eye which Nature bestows only on a poet; the eye that distinguishes, in everything presented to its view, whatever there is on which imagination can delight to be detained, and with a mind that at once comprehends the vast and attends to the minute. The reader of *The Seasons* wonders that he never saw before what Thomson shows him, and that he never yet has felt what Thomson impresses.   (III, 299)

The same cannot be said, however, for the later generation of poets that it was once usual to term the 'pre-romantics', Thomas Gray and William Collins in particular. The extravagances of their style, unlike Thompson's, are not justified by their subject-matter. Johnson attacks Gray's 'poetic diction', it is interesting to see, with the same vigour as Wordsworth would in the Preface to *Lyrical Ballads*, finding it an offence against decorum rather than in keeping with it, and hence decadent. These odes are:

> marked by glittering accumulations of ungraceful ornaments; they strike rather than please; the images are magnified by affectation; the language is laboured into harshness. The mind of the writer seems to work with unnatural violence. 'Double, double, toil and trouble.' He has a kind of strutting dignity, and is tall by walking on tiptoe. His art and his struggle are too visible, and there is too little appearance of ease and nature.   (III, 440)

Again in contrast to Thompson's, Johnson finds the 'imagination' of these poets an indulgence in fancy, an escape from truth rather than a special way of realizing nature: Collins:

> had employed his mind chiefly upon works of fiction and subjects of fancy; and by indulging some peculiar habits of thought, was eminently delighted with those flights of imagination which pass the bounds of nature. . . . He loved fairies, genii, giants and monsters; he delighted to rove through the meanders of enchantment, to gaze on the magnificence of golden palaces, to repose by the waterfalls of Elysian gardens.   (III, 337)

In making such criticisms Johnson was going against the literary fashions of the day, as he very well knew, and he incurred considerable hostility in some quarters. It is only with hindsight that we call this 'The Age of Johnson'. In literature as in politics Johnson felt himself an embattled figure in some respects. The various new trends discussed in the section on Shakespeare had come to fruition now. Johnson had at first welcomed his friend Joseph Warton's *Essay on the Genius and Writings of Pope* (1756), but the implications and general tenor of the book had become clearer over the years and it had contributed to a certain downgrading of Pope's major work in comparison with the ideals of the new school. This specific literary controversy is itself clearly a reflection of much wider ideological issues. To Johnson poets such as Gray and Collins come to stand for the excesses of the sentimental movement and the growing subjectivity of the period, and he opposes these symptoms with great vigour whilst conceding at times the incidental beauties of their work.

Yet, as Alvin Kernan says, we should not allow the controversies and the apparent randomness of the *Lives* to obscure 'Johnson's real achievement . . . of combining the hitherto scattered pieces of English literary lore, and working them into a structure of biography, social history and criticism sufficiently firm to constitute for the first time a history of English letters' (*Printing, Technology, Letters & Samuel Johnson*, p. 275). His great predecessor, Dryden, from whom he learned so much, writes criticism as a practising artist and addresses it to a small élite. Johnson writes as *a reader*, and builds on Addison's achievement to address a general public. He thinks of his audience as people who buy books and who, quite rightly, expect to enjoy them, but in invoking their responses as the authority for his own criticism he is in reality also seeking to improve their tastes by implying what their norms of judgement should be. He is 'both appealing to and calling into being their good sense, their fundamental humanity, their awareness of permanent social and experiential truths', as Kernan puts it. He thus achieves, in the words of another commentator, an 'impressive compromise' between the values of excellence and the literary hierarchy and the values of the marketplace (Patrick Parrinder, *Authors and Authority*, 1977, p. 31).

129

8 Language

The Renaissance boosted interest not only in the classical languages but also in the modern European vernaculars, and highlighted the humanist view that language was central to the social, cultural and political life of human beings. Language was the 'great Instrument, and common Tye of Society' in the words of Locke (*Essay concerning Human Understanding*, III, i.i). It was therefore of the greatest importance to the cultural health of the nation, for 'the language of any people is an exact index of the state of their minds' (*Encyclopaedia Britannica*, 1787–97).

As we have seen, the revival of interest in classical literature in the Renaissance was not a matter of slavish imitation. For most writers the point was rather to attempt to emulate that greatness for one's own nation in the modern age. The requirement, therefore, was to raise the vernacular languages as much as possible to the same quality and status as the classical languages.

Early in the sixteenth century the poet John Skelton complained feelingly about the inadequacy of English:

> Our natural tongue is rude,
> And hard to be enneude [renewed]
> With polished terms lusty;
> Our language is so rusty.
> (*Booke of Phyllyp Sparowe*, 769–73)

One way of attempting to deal with the problem was to fill English with Latin and Greek words, like Shakespeare's pedantic schoolmaster Holofernes in *Love's Labour's Lost,* who 'has been at a great feast of languages' and now has only 'the scraps' remaining. In the so-called 'Ink-horn controversy' of the late sixteenth century the debate was entered between supporters of classical diction in English and those who preferred instead to try to develop native resources. Of the two greatest British epic writers of the Renaissance, Spenser in the Elizabethan period chose on the whole the native model, whereas Milton in the next century may in the very broadest terms be said to have chosen the classical.

The most ambitious poets in Renaissance traditions were

especially worried about the instability of the modern languages compared to the classics. It was a genuine question at first whether it was worth trying to write in the native language at all. As late as the seventeenth century Edmund Waller says that he who writes in English 'writes in sand', and Pope was later to comment that the English language changes so fast that 'Such as Chaucer is, shall Dryden be' (i.e. difficult for the general reader to understand). There was also the concern caused by theories of inevitable cyclic decline into over-refinement and corruption that were popular at the Renaissance through the influence of classical historians. Johnson himself reflects such theories when he writes in the 'Preface' to his *Dictionary* that 'every language has a time of rudeness antecedent to perfection, as well as a false refinement and declension'.

Such concerns combine with social considerations in the growing desire to achieve correctness and 'fix' the language. To write and speak properly is always regarded as the mark of having been properly brought up, and issues of class and education are inevitably bound up together. In the early Renaissance the centralization of national power required a new educated bureaucracy, and the growth of town life and the new prosperity produced a new social mobility. The new groupings were anxious to improve and assert their status by the way they wrote and spoke, but more conservative influences were naturally anxious to reassert their own status in ways that would exclude such social climbers.

There was also an increased awareness of other more exotic languages throughout the Renaissance period. New directions in biblical study after the Reformation led more scholars to learn Hebrew. The missionary work of the Catholic Counter-Reformation and the voyages of discovery meanwhile brought knowledge of a wide range of languages that were virtually unknown to Europeans before.

As Murray Cohen summarizes it in *Sensible Words* (1977), seventeenth-century linguistics were dominated 'by assumptions of divine origin, prospects of renewed universal language, and faith in the correspondence between words and the order of things'. The biblical perspective and the increased recognition of the diversity of human languages brought the question of the origins of language to the fore, and there was a great deal of speculation and theorizing on the subject. Most thinkers of the time followed biblical orthodoxy in seeing language as God's direct gift. Adam was originally granted the authority to confer on everything its proper name, but this perfect correspondence had been broken by the fall. The story of the Tower of

Babel completed the disharmony and created the bewildering diversification of human language, which henceforth made communication difficult.

In the middle ages the original language had been assumed to be Hebrew. The idea continued to have its supporters, but other theorists, of a mystical or rationalist bent, sought not to rediscover this universal language but to re-invent one that would have a proper correspondence between word and thing. The need seemed the more urgent since Latin was declining as the standard European language for learning because of the Reformation and because of the new science, for the purposes of which it was clearly inadequate. Scientists obviously needed to communicate across national boundaries and they had to establish an appropriate symbolic language for experimental purposes. Yet, as Bacon pointed out, confusions of languages were widespread and words could not always be taken as referring to real things. He himself proposed a special system of 'real' characters – symbols that would have an immediately obvious connection to the thing they described – to remedy the situation.

Others, imbued with the ambitious rationalism of some seventeenth-century philosophy, proposed a language system that in its own complex internal relationships would mirror the relationships between things in the world. In England the Royal Society expressed grave concern about the inaccuracy of current language, and Thomas Sprat made a famous recommendation to exact from its members (at least for scientific purposes) 'a close, naked, natural way of speaking; positive expressions; clear senses, a native easiness; bringing all things as near to the mathematical plainness, as they can: and preferring the language of artisans, countrymen and merchants, before that of wits, or scholars'. More radically, the Society also sponsored John Wilkins's remarkable project to formulate a philosophic language. He produced a hierarchy of conventional signs that was supposed to reflect natural order, writing confidently in the 'Dedication' that 'the reducing of all things and notions, to such kind of Tables, as are here proposed . . . would prove the shortest and plainest way to the attainment of real knowledge that hath been yet offered to the World'.

The philosophy of John Locke in the late seventeenth century had important things to say about the way language *signifies*. He explains in the *Essay concerning Human Understanding* that most people do not assign meaning in an objective and logical way but allow words to be coloured with associations that are purely subjective. Thus words do not follow 'natural correspondences', and definitions vary from speaker to speaker. As Johnson, following Locke, puts it in the 'Preface' to the *Dictionary*: 'Words are but the signs of ideas. ...' Locke himself, though, is still sufficiently of his period to hope that his explanation of the irrationality of human language would help to rectify the situation and bring about a new, more logical type of definition. He suggests that terms be broken down into separate sense impressions, 'simple ideas', that are the basic building bricks of more complex ideas.

Post-Restoration concerns for English

In Chapter 5 of the third book of *Gulliver's Travels* Swift has some marvellous satire on the seventeenth-century linguistic reformers and their attempts to produce a universal language in which there would be a perfect correspondence between words and things. One project calls, for example, for the abolition of words altogether and requires carrying about a great sack of things with which to communicate:

> which hath only this inconvenience attending it, that if a man's business be very great, and of various kinds, he must be obliged in proportion to carry a greater bundle of *things* upon his back, unless he can afford one or two strong servants to attend him. I have often beheld two of those sages almost sinking under the weight of their packs, like pedlars among us; who when they met in the street would lay down their loads, open their sacks and hold conversation for an hour together; then put up their implements, help each other to resume their burthens, and take their leave.

Older ideas about the origins of language certainly did not disappear in the eighteenth century. On the whole, though, there is less interest in the more ambitious speculations and the universal projects of reform and more attention to the needs of the *English* language as such. An intensified post-Restoration concern for improvement, refinement and stability lies behind such considerations, and it is reinforced by a growing national pride. There was anxiety, for example, that the English language would be contaminated by too many French loan words. Addison in the *Spectator* No. 165 wondered whether 'superintendents of our language' might not be required to prevent this. The needs of a new, broader based élite are also reflected in the increasing concern with language, for such a grouping would obviously be anxious to establish its own status in this way and mark itself off from the 'the vulgar'.

For half a century or so after the Restoration various writers thought that the only solution lay in an Academy on the lines of the several Italian Academies and the French Academy, which had been founded in 1635 to act as an authority for the language. Dryden was one of the most prestigious of those who argued for such a measure, and Defoe took the same view. Swift was the last major advocate in 1712, regarding it as the best method for '*ascertaining* and *fixing* our language for ever, after such alterations are made in it as shall be thought requisite'.

The question of English grammar was also especially relevant here. Johnson describes the English language in the 'Preface' to his *Dictionary* as being 'copious without order, and energetic without rules'. Traditional upper-class education was so dominated by the classics that 'illiterate' often meant 'ignorant of Latin and Greek' in the period. But Locke declared in *Some Thoughts Concerning Education* (1693) that 'it will be a matter of wonder why young gentlemen are forced to learn the grammars of foreign and dead languages, and are never once told of the grammar of their own tongues: they do not so much as know there is any such thing, much less make it their business to be instructed in it'. He goes on to say that a gentleman must study English grammar since 'the want of propriety and grammatical exactness is thought very misbecoming to one of that rank, and usually draws on one guilty of such faults the censure of having had a lower breeding and worse company than suits with his quality'. It was the new schools and colleges for the Protestant dissenters, who were debarred from the traditional universities, that began to pioneer the practical teaching of English grammar. Titles such as James Greenwood's *An Essay Towards a Practical Grammar of the English Language* (1711) proliferated in the eighteenth century.

As the century progressed, however, the very desire for correctness in English grammar and the social anxiety about mistakes had the paradoxical effect of reaffirming the domination of the model of *Latin* grammar because it was easier to draw orderly rules on that basis. This reaches its climax with Lindley Murray's highly influential *English Grammar* of 1795, which was based to an extraordinary degree on rules analogous to Latin.

English spelling was also a matter of special concern. It was dependent on pronunciation, and this in turn varied in accordance with the class, education and regional dialect of the speaker. One writer (George Harris) went so far in his attempt to rectify the situation as to argue that parliament should make correct spelling a matter of law!

What was becoming obvious was that English needed not

so much an Academy on the continental model as a proper dictionary. The lack of such a resource when the major continental countries already had one was becoming a constant rebuke to English intellectual life. Dryden complained forcefully in 1693, for example, that 'we have yet . . . not so much as a tolerable dictionary . . . so that our language is in a manner barbarous' (*Discourse Concerning Satire*). The same complaint was repeated in 1724 by the anonymous authors of *The Many Advantages of a Good Language*, who said that a dictionary was needed to bring English 'into method, with an account of the Derivations, and Senses and Uses of Words', and by many other writers.

It was not, as is still sometimes popularly asserted, that there was no such thing as a dictionary in English at all before Johnson. In the sixteenth century bilingual lists of words – French–English, Welsh–English, Spanish–English – had appeared. From the beginning of the seventeenth century there were dictionaries devoted solely to the English language, but they were concerned with so-called 'hard words', the vocabulary of learning, technical words, and acclimatised foreign words. It was not until 1702 that the first dictionary appeared that included the basic 'core' words of English. The revised edition of Nathaniel Bailey's dictionary in 1736 contained nearly sixty thousand words, but there was still confusion between the roles of a dictionary and an encyclopaedia, so that proper names such as the mythological figure Actaeon, for example, were included.

The later eighteenth century was to see the first signs of a major shift in language study. Lord Momboddo's notorious speculations on the origins of language as an evolution from the most primitive forms of communication which human beings share with the animals were mocked by Johnson, but they reveal an understanding that change is the essence of language. Otherwise disparate figures such as Adam Smith, Joseph Priestley and Sir William Jones also came to see their primary function as that of *describing* language and *recording* change, and this marks the real beginning of scientific linguistics in Britain.

Such a view was very much in its infancy, however, and held only by a small minority. Most writers on the language, most schoolmasters and almost the whole of the general educated public continued to be dominated by rule-bound, prescriptive linguistics. Johnson's *Dictionary* obviously itself arises out of the general context of the desire for correctness and stability. Yet its main significance in the history of language study in Britain is the way that Johnson painfully and with great ambivalence comes to recognize that rules cannot hold back linguistic change.

Johnson's Dictionary

If it is a mistake to think of Johnson's as the *first* English dictionary, it is undoubtedly the first one that could be taken as meeting the real needs already described, the first, as H.W. Wheatley writes, that 'could in any way be considered as a standard. . . . For a century at least literary men had been sighing for some standard, and Johnson did what Dryden, Waller, Pope, Swift and others had only talked about' (*Antiquary*, XI, 1885). Johnson spends no time on the speculations about the origins of language that were so popular in the seventeenth century. His views throughout seem resolutely anti-theoretical, even secular. 'Speech', he announces in the *Plan of a Dictionary of the English Language*, 'was not formed by an analogy sent from heaven. It did not descend to us in a state of uniformity and perfection. . . .' 'I am not yet so lost in lexicography', he says in the 'Preface', 'as to forget that *words are the daughters of earth, and that things are the sons of heaven.*' His is an eminently practical work, a dictionary for use. Despite the beautiful rhetorical self-depreciation of the 'Preface' he said without any undue modesty to Boswell, 'I knew very well what was to be done and have done it very well.'

The choice of words and the definitions are themselves a major improvement on what had gone before. As pointed out in the biographical section, too much attention (even if this is almost irresistible) has been paid to the humorous or self-depreciating definitions such as *oats* or *lexicographer* and to the elaborate Latinate explanations of words like *cough* – 'a convulsion of the lungs, vellicated by some sharp serosity' – or *network* – 'anything reticulated or decussated at equal distances with interstices between the intersections'. Johnson's own style, of course, has always been notorious for 'hard words'. One contemporary said rudely that Johnson wrote the *Rambler* to make the *Dictionary* necessary and the *Dictionary* to explain the *Rambler*. It is true that he introduces some words of classical origin in the *Dictionary* that never became acclimatized, though these, as W.K. Wimsatt has shown, are words chosen for their scientific and medical precision, not their classicism. Johnson is not an exponent of 'ink-horn' classicism for its own sake, and, as we have seen, he is not afraid of plain English where necessary. Like the famous jokes and personal references, elaborate definitions are rare. Even the version of *cough* has

LE'WDSTER. *n. f.* [from *lewd.*] A lecher; one given to criminal pleafures.

> Againſt ſuch *lewdſters*, and their lechery,
> Thoſe that betray them do no treachery.   *Shakeſpeare.*

LE'WIS D'OR. *n. f.* [French.] A golden French coin, in value twelve livres, now ſettled at ſeventeen ſhillings.   *Dict.*

LEXICO'GRAPHER. *n. f.* [λεξικὸν and γράφω; *lexicographe,* French.] A writer of dictionaries; a harmleſs drudge, that buſies himſelf in tracing the original, and detailing the ſignification of words.

> Commentators and *lexicographers* acquainted with the Syriac language, have given theſe hints in their writings on ſcripture.   *Watts's Improvement of the Mind.*

LEXICO'GRAPHY. *n. f.* [λεξικὸν and γράφω.] The art or practice of writing dictionaries.

LE'XICON. *n. f.* [λεξικὸν.] A dictionary; a book teaching the ſignification of words.

> Though a linguiſt ſhould pride himſelf to have all the tongues that Babel cleft the world into, yet if he had not ſtudied the ſolid things in them as well as the words and *lexicons*, yet he were nothing ſo much to be eſteemed a learned man as any yeoman competently wiſe in his mother dialect only.   *Milton.*

LEY. *n. f.*

> *Ley, lee, lay,* are all from the Saxon leaᵹ, a field or paſture, by the uſual melting of the letter ᵹ or g. *Gibſon's Cam.*

LI'ABLE. *n. f.* [*liable*, from *lier*, old French.] Obnoxious; not exempt; ſubject.

> But what is ſtrength without a double ſhare
> Of wiſdom? vaſt, unwieldy, burthenſome,
> Proudly ſecure, yet *liable* to fall
> By weakeſt ſubtleties.   *Milton's Agoniſtes.*

> The Engliſh boaſt of Spenſer and Milton, who neither of them wanted genius or learning; and yet both of them are *liable* to many cenſures.   *Dryden's Juvenal.*

> This, or any other ſcheme, coming from a private hand, might be *liable* to many defects.   *Swift.*

LIAR. *n. f.* [from *lie.* This word would analogically be *lier*; but this orthography has prevailed, and the convenience of diſtinction from *lier*, he who lies down, is ſufficient to confirm it.] One who tells falſhood; one who wants veracity.

> She's like a *liar*, gone to burning hell!
> 'Twas I that kill'd her.   *Shakeſpeare's Othello.*

> He approves the common *liar*, fame,
> Who ſpeaks him thus at Rome.   *Shakeſp. Ant. and Cleop.*

> I do not reject his obſervation as untrue, much leſs condemn the perſon himſelf as a *liar*, whenſoever it ſeems to be contradicted.   *Boyle.*

> Thy better ſoul abhors a *liar's* part,
> Wiſe is thy voice, and noble is thy heart. *Pope's Odyſſey.*

A section from the Dictionary

been shown to be an attempt to avoid an evasive definition by Bailey and at the same time to rationalize and simplify Johnson's other sources in encyclopaedias.

Johnson is in fact remarkably acute in discriminating grammatical usage and shades of meaning in everyday English words. He offers sixty definitions for *make* and over twenty different senses for *up*, for example, and these are unparalleled in earlier dictionaries. Overall, to quote H.W. Wheatley again, Johnson's 'definitions are full, clear, and above all praise for their happy illustration of the meaning of words. These can never be superseded, and the instances in which Johnson's successors have been able to improve upon his work in this respect are singularly few.' A real sense of the justice of these remarks can only be gained by students who dip into this great dictionary for themselves, but a recent commentator J.P. Hardy has cited as a brief example of one of Johnson's entirely unstartling but clear and felicitous definitions *tawdry* – 'meanly showy; splendid without cost; fine without grace; showy without elegance'.

A major innovation as far as English dictionaries are concerned is Johnson's inclusion of quotations as an integral part of the work, though this practice had been anticipated on the continent. There are about 116,000 quotations in all, an indication of Johnson's massive reading not only in literary texts but in historical, theological and scientific works. Among the most frequently cited authors are not only Shakespeare, Spenser and Milton, as we might expect, but also Richard Hooker and Archbishop Tillotson, Bacon, Locke and Newton.

Johnson had originally intended that every single quotation would serve more than a purely linguistic function: 'I therefore extracted from philosophers principles of science; from historians remarkable facts; from chemists complete processes; from divines striking exhortations; and from poets beautiful descriptions.' As the work grew it became clear that this was too optimistic an aim, but enough survives of it to turn the work into a great anthology of English culture from the Elizabethan period to the mid-eighteenth century, enriched, as W.K. Wimsatt says, with numerous aphorisms and anecdotes, literary and critical judgements, nuggets of morality and religious sentiment and doctrine, and historical, natural and scientific facts.

The primary function of the quotations remains, of course, their relationship to the meaning of the words to which they are appended. Johnson is attracted by the idea of determining meaning philosophically, as it were, by logic or analogy or by the strict derivation of words. On occasions he cannot restrain himself from condemning writers from whom he quotes for going against these criteria. By and large, though, he has come to recognize that usage not logic or linguistic rule is the primary determinant of meaning. Even in this respect, however, an ambivalence remains that is at the heart of Johnson's attitudes to language, an uncertainty about whether his job is to record language or to fix it.

For the *Dictionary*, as we have said, obviously has a paramount place in the movement for correctness and stability in the period. Johnson is influenced by anti-French sentiment in his desire to keep French loan words out. He appears, as we have seen, to believe in a cyclic theory of the development of languages, which makes the threat of degeneration a powerful one to be resisted as much as possible. Yet, as is well known, he rejects the idea of a linguistic academy not only because it is authoritarian, and hence alien to the genius of the British people, but also because he knows language can never be completely bound by rules: 'sounds are too volatile and subtle for legal restraints; to enchain syllables, and to lash the wind, are equally the undertakings of pride, unwilling to measure its desires by its strength.'

Johnson has always understood, as he puts it in his original *Plan*, that 'language is the work of man, of a being from whom permanence and stability cannot be derived'. As he presents it characteristically in the 'Preface' his hopes have changed further in the very course of compiling his materials:

> When first I engaged in this work, I resolved to leave neither words nor things unexamined, and pleased myself with a prospect of the hours which I should revel away in feasts of literature, the obscure recesses of northern learning, which I should enter and ransack, the treasure with which I expected every search into those neglected mines to reward my labour, and the triumph with which I should display my acquisitions to mankind. When I had thus enquired into the original of words, I resolved to show likewise my attention to things: to plunge deep into every science, to enquire the nature of every substance of which I inserted the name, to limit every idea by definition strictly logical, and exhibit every production of art or nature in an accurate definition, that my book might be in place of all other dictionaries whether appellative or technical. But these were the dreams of a poet doomed at last to wake a lexicographer.

The later eighteenth century, as we have noted, was to see the emergence of highly rule-bound grammars. A symptom of

a similar trend was the pronunciation dictionary of Thomas
Sheridan (*Complete Dictionary*, 1780). But the English grammar
Johnson provides at the beginning of his work is an unambitious
one, and he takes the decision to mark the accentual stress on
words but not the punctuation as such. Even in the realm of
spelling he errs on the side of caution and usage:

> I hope I may be allowed to recommend to those whose
> thoughts have been, perhaps, employed too anxiously on
> verbal singularities, not to disturb, upon narrow views, or
> for minute propriety, the orthography of their fathers. . . .

Johnson's appreciation of the inevitability of linguistic change
and his careful recording of it is in some senses a stage in the
progress towards modern linguistics. But he also *regrets* the
change and records it, paradoxically, in the hope of arresting
it. His attention to usage rather than to linguistic rules as such
thus remains a double-edged one. His focus is on *literary* rather
than spoken usage, and he records it selectively and with the
hope that the best usage will itself assume prescriptive force.
Although he rejects the authority of an academy, he implicitly
suggests a kind of alternative in the examples he provides from
the best writers. As George Watson says, to Johnson 'a word
means, not what most men suppose it to mean, but what the
finest authors have made it mean. Like his critical theory,
Johnson's theory of language is only superficially democratic:
it is not content to count heads' (*The Literary Critics*, Penguin,
1963, p. 89).

Yet Johnson's own prescriptiveness and the prescriptiveness
he confers upon the authors he selects is both masked and
modified by his self-deprecation in the great 'Preface' and by
his melancholy sense of the inadequacy of *all* prescriptions in
the face of time. He knows that there is no permanent victory
to be won. At the same time this does not mean that we should
give up trying. *Something* at least can be done in the face of time
and something of great importance, as Johnson knew, had been
done in his own work:

> If the changes we fear be thus irresistible, what remains but
> to acquiesce with silence, as in the other insurmountable
> distresses of humanity? It remains that we retard what we
> cannot repel, that we palliate what we cannot cure. Life may
> be lengthened by care, though death cannot be ultimately
> defeated: tongues, like governments, have a natural tendency
> to degeneration; we have long preserved our constitution, let
> us make some struggles for our language.

In the hope of giving longevity to that which its own nature forbids to be immortal, I have devoted this book, the labour of years, to the honour of my country, that we may no longer yield the palm of philology without a contest to the nations of the continent. . . .

The dictionary Johnson finally produced was, after all, incomparably better than what had preceded it, and it was to remain the best English dictionary for many years to come. It is a fine embodiment of eighteenth-century culture and ideas of language. In the words of Walter Jackson Bate, it is also without any exaggeration 'one of the greatest single achievements of scholarship, and probably the greatest ever performed by one individual who laboured under anything like the disadvantages in a comparable length of time'.

Part Two
Critical Survey

Johnson's range

As a professional writer with an urgent need to make a living Johnson wrote a considerable body of material on a vast range of subjects, including a review of a book on the evil effects of drinking tea, a dedication to a book on draughts and a preface to one on Chinese buildings. He wrote in an extraordinary range of genres that includes, as we have seen, a tragedy, prose allegories and fictions, moral essays, biography and satire. He used modes such as the sermon and the fairy story as well as the more conventional forms of literature. Despite his famous assertion that 'no man but a blockhead ever wrote but for money', he often wrote with no thought of reward to help deserving cases. He also wrote his most intimate thoughts with no intention of publication in his *Diaries, Prayers and Annals*, and he expressed himself for pure fun, as in some of his occasional poems, which include titles such as 'To Miss ------ On Her Playing upon the Harpsichord' and are sometimes produced completely impromptu.

Almost all of Johnson's work, whatever the subject on which he is writing, is marked, of course, by a certain moral seriousness and a very distinctive style. As the following representative extracts will show, however, the same basic moral themes are expressed not only in a wide range of different contexts but also with a great variety of techniques, and the style itself is far more flexible than is commonly supposed.

Johnson the poet

Although the proportion of Johnson's poetry is small compared to his prose, he writes in a variety of metres and stanza forms. He keeps the heroic couplet for his high public poetry and used these other forms as a mark of relaxation or an occasional quality, as with his parodies of ballads and an alphabetical poem on Mrs Thrale's birthday. His two best shorter poems are both in the four-line stanza form called quatrains, a metre that itself seems to imply a certain seriousness to him, whether the full moral seriousness of the elegy for Robert Levet, for example, to be discussed below, or the sardonic 'Short Song of Congratulation' to Mrs Thrale's nephew Sir John Lade on reaching his twenty-first birthday:

> Wealth, Sir John, was made to wander,
>   Let it wander as it will;
> See the jockey, see the pander,
>   Bid them come and take their fill.
>   . . .
> If the guardian or the mother
>   Tell the woes of wilful waste,
> Scorn their counsel and their pother,
>   You can hang or drown at last.

The heroic couplet form is itself a metre capable of a wide variety of tones, as Pope's work shows. It can be used for racy colloquial effects as well as the high solemnity that makes it suitable for epic translation. Johnson writes lighter colloquial couplets at times in *London,* and often reveals a special ironic wit even at his most solemn. Yet a certain weightiness is undoubtedly Johnson's special note in this metre. We would perhaps expect a more chatty intimacy from theatrical prologues than from a poem called *The Vanity of Human Wishes.* Yet Johnson begins his prologue to his friend Oliver Goldsmith's comedy *The Good-Natured Man,* for example, rather off-puttingly with:

> Pressed by the load of life, the weary mind
> Surveys the general toil of human kind.

In *The Vanity of Human Wishes* itself this moral weight is built up in every single paragraph and sustained inimitably through the whole, though by no means to the detriment of wit, irony and lively local detail.

FROM *The Vanity of Human Wishes*

> When first the college rolls receive his name,
> The young enthusiast quits his ease for fame;
> Through all his veins the fever of renown
> Burns from the strong contagion of the gown;
> O'er Bodley's dome his future labours spread,
> And Bacon's mansion trembles o'er his head.
> Are these thy views? proceed, illustrious youth,
> And virtue guard thee to the throne of Truth!
> Yet should thy soul indulge the gen'rous heat,
> Till captive Science yields her last retreat;
> Should Reason guide thee with her brightest ray,
> And pour on misty Doubt resistless day;
> Should no false Kindness lure to loose delight,
> Nor Praise relax, nor Difficulty fright;
> Should tempting Novelty thy cell refrain,

And Sloth effuse her opiate fumes in vain;
Should Beauty blunt on fops her fatal dart,
Nor claim the triumph of a letter'd heart;
Should no disease thy torpid veins invade,
Nor Melancholy's phantoms haunt thy shade;
Yet hope not life from grief or danger free,
Nor think the doom of man revers'd for thee:
Deign on the passing world to turn thine eyes,
And pause awhile from letters, to be wise;
There mark what ills the scholar's life assail,
Toil, envy, want, the patron, and the jail.
See nations slowly wise, and meanly just,
To buried merit raise the tardy bust.
If dreams yet flatter, once again attend,
Hear Lydiat's life, and Galileo's end.   (ll.135–64)

Context   The account of the scholar's life follows a passage on the desire for political power and precedes one on military achievement, so that its less *active* ambitions are neatly contrasted with both and Johnson is able to give the impression of canvassing all the main options and human aspirations. Broadly speaking he follows the scheme of the poem he is imitating, Juvenal's 'Satire X'. But an 'imitation' is more than a translation. It is a creative taking off from a classical text that highlights differences as well as similarities. Here Johnson is expanding on a mere four lines in the Latin poem about the life of orators, clear evidence both of his own special interest in this lifestyle and of the originality of his own poem.

Criticism   The passage is highly logical in its progression. Johnson begins by describing the first hopes of the young 'enthusiast' at the start of his career. (The word is itself pejorative or at least condescending in the period, because of its association with the Puritans' claims to inspiration. Johnson gives three definitions in the *Dictionary*, of which only the third does not carry this unfavourable sense). Fired with the hope of fame he expects the books he will publish to fill the shelves of the Bodleian library in Johnson's old university and to fulfil the Oxford tradition that the 'mansion' of the great medieval scholar Friar Roger Bacon would collapse when a greater scholar passed beneath it. Johnson, we note, does not condemn these hopes out of hand, but there is an almost mock-heroic note in 'Proceed, illustrious youth', as well as a genuine feeling of wishing him well in his search for 'Science' [Knowledge] and 'the throne of Truth'. But the progress will not be an easy one. There is an enormous list of potential dangers and temptations

147

to get through first: Sloth, the seductiveness of those beauties (if there are any) who prefer scholars to fops, melancholy (traditionally associated with the solitary and sedentary life of scholars, as in one of Johnson's favourite books *The Anatomy of Melancholy* by Robert Burton [1621]).

The real point is, though, that even if the scholar does surmount all these obstacles he should certainly not expect peace or any rewards for his labours while he is still alive to enjoy them. The line 'And pause awhile from letters [book learning], to be wise' invokes the ancient theme of authority versus experience, the idea, central to Johnson's own sense of himself, that theoretical learning is all very well, but that it has to be backed up with practical experience. Experience will serve to show that scholars have not lived in prosperity and honour, but in poverty, the objects of envy and persecution, and Johnson could not resist a reference to his quarrel with Lord Chesterfield by ironically introducing 'the patron' as one of the 'ills' of a scholar's life (replacing 'the garret' in the first edition). The irony in 'To buried merit raise the tardy bust' is of the deeper 'Vanity of Human Wishes' kind that implies the futility of posthumous renown on earth. He ends with the examples of two scholars, the writer on chronology Lydiat and the great scientist Galileo, who was imprisoned by the Inquisition, to prove the point he has been making throughout.

The powerful logic of Johnson's argument is enforced by his style. He thinks, it has been said, in paragraphs. The rhetoric of his couplet form is cumulative, with heavy rhetorical repetition (the technical name for which is 'anaphora') to ram home his points – the repeated 'Should . . . Should', for example. Juvenal works by racy detail and proper names. Johnson presents a representative, typified figure, almost an allegorical one on his pilgrimage to the throne of truth, but threatened, like Christian in Bunyan's *Pilgrim's Progress*, by a whole series of personified evils. 'Reason', for example, is a full-scale, if conventionally pictured, personification, who guides the hero with the 'brightest ray' of her lamp; 'Sloth' breathes out 'opiate fumes' and even 'Novelty' is a tempting visitor to the scholar's cell. The constant use of 'the' – 'the young enthusiast', 'the fever of renown' – is itself generalizing in effect, and the generalizing movement of the passage throughout culminates in a line on the experience of the whole human race, 'Nor think the doom of man revers'd for thee'. The scholar's mistake, indeed, as so often in Johnson, is to think that he can be an exception to these general rules.

If on the whole we do not expect to find the constant wit
and brilliance of Pope in Johnson's couplet work we do find
a considerable weight and logical balance – 'Nor Praise relax,
nor Difficulty fright'; 'Hear Lydiat's life, and Galileo's end'.
The phrasing of the individual lines and the couplets as a unit
both contribute to the accumulated weight of experience that
Johnson packs behind the lines. This is the abiding impression
that most readers take away and Johnson's most characteristic
note. The sombre generalizing tone, the personifications, the
heavy couplets combined with the sharp touches of wit and
irony ('Toil, envy, want, *the patron* and the jail') convey enormous
authority. These, we come to realize, are not empty generalizations, theories untested by experience. This is a man who
has himself deigned 'on the passing world' to turn his eyes and
paused 'awhile from letters to be wise'.

Emotion lies behind these lines too. Clearly this passage
relates to some degree to Johnson's own experience and
aspirations. On one famous occasion when he read these lines in
public he was unable to hold back tears. Yet any purely personal
note, obviously, has been ironed out of the passage (even the dig
at 'patron', which took off from a personal experience, is still a
general point). When Johnson cried he was not crying *for himself*,
but from *identification* with the passage, a very different matter.
There is enormous compassion here for this, after all *relatively*
noble and harmless aspiration, which is nevertheless bound to
be disappointed. It is in this respect an instance of all human
aspirations, of the human fate in general, the 'human affairs'
which, as Virgil said, 'touch the heart'. It is this tremendous
sense of compassion which W.J. Bate says prevents Johnson
from being, in the last analysis, a satirist. There *is* satire, of
course, of the 'young enthusiast,' the 'illustrious youth' with his
exaggerated ambitions, but in a more general sense none of us
can afford to satirize him since he is but one general instance
of that which we all suffer from ourselves.

'On the Death of Dr. Robert Levet'

Condemned to hope's delusive mine,
As on we toil from day to day,
By sudden blasts, or slow decline,
Our social comforts drop away.

Well tried through many a varying year,
See LEVET to the grave descend;

Officious, innocent, sincere,
Of ev'ry friendless name the friend.

Yet still he fills affection's eye,
Obscurely wise, and coarsely kind;
Nor, lettered arrogance, deny
Thy praise to merit unrefined.

When fainting nature called for aid,
And hov'ring death prepared the blow,
His vig'rous remedy displayed
The power of art without the show.

In misery's darkest caverns known,
His useful care was ever nigh,
Where hopeless anguish poured his groan,
And lonely want retired to die.

No summons mocked by chill delay,
No petty gain disdained by pride,
The modest wants of ev'ry day
The toil of ev'ry day supplied.

His virtues walked their narrow round,
Nor made a pause, nor left a void;
And sure th' Eternal Master found
The single talent well employed.

The busy day, the peaceful night,
Unfelt, uncounted, glided by;
His frame was firm, his powers were bright,
Tho' now his eightieth year was nigh.

Then with no throbbing fiery pain,
No cold gradations of decay,
Death broke at once the vital chain,
And freed his soul the nearest way.

Context   Robert Levet was an unqualified medical practitioner
who worked among the poor. Johnson had great respect for
him and allowed him to live for many years in an apartment
in his house. Boswell reports that 'I have heard him say he
should not be satisfied, though attended by all the College of
Physicians, unless he had Mr. Levet with him'. He died on
17 January 1782, aged seventy-seven. Johnson wrote the poem
in his memory a few months afterwards, and it was published
only just over a year before his own death.

Criticism Levet was not only a personal friend of Johnson's but also a very particular instance of his increasing sense of bereavement and personal loneliness as he grew older: 'By sudden blasts, or slow decline,/Our social comforts drop away.' Yet Johnson does not write 'Yet still *I* affectionately remember him', but the curiously clumsy 'Yet still he fills affection's eye'. Personal emotion and personal bereavement are subsumed into a more general sense of the pain of being human, yet in such a way that we become even more aware of the deep feeling behind and in the lines. For Johnson we are all labourers in 'Hope's delusive mine', the goldmine in which we constantly expect to strike lucky. Similar imagery recurs poignantly in lines that generalize Levet's work into a powerful reminder of all human misery and that are filled with Johnson's deep compassion for the poor:

> In misery's darkest caverns known,
> His useful care was ever nigh,
> Where hopeless anguish poured his groan,
> And lonely want retired to die.

Like Levet we have to do what we can to help each other. His businesslike virtue is celebrated without sentimentality. He is 'obscurely wise', i.e. wise in ways that are not immediately obvious and perhaps wise in obscure medical lore rather than in fashionable medicine. Certainly he is very different from other doctors – 'No summons mocked by chill delay'. He is on the side of experience rather than 'authority' ('lettered arrogance'). He is 'coarsely kind' (almost an oxymoron). 'Levet', said Johnson once, 'is a brutal fellow . . . but his brutality is in his manners, not in his mind.' His is 'merit unrefined'. His virtues form a traditional circle of harmony, but it is a *'narrow* round' (the doctor's round is also suggested). All his life Johnson was obsessed with the parable of the talents, in which Christ tells the story of a master who leaves different sums of money (the literal meaning of 'talents') with three servants, and expects them to have made a profit for him on his return. Levet, unlike Johnson and presumably most of his readers, had only one talent, but in contrast to the servant in that position in the parable, he has used it to the very full.

Levet is the epitome of the Johnsonian hero, the hero of experience and steady work, the hero of the private rather than the public sphere, anti-aristocratic in his uncultivated manners (we remember that Johnson wrote of Lord Chesterfield's *Letters* that they taught the 'manners of a dancing master and the morals of a whore') and almost anti-heroic in his Christian humility. Death, in respect for his worthy and businesslike opponent, has 'freed' his soul from the pains and toils of life in an equally businesslike way (compare 'And hov'ring death prepared the blow' earlier) and Levet has gone to his reward. But his example can also teach us to be as happy as we can here, busy, virtuous, and with as little self-concern as it is humanly possible for us to have:

> The busy day, the peaceful night,
> Unfelt, uncounted, glided by;
> His frame was firm, his powers were bright,
> Tho' now his eightieth year was nigh.

Johnson's style here is the perfect accompaniment to his meaning. His quatrains mark a less public occasion than the heroic couplet would be used for. They are in the tradition of Thomas Gray's famous *Elegy Written in a Country Churchyard*, one poem of Gray's that Johnson unreservedly admired and that was analogous to his own poem in its celebration of humble virtues that would otherwise have remained unsung (though Gray is much more sentimental). The sombre repeated pattern of Johnson's quatrains acts out the relentless movement of time – 'As on we toil from day to day' – but also the steady daily work of Levet, 'The modest wants of ev'ry day/The toil of ev'ry day supplied'. The rhetoric and diction are in deliberate contrast to the elaborations of upper-class elegy and funereal art. Johnson's personifications, it is true, generalize the significance of the whole, but they do so without making unconvincing claims for the superhuman and angelic virtues of the deceased: 'the *single* talent'. There is no sentimentality here. Just as Levet's medicine is 'The power of art without the show', so is the poet's art here, 'merit unrefined' and unadorned with conventional decorations and the polite and pious platitudes expected on such occasions. The diction can be movingly bare and plain, 'Of ev'ry friendless name the friend', though it has its own clear dignity and remains, as we have seen, 'literary' rather than purely and simply personal and 'sincere' in any simplistic sense. In the way that he weds style and content here, sound and meaning, emotion and artistic control Johnson achieves a marvellously concise concentration of his whole moral teaching.

Johnson's prose style

Johnson's prose is far more extensive than his poetry but here too it would be true to say that even on the slightest

subject his work is marked by moral seriousness and a
distinctive style. The latter is commonly characterized by
its frequent use of parallel and antithetical syntax, long
sentences and Latinate and learned diction. Elements of
such a style are evident even in Johnson's earliest published
work, the translation of Father Lobo's *Voyage to Abyssinia*. It
seems to have come to Johnson partly from the influence of
Latin prose – a combination of the long sentences of Cicero
with the terser clauses of Seneca and Tacitus – and partly
from the influence of sixteenth- and seventeenth-century
English writers such as Richard Hooker, Francis Bacon
and the meditative and eccentric writer on antiquarian and
religious topics Sir Thomas Browne, whose life Johnson
wrote. He himself also attributed influence to Swift's mentor,
Sir William Temple, a retired seventeenth-century diplomat.
Temple's style, like Swift's own, is much simpler than
Johnson's, but Johnson says that he had a special care for
the musical harmony of sentence construction and especially
for the way sentences ended, the 'cadence'.

It is easy to over-simplify in describing Johnson's style and
it is a style, of course, that is easy to parody. An anonymous
magazine writer of the time has Johnson wooing Mrs Thrale in
verse such as the following:

> Cervisial coctor's viduate dame,
> Opins't thou this gigantick frame,
> Pronuming at thy shrine;
> Shall, catenated by thy charms,
> A captive in thy ambient arms,
> Perennially be thine.

Horace Walpole talks of the 'teeth-breaking diction' of Johnson,
and even Oliver Goldsmith, when Johnson discussed writing a
fable about fishes, said that he would make them speak like
whales!

The point is, though, that Johnson's style is the necessary
and appropriate vehicle for his moral concerns. He uses his
elaborate rhythms to create a sense of dignity, intellectual
control and authority, but also because of the need to compare
and contrast one thing with another, to weigh and adjudicate.
His parallels and antitheses are not just there for decoration.
The maxims of many moralists, he says in *Rambler* 2, are
'enforced with too little distinction'. Johnson compares theory
with experience or one theory with another. As his early biographer Sir John Hawkins describes it, 'he frequently raises
an edifice, which appears founded and supported to resist any

attack; and then, with the next stroke annihilates it'. Yet he also often finds some truth in what he has, in the last analysis, to reject, so that there is 'a certain even-handed justice'. When Johnson does finally decide between the alternatives, as he almost always does, he has gained immense authority, like a judge weighing precedents, from the careful procedures he has gone through.

It is in the interests of a similar precision that Johnson uses his learned diction. He claims in his famous last *Rambler* essay, No. 208, to have improved the language by adding something to the 'elegance of its construction, and something to the harmony of its cadence', but he also says that 'When common words were less pleasing to the ear, or less distinct in their signification, I have familiarized the terms of philosophy, by applying them to popular ideas, but have rarely admitted any word not authorized by former writers. . . .' By 'terms of philosophy' Johnson means learned words in general, from medicine, science and theology as well as from what we call philosophy as such. W.K. Wimsatt has shown in his important book on the *Rambler, Philosophic Words* that Johnson uses such words not only for the authority that they confer on him but also because they enable precise distinctions to be made. Johnson is keen as well to transfer literal scientific and medical words into the moral and psychological realm, thus producing new metaphorical usages. As will be apparent throughout his published work and conversations he is at the same time never afraid of being down-to-earth where necessary, and he is always aware of the effect of juxtaposing learned vocabulary with the most basic Anglo-Saxon monosyllables.

For Johnson has a strong sense of literary and linguistic decorum, and this is the final general point that needs to be made about his prose style before we go on to look at some examples in more detail. The diction and sentence structure of the essays in the *Rambler* on more general topics, for example, are very different from the barer diction and shorter sentences of the biographical portions of the *Lives of the Poets*. This is not, as once used to be argued, because Johnson has grown more relaxed as he got older but because he has a sense that different styles are more appropriate for the different modes. As Robert Folkenflik has pointed out, the full-blown *Rambler* style can be found at places in the *Lives*, especially when Johnson is defining the general moral and artistic character of a great poet. But the main body of the work, especially the factual parts of the narrative, suits Johnson's anti-heroic, realistic norms for biography. In Folkenflik's words, which apply to all Johnson's work as well as to the *Lives*, there is 'a repertoire of styles which gives expressive variety to the whole' (*Samuel Johnson, Biographer*, 1978, p. 187).

Johnson the fiction writer and moralist

FROM *Rasselas*

Chapter XVII: *The Prince associates with young men of spirit and gaiety*

Rasselas rose next day, and resolved to begin his experiments upon life. 'Youth', cried he, 'is the time of gladness: I will join myself to the young men whose only business is to gratify their desires, and whose time is all spent in a succession of enjoyments.'

To such societies he was readily admitted, but a few days brought him back weary and disgusted. Their mirth was without images ['an idea; a representation of anything to the mind', *Dictionary*], their laughter without motive; their pleasures were gross and sensual, in which the mind had no part; their conduct was at once wild and mean; they laughed at order and at law, but the frown of power dejected, and the eye of wisdom abashed them.

The prince soon concluded that he should never be happy in a course of life of which he was ashamed. He thought it unsuitable to a rational being to act without a plan, and to be sad or cheerful only by chance. 'Happiness', said he, 'must be something solid and permanent, without fear and without uncertainty.'

But his young companions had gained so much of his regard by their frankness and courtesy that he could not leave them without warning and remonstrance. 'My friends,' said he, 'I have seriously considered our manners and our prospects, and find that we have mistaken our own interest. The first years of man must make provision for the last. He that never thinks can never be wise. Perpetual levity must end in ignorance; and intemperance, though it may fire the spirits for an hour, will make life short or miserable. Let us consider that youth is of no long duration, and that in maturer age, when the enchantments of fancy shall cease, and phantoms of delight dance no more about us, we shall have no comforts but the esteem of wise men, and the means of doing good. Let us, therefore, stop, while to stop is in our power: let us live as men who are sometimes to grow old, and to whom it will be the most dreadful of all evils not to count their past years but

155

by follies, and to be reminded of their former luxuriance of health only by the maladies which riot has produced.'

They stared a while in silence one upon another, and, at last, drove him away by a general chorus of continued laughter.

The consciousness that his sentiments were just, and his intentions kind, was scarcely sufficient to support him against the horror of derision. But he recovered his tranquillity, and pursued his search.

Context   Rasselas, Prince of Abyssinia, is brought up in a 'Happy Valley' of pleasure and delight, but he finds himself profoundly bored there and longs to escape. Accompanied by his sister and her maidservant and the sage, Imlac, who has previously lived in the world, they succeed in their endeavours. They come to Cairo and, after a time of preparation, the Prince begins his determined search for the ideal lifestyle that will bring happiness, despite the warnings of Imlac that such a thing is nowhere to be found.

Criticism   Rasselas, young himself, begins his search for happiness, sensibly enough it might seem, among the young, since 'youth' is, after all, 'the time of gladness'. He soon finds, however, that their apparent joy is empty and futile, heading for disaster in the future. Human beings are creatures endowed with reason, and it is inappropriate therefore to 'live without a plan'. Surely, he decides, 'happiness must be something solid and permanent, without fear and without uncertainty'.

Johnson obviously agrees with Rasselas here, yet the hero's sentiments are still surrounded with dramatic irony. True happiness must be as Rasselas describes it, not the empty frolics of pleasure he sees the young men engaged in, but the whole thrust of the book is to show that solid and permanent happiness of this kind cannot be expected on earth at all.

The structure of the book reflects this. It does not have the progressive linear narrative of a novel, but the circular, patterned one of a parable or a satire. In a sense the characters come back, disappointed, to where they started from (though this is not all there is to it). If the work as a whole is a narrative of anti-climax, so are many of the chapters. In the next chapter, for example, Rasselas will hear a sage, a 'wise and happy man' as the heading ironically says, discourse on the necessity for overcoming all passion and bearing worldly disasters stoically, only to be disappointed by the despair he expresses when he hears that his daughter has died. In this brief present chapter of the Prince's encounter with 'young men of youth and gaiety' Rasselas has two major disappointments and anti-climaxes: his initial hope of finding youth and pleasure a source of true happiness, and his expectation that the young men will gratefully welcome his wise and eloquent words and reform. With the best of intentions he preaches a kind of sermon to his former companions. There is nothing wrong with the things he says. Yet he comes across as priggish, not so much in his sentiments as in his inexperience and idealism in expecting anyone to take any notice of them. We are not on the side of his disrespectful hearers and he is certainly in the right. But if human beings are in possession of reason and should act as rational creatures, Johnson well knows, of course, that in practice they usually do not. We feel sympathy with Rasselas's experience of the 'horror of derision', but in another sense he has brought it upon himself by his hopelessly unrealistic idealism. His lesson really begins here, but it will take him a long time to learn it, and, as we have said, it is never really complete.

Although *Rasselas* does not create the narrative structure we associate with novels, there is a certain suspense and surprise in the anti-climaxes as well as a degree of ironic amusement. We feel some emotional identification with Rasselas (though not so much as we might in a realistic novel) but we are to some extent thereby manipulated into sharing his 'fall'. Johnson creates a remarkable distancing effect overall. He puts something of himself into Rasselas's moral teaching, which is, after all, correct. At the same time he avoids direct moralizing in his own voice. Rasselas serves as a kind of literary persona, and Johnson stands back from his naivety and priggishness. He gets the best of both worlds here with remarkable strategic skill, putting forward genuine moral teaching and yet at the same time indicating the uselessness of mere admonition and the difficulty of bringing about change. Through Johnson's manipulation of the interplay between these different viewpoints we are ourselves educated into a position between the two extremes, siding with Rasselas's morality against the young men, yet with a greater sense of realism than he displays.

The style, of course, is part of the secret. Its main mode is elegant, extremely organized and rhythmic, so that the narrative base of the passage reads, as already mentioned, like a parable or semi-allegory rather than the relatively realistic texture that we expect of a novel. It is dignified and impersonal. General moral reflections arise readily from it, and the prose is organized in such a way as to suggest that the weight of experience and logic lies behind such thinking (for 'He that thinks reasonably must think morally'): 'their conduct was at once wild and mean ...'. But Johnson also parodies such moralism at the same time. The carefully balanced way that *Rasselas* speaks suggests that moral truths are clear (as indeed in a sense they are) and that all we have to do is to state them for their obviousness and truth to become apparent and we will then follow them. He thinks and speaks in aphorisms, as Johnson himself often does – 'The first years of man must make provision for the last. He that never thinks never can be wise' – and in careful rhetorical repetitions (*anaphora*): 'Let us ... Let us ...' But in his visit to the stoic in the next chapter the Prince will come to learn more clearly 'the emptiness of rhetorical sound, and the inefficacy of polished periods and studied sentences'.

FROM *Rambler*, No. 129

... It can, indeed, raise no wonder that temerity has been generally censured; for it is one of the vices with which few can be charged, and which therefore, great numbers are ready to condemn. It is the vice of noble and generous minds, the exuberance of magnanimity, and the ebullition of genius; and is therefore not regarded with much tenderness, because it never flatters us by that appearance of softness and imbecility which is commonly necessary to conciliate compassion. But if the same attention had been applied to the search of arguments against the folly of presupposing impossibilities, and anticipating frustration, I know not whether many would not have been roused to usefulness, who, having been taught to confound prudence with timidity, never ventured to excel, lest they should unfortunately fail.

It is necessary to distinguish our own interest from that of others, and that distinction will perhaps assist us in fixing the just limits of caution and adventurousness. In an undertaking that involves the happiness or the safety of many, we have certainly no right to hazard more than is allowed by those who partake the danger; but where only ourselves can suffer by miscarriage, we are not confined within such narrow limit; and still less is the reproach of temerity, when numbers will receive advantage by success, and only one be incommoded by failure.

Men are generally willing to hear precepts by which ease is favoured; and as no resentment is raised by general representations of human folly, even in those who are most eminently jealous of comparative reputation, we confess, without reluctance, that vain man is ignorant of his own weakness, and therefore frequently presumes to attempt what he can never accomplish; but it ought likewise to be remembered that man is no less ignorant of his own powers, and might perhaps have accomplished a thousand designs, which the prejudices of cowardice restrained him from attempting.

It is observed in the golden verses of Pythagoras, that 'Power is never far from necessity'. The vigour of the human mind quickly appears, when there is no longer any place for doubt and hesitation, when diffidence is absorbed in the sense of danger, or overwhelmed by some resistless passion. We then soon discover that difficulty is, for the most part, the daughter of idleness, that the obstacles with which our way seemed to be obstructed were only phantoms, which we believed real, because we durst not advance to a close examination; and we learn that it is impossible to determine without experience how much constancy may endure, or perseverance perform.

But whatever pleasure may be found in the review of distresses when art or courage has surmounted them, few will be persuaded to wish that they may be awakened by want, or terror, to the conviction of their own abilities. Every one should therefore endeavour to invigorate himself by reason and reflection, and determine to exert the latent force that nature may have reposed in him, before the hour of exigence comes upon him, and compulsion shall torture him to diligence. It is below the dignity of a reasonable being to owe that strength to necessity which ought always to act at the call of choice, or to need any other motive to industry than the desire of performing his duty.

Reflections that may drive away despair, cannot be wanting to him who considers how much life is now advanced beyond the state of naked, undisciplined, uninstructed nature. Whatever has been effected for convenience or elegance, while it was yet unknown, was believed impossible; and therefore would never have been attempted, had not some, more daring than the rest, adventured to bid defiance to prejudice and censure. Nor is there yet any reason to doubt that the same labour would be rewarded with the same success. There are qualities in the products of nature yet undiscovered, and combinations in the power of art yet untried. It is the duty of every man to endeavour that something may be added by his industry to the hereditary aggregate of knowledge and happiness. To add much can indeed be the lot of few, but to add something, however little, every one may hope;

and of every honest endeavour, it is certain, that, however unsuccessful, it will be at last rewarded.

Context   In this *Rambler* essay, called 'The Folly of Cowardice and Inactivity' by one editor, Johnson not only presents a characteristic moral but also displays a characteristic manner of proceeding. As so often he differentiates himself from the moralists of the past by an adjudication between what they say and what he presents as the truths of experience. Most moralists, he begins the essay by saying, take their teaching from books rather than 'casting their eyes abroad in the living world' and expect veneration simply for repeating received ideas. It is for this reason, says Johnson, that so much attention has been devoted to condemning the vice of rash undertakings and so little to the opposite extreme, the vice of inactivity and undue, timid caution. Certainly, he concedes, we should try to consider what we are about to do before any great endeavour and see if our resources are adequate, but it is also possible to err on the side of too much caution, and this is both much more common and, in the most general sense, more harmful.

Criticism   Johnson has an unrelenting and ironic realism about human motives that, in a lesser man, would have turned to complete cynicism. He begins the extracted portion of the essay by explaining that one reason for the general condemnation of those who attempt what is beyond them is that it is quite a rare vice, and therefore all those people who are unlikely to be accused of it are delighted to attack it. Johnson's own secret sympathy with 'temerity' (rash boldness) is implied in the rich Latinate diction he uses to describe it, 'the exuberance of magnanimity', 'ebullition', and he is equally clear in his disdain for the weakness that is more likely to gain our compassion. The style here is not an immediately inviting one in its relative abstraction and its intellectual rigour, but then Johnson is dealing with abstract moral qualities and enforcing careful distinctions. If the moralists of the past had turned their attention to the opposite danger of undue caution (as Johnson himself is now) it might have been more encouraging to their readers. Prudence, a necessary virtue, is not at all the same as 'timidity', though those who lack the moral and intellectual discipline that Johnson's style enacts and inculcates may easily confuse them with one another.

For what Johnson produces in essays of this kind is a secular version of the Christian tradition of moral casuistry, the art of finding solutions to knotty moral problems. It was the Jesuits that made 'casuistry' notorious, but it had also been cultivated by Anglican writers such as Jeremy Taylor whom Johnson admired. It is from that tradition that he draws the criteria he uses in the second paragraph: the idea, for example, that to take risks that only involve oneself is more legitimate than to 'hazard' the 'happiness or safety of many'. He is supremely confident, we notice, of the existence of moral guidelines, if only we can think clearly enough, that will enable us to find the exact balance between the different qualities and the permissible deviations from that exact balance according to different circumstances, 'just limits of caution and adventurousness'. The moral standard itself remains absolute, as the abstract and general words suggest, but they have to be applied differently as the situation changes. The careful balance and antitheses with which Johnson's sentences are constructed – the lengthy second sentence of this paragraph, for example – act out the necessary distinctions. The syntax carefully weighs the first clause, which involves responsibility for many people, against the second, which involves responsibility only for oneself. The third clause introduces another alternative again, which logically, morally and syntactically combines elements from both the preceding: 'and still less is the reproach of temerity, when numbers will receive advantage by success, and only one be incommoded by failure'.

Despite the necessary level of abstraction and generality in this kind of discourse Johnson succeeds in drawing the reader in. He uses inclusive personal pronouns and adjectives like 'us' and 'our' and 'we'. These issues do concern us in practical ways, and he is not preaching at us as though he is not included in these struggles himself. The style itself, of course, makes the reader work to understand, and since the complexity of syntax and diction enacts a genuine moral complexity, the very process of reading and following the necessary distinctions is itself a kind of moral education.

The next paragraph begins with another statement about human motives that is so realistic as to verge on cynicism and so generalized and authoritative as to sound like an aphorism or axiom: 'Men are generally willing to hear precepts by which ease is favoured.' Yet this generalization itself leads into an attack on superficial generalizations and 'representations of human folly', to which we are all complacently ready to listen because we do not really feel they concern us. The paragraph consists of one long sentence, which achieves an effect of authority and intellectual control, and the final section once again sets up an antithesis to the commonly received opinion. Here the generalization that 'man' is 'ignorant of his powers' and of what he could achieve if he exerted himself gains strength by being set in opposition to more superficial generalizations that only encourage inertia.

Despite the way he rejects the repetition of the moral axioms of the past for their own sake, Johnson is delighted to have the authority of the classical moralists when it suits him and he moves into the next phase of his argument by citing the Greek philosopher Pythagoras. Johnson's respect for the innate powers of the human mind comes out clearly in his claim that when we are under pressure we often achieve far more than we could have imagined possible. Once again it is experience not theory that is our true teacher. The whole argument is enlivened by a constant, if low-key, imagery that turns the abstract into concrete by a kind of personification: 'how much constancy may endure, or perseverance perform' or even short allegory, 'difficulty is, for the most part, the daughter of idleness'.

The next paragraph is centred around Johnson's noble appeal to what he calls the 'dignity of a reasonable being'. He is entirely confident that this is our proper status and that it must therefore be possible for us 'to invigorate' ourselves 'by reason and reflection' so that we act in accordance with the highest norms of our status. Yet he is equally aware of the sad irony that we are more inclined to act under the domination of passion and circumstance. What certainly is important is that we do not allow ourselves to be lulled into complacency and inertia by trite moral reflections that discourage us from doing the best we can. The urgency comes out especially in the violent personification imagery of 'compulsion shall torture him into diligence'.

The theme widens out remarkably in the final paragraph into a survey of the whole history of human civilization. We see once again how far Johnson is from the sentimentality of romantic primitivism. Life in the state of nature is 'naked, undisciplined, uninstructed'. On the other hand there is a firm optimism and sense of progress behind the assertion that human effort in the arts and sciences has gradually improved things. None of these improvements would have occurred had some bold spirits not tried what had never been attempted before. There is still much more that can be achieved, and Bacon's ideal of cooperative scientific endeavour obviously underlies Johnson's phrasing here: 'There are qualities in the products of nature yet undiscovered . . . the hereditary aggregate of knowledge and happiness.' The characteristically Johnsonian combination of pessimism and optimism or, more precisely, the use of what at first seem pessimistic reflections as a source of encouragement is underlined again in the fine concision and balance of the last sentence, and its resolute honesty and courage is enhanced by a noble simplicity of diction compared to much of the rest of the passage. Only a few great spirits, Johnson suggests, can expect to make great discoveries and add greatly to human progress, but we can all expect to make some contribution, however humble, if we do not allow ourselves to be discouraged in advance. With an especial sense of decorum Johnson introduces the religious dimension only at the end of the passage in the careful and understated paradox of efforts that are 'unsuccessful' on earth but 'at last rewarded' (i.e. in heaven).

Johnson as writer on society

FROM *Thoughts on the Late Transactions Respecting Falkland's Islands*

As war is the extremity of evil, it is surely the duty of those whose station entrusts them with the care of nations, to avert it from their charge. There are diseases of animal nature which nothing but amputation can remove; so there may, by the depravation of human passions, be sometimes a gangrene in collective life for which fire and sword are the necessary remedies; but in what can skill or caution be better shewn than preventing such dreadful operations, while there is yet room for gentler methods?

It is wonderful with what coolness and indifference the greater part of mankind see war commenced. Those that hear of it at a distance, or read of it in books, but have never presented its evils to their minds, consider it as little more than a splendid game, a proclamation, an army, a battle, and a triumph. Some indeed must perish in the most successful field, but they die upon the bed of honour, 'resign their lives amidst the joys of conquest, and, filled with England's glory, smile in death'.

The life of a modern soldier is ill represented by heroic fiction. War has means of destruction more formidable than the cannon and the sword. Of the thousands and ten thousands that perished in our late contests with France and Spain, a very small part ever felt the stroke of an enemy; the rest languished in tents and ships, amidst damps and putrefaction; pale, torpid, spiritless, and helpless; gasping and groaning, unpitied among men made obdurate by long continuance of hopeless misery; and were at last whelmed in pits, or heaved into the ocean, without notice and without remembrance. By incommodious encampments and unwholesome stations, where courage is useless, and enterprise impracticable, fleets are silently dispeopled, and armies sluggishly melted away.

Thus is a people gradually exhausted, for the most part with little effect. The wars of civilized nations make very slow changes in the system of empire. The public perceives scarcely any alteration but an increase of debt; and the few individuals who are benefited, are not supposed to have the clearest right to their advantages. If he that shared the danger enjoyed the profit, and after bleeding in the battle grew rich by the victory, he might shew his gains without envy. But at the conclusion of a ten years war, how are we recompensed for the death of multitudes and the expence of millions, but by contemplating the sudden glories of paymasters and agents, contractors and commissaries, whose equipages shine like meteors, and whose palaces rise like exhalations.

Context Thoughts on the Late Transactions Respecting Falkland's Islands discusses the conflicting claims of England and Spain to the islands (later, of course, the Spanish claim was taken up by Argentina). The Spanish had recently ejected a small British garrison there by force. After lengthy negotiations, however, Spain had promised satisfaction for the injury, but had not agreed to cede claims to sovereignty. The opposition in Britain were continuing to urge war, but Johnson argues that the British government had already gained all that was asked and that the evils of war are such that it should only ever be a last resort.

Criticism This passage must be judged first and foremost as political rhetoric: by its ability to persuade its particular readership that the government of the time had acted rightly in deciding to accept Spanish representations and to refuse to go to war. Johnson is in fact enormously persuasive. He uses all the traditional devices of rhetoric from rhetorical questions to sarcastic understatement. Each paragraph represents a different kind of tone and a different method of argument, ranging from an appeal to the law of nations that war is to be the last resort to an ironic realism about the profiteering that war brings. His prose style confers enormous authority on what he says through his weighty Latinate diction and sharp aphoristic wisdom, and the remarkable balanced rhythm of his sentences can at one time be sonorous and compassionate and at another be used to point out ironic discrepancies.

Johnson begins by an appeal to the consensus of nations that war is the 'extremity of evil' and therefore to be avoided if at all possible. This, he implies, is what the British government has done, and his phrasing is contrived to confer upon the government all the general respect that is its due for carrying out its responsibility of protecting those in its care as well as a specific approval for the way that it has used 'gentler methods' in this particular instance. Johnson clearly is not a pacifist and his strong sense of original sin comes across in his concession that the 'depravation of human passions' may sometimes necessitate war, but his choice of metaphor is a brilliant one, for who would not wish, as he asks rhetorically, to avoid the terrible operation of amputation (we remember the eighteenth century had no anaesthetics!) if it were at all possible?

The next paragraph is more of an assault upon the audience than an appeal to them, although there could be said to be an element of implicit, flattering appeal that they should separate themselves from the folly of the 'greater part of mankind'. There is a satiric sense of marvelling at human self-deception and ignorance in 'It is wonderful to see with what coolness and indifference . . .'. Johnson, as so often, presents himself as one with the authority of experience not books behind what he says, and he ironically evokes the succession of events that those who hear of war at a distance or read about it imagine, 'a splendid game, a proclamation, an army, a battle, and a triumph'. The parody is strengthened by a specific quotation (in fact misquotation) from an early eighteenth-century poem, Addison's *The Campaign*, that glorifies war.

The theme is expanded upon in the next paragraph with the contrast between 'heroic fiction' and the realities of war, with Johnson once again presenting himself as the spokesman for realism against theory, imagination and fiction. The tone of the prose begins to change with the two remarkable sentences that follow. 'Thousands and ten thousands' raises the emotional temperature, and the irony that develops is of a different kind to what precedes, a bitter but also sad irony about the very nature of wars in human history, the fact that far more of the combatants die from disease than in actual battle. The main part of the paragraph is taken up with a long sentence with emotionally expansive and yet balanced clauses that describes the progress of these victims towards their fates and expresses with the greatest eloquence both righteous indignation and tremendous compassion. The diction itself combines Latinate dignity – 'obdurate', 'continuance' – with concrete realism – 'gasping and groaning', 'whelmed in pits'. The idea is summarized and reinforced in more general form in the final sentence to bring home the irony and the enormity of a situation in which whole 'armies' are 'sluggishly melted away'.

Another kind of irony again appears in the final paragraph of the extract. For all their terrible cost in human suffering wars make very little difference to the course of events. The only people who actually profit from them, says Johnson, with satiric understatement, 'are not supposed to have the clearest right to their advantages'. The aphorisms that follow enforce the irony: 'If he that shared the danger enjoyed the profit . . .'. The balance of the syntax indicates what would be logical and just, but does so only as a means of implying that the real state of affairs is in fact the opposite. The real benefits of war go to 'paymasters, and agents, contractors and commissaries,' who sit happily at home computing their profits. This is the traditional eighteenth-century Tory dislike of expensive wars because of the way they necessitated government borrowing and encouraged the growth of middlemen, suppliers, bankers and so on. The rapid and reprehensible rise of the latter to wealth is itself expressed in ominous metaphors full of a traditional dislike of social mobility and the instability of new wealth (an exhalation is a vapour associated with meteors, according to the *Dictionary*, and meteors were themselves, of course, considered as heralds of ill fortune).

For effectiveness as political rhetoric this passage could hardly be bettered. But Johnson's style, rhetorical to persuade, weighty to give authority to that persuasion, is such that he is also able to transcend its particular occasion and turn a political pamphlet into literature. He relates a specific situation to general moral principles while at the same time preserving a hard-headed realism about political facts. His deeply compassionate sense of the evils of war has hardly lost its relevance.

FROM *A Journey to the Western Islands of Scotland*

The art of joining squares of glass with lead is little used in Scotland, and in some places is totally forgotten. The frames of their windows are all of wood. They are more frugal of their glass than the English, and will often, in houses not otherwise mean, compose a square of two pieces, not joined like cracked glass, but with one edge laid perhaps half an inch over the other. Their windows do not move upon hinges, but are pushed up and drawn down in grooves, yet they are seldom accommodated with weights and pulleys. He that would have his window open must hold it with his hand, unless, what may be sometimes found among good contrivers, there be a nail which he may stick into a hole, to keep it from falling.

What cannot be done without some uncommon trouble or particular expedient will often not be done at all. The incommodiousness of the Scotch windows keep them very closely shut. The necessity of ventilating human habitations has not yet been found by our northern neighbours; and even in houses well built and elegantly furnished, a stranger may sometimes be forgiven if he allows himself to wish for fresher air.

These diminutive observations seem to take away something from the dignity of writing, and therefore are never communicated but with hesitation, and a little fear of abasement and contempt. But it must be remembered that life consists not of a series of illustrious actions, or elegant enjoyments; the greater part of our time passes in compliance with necessities, in the performance of daily duties, in the removal of small inconveniences, in the procurement of petty pleasures; and we are well or at ease as the main stream of life glides on smoothly, or is ruffled by small obstacles and frequent interruption. The true state of every nation is the state of common life. The manners of a people are not to be found in the schools of learning, or the palaces of greatness, where the national character is obscured or obliterated by travel or instruction, by philosophy or vanity; nor is public happiness to be estimated by the assemblies of the gay, or the banquets of the rich. The great mass of nations is neither rich nor gay: they whose aggregate constitutes the people are found in the streets, and the villages, in the shops and farms; and from them collectively considered must the measure of general prosperity be taken. As they approach to delicacy a nation is refined, as their conveniencies are multiplied, a nation, at least a commercial nation, must be nominated wealthy.

(IX, 21–3)

Context   After visiting the town and university of Aberdeen on their great tour of Scotland and the Hebridean islands, Johnson and Boswell come to the ancient town of Banff.

Criticism   Although there is certainly evidence in *A Journey to the Western Islands of Scotland* of Johnson's interest in wild scenery and the impressiveness of ancient buildings, the reader who approaches the work expecting an exciting travelogue will be disappointed. Johnson is determined to be as factual and realistic as possible, and his main interest is what we would term a sociological one today.

Yet the degree of attention devoted to the inadequacies of Scottish windows still seems surprising, and the modern reader may find the first paragraphs of the extract mundane, even verging on the ridiculous. Johnson was well aware of this reaction and well aware of what he was doing. His last paragraph both justifies his procedure and expands out remarkably from the details with which he begins. His style at first, though, is as bare and factual as he can make it, in keeping with his close eye to the detail of his unglamorous subject-matter – 'with one edge laid perhaps half an inch over the other . . . a nail which he may stick into a hole'. There is one sign of Johnson's more usual habits of style, however, in the curious generalized phrasing of 'He that would have his window open . . .'. But the paragraph as a whole is the product not only of Johnson the sociologist, fascinated by the details of the way that people in other societies live, but of Johnson the practical man, Johnson the technologist, knowledgeable about all the details of agriculture, brewing, etc. – 'Their windows do not move upon hinges, but are pushed up and drawn down in grooves, yet they are seldom accommodated with weights and pulleys.'

The change of style towards more elaborate diction in the next paragraph marks a widening out of the passage into more general reflections. It begins with a characteristically Johnsonian, realistic, almost cynical, general statement about the inertia of human beings. The implication is not condemnatory, however, but resigned, and the suggestion is clearly that the fault lies with those who have not made provision for this side of human nature. Anti-Scots prejudice or at least a tendency to patronize the Scots is apparent here, and there is a sarcastic note in 'the necessity of ventilating human habitations has not yet been found by our northern neighbours'. We see once again Johnson's distance from any tendency to romanticize lifestyles divorced from what he regards as the conveniences of civilization.

The next paragraph justifies Johnson's use of these 'diminutive observations' and in so doing generalizes out from them into a remarkable meditation on human life and human society. The style rises to an even higher level in order to accomplish this, and the sentence units become much more elaborate, with a careful rhetorical arrangement of balance, antithesis and repetition with variation. A brief example of the last point is:

'in the removal of small inconveniences, in the procurement of petty pleasures', which obviously repeats the same syntactical pattern, but varies it by contrasting 'removal' with 'procurement' and 'inconveniencies' with 'pleasures' and avoids repetition by replacing 'small' with 'petty'. Similar methods are used throughout the sentence construction of the whole paragraph, and they create a matchless sense of dignity, intellectual control and objective authority.

Indeed, the phrasing in this paragraph is impersonal from the first, which contributes to the sense of authority. Johnson does not say that *he* was afraid he was writing in too mundane a fashion, but that there is a danger that such a subject-matter will detract from 'the dignity of writing'. There is a neo-classical conviction of the need for what Johnson calls elsewhere 'the grandeur of generality' behind this fear. But, as we have seen, Johnson's own generalizations always arise out of particulars, and he refuses to withdraw here. There is anti-heroic sentiment in his assertion that life does not consist in 'illustrious actions' and perhaps a middle-class, anti-aristocratic note in the idea that is not a matter of 'elegant enjoyments' either. What is most noticeable, though, is a characteristic realism about life, a recognition that most of it is undramatic and unglamorous and that we are all contingent creatures inevitably dominated by 'small inconveniencies' and 'petty pleasures'.

The second half of the paragraph follows on logically from the preceding argument, but represents a change of tack into a more specific socio-economic point. It represents Johnson's broad allegiance to the social, political and economic changes of his own time, despite his conservatism in other regards. The sentence 'The true state of every nation is the state of common life' is the shortest in the paragraph and carries an epigrammatic weight. It leaves no doubt that Johnson, without being a democrat in the modern sense, is entirely in favour of the broadening of the political nation and the great rise of middle-class culture and prosperity that are among the most marked developments of the time. There is a broad sweep of realistic human sympathy in the idea that the small conveniencies of life brought about by commercial society improve the lot of the majority of people, and Johnson's own belief in the superiority of such a society is clearly suggested. Indeed it is this, whether intended from the start or not, that seems to become the main theme of *A Journey to the Western Islands of Scotland*. What is most notable, however, is the way that it emerges, as here, out of a rigorous attention to all the practical, almost mundane details of life in Scotland.

Critical Survey

Johnson the biographer

From *Life of Savage*

It must therefore be acknowledged, in justification of mankind, that it was not always by the negligence or coldness of his friends that Savage was distressed, but because it was in reality very difficult to preserve him long in a state of ease. To supply him with money was a hopeless attempt, for no sooner did he see himself master of a sum sufficient to set him free from care for a day, than he became profuse and luxurious. When once he had entered a tavern, or engaged in a scheme of pleasure, he never retired till want of money obliged him to some new expedient. If he was entertained in a family, nothing was any longer to be regarded there but amusements and jollity; wherever Savage entered, he immediately expected that order and business should fly before him, that all should thenceforth be left to hazard, that no dull principle of domestic management should be opposed to his inclination, or intrude upon his gaiety.

His distresses, however afflictive, never dejected him; in his lowest state he wanted not spirit to assert the natural dignity of wit, and was always ready to repress that insolence which the superiority of fortune incited, and to trample the reputation which rose upon any other basis than that of merit: he never admitted any gross familiarities, or submitted to be treated otherwise than as an equal. Once, when he was without lodging, meat, or clothes, one of his friends, a man not indeed remarkable for moderation in his prosperity, left a message, that he desired to see him about nine in the morning. Savage knew that his intention was to assist him, but was very much disgusted that he should presume to prescribe the hour of his attendance, and, I believe, refused to visit him, and rejected his kindness.

(Tracy (ed.), 1971, pp. 98–9)

Context Richard Savage the poet believed himself the illegitimate son of the Countess of Macclesfield but was rejected by his supposed mother. After a period of patronage by Lord Tyrconnell, Savage quarrelled with him and was left to his own devices, soon falling on very hard times and virtual destitution. Many people tried to help him, but their efforts achieved little success because of Savage's bitter resentment of anything that seemed like condescension and because of his own incurable extravagance and refusal to make provision for himself.

Criticism   The facts of Savage's life were sensational, including the mystery of his birth, his trial for murder and the whole low-life drama of a man of genius reduced to destitute circumstances. Johnson clearly understands that to tell the story of a life of this kind requires a different style to that of moral essays, for example. His narrative is lively, his sentences shorter than in (say) *Rambler* and his diction plainer. Yet his tone is certainly not a sensational one itself, but relatively even and sombre. He reveals a strenuous and scrupulous concern for the truth: his 'I believe' in the last sentence is symptomatic of his refusal to commit himself if there is the slightest doubt about the facts.

As noted before, though, Johnson does not really collect facts for their own sake. Earlier biographies had allowed exemplary moral purposes to shape the facts completely. Johnson gave the impression of letting details coalesce into generalization and moral order. Much of this passage consists of facts that have already been assimilated and organized into a pattern prior to the process of writing, and the very markedly balanced rhythms of the prose reflect that pattern. Only at the end of the two paragraphs is the previously established general truth in turn illustrated and made more vivid by an interesting anecdote about Savage's defiance of anything that could remotely be construed as being patronizing.

Yet the tone of judicious generalization has obviously had to be worked for. As the concluding story suggests, Johnson identifies with Savage to a considerable extent, and the man was, after all, his intimate friend for a time. Johnson, too, found patronizing charity intolerable, and threw a well-meaning donor's shoes down the stairs at Oxford. He, too, in the first half of his career had experienced the 'melancholy truth' that Savage's life so well illustrated, 'SLOW RISES WORTH BY POVERTY DEPRESS'D' and was angry against 'that insolence which the superiority of fortune incited' and sceptical of a 'reputation which rose upon any other basis than that of merit'. His sympathy for Savage is apparent throughout and, indeed, his genuine admiration: 'His distresses, however afflictive, never dejected him; in his lowest state he wanted not spirit to assert the natural dignity of wit. . . .'

At the same time there is criticism. His personal devotion to his friend is not allowed to swamp his greater commitment to the facts of the case and the moral truth that arises, as it always will, when those facts are carefully presented and considered. We get the feeling that Savage's extravagance amounts to self-destructiveness, and there are slight touches of irony at times when things are stated in the way Savage views them: 'no dull principle of domestic management should be opposed to his inclination . . . should presume to prescribe the hour of his attendance.'

The net result is a magisterial balance of assessment. As always Johnson's style adjudicates, qualifies, makes concessions. It would be almost impossible to exaggerate the care he takes to be just both to Savage and to those who tried to help him. The first sentence, for example, sets Savage against 'his friends' and speaks for the latter as an example of and in justification of the general category 'mankind'. Yet the word 'always' in 'it was not always by the negligence or coldness of his friends' goes a long way on Savage's behalf, despite the statement in the next sentence that 'To supply him with money was a hopeless attempt'. The friend who asks Savage to attend him at nine in the morning similarly has 'kindness' attributed to him, and we have already noted an element of sarcasm in the account of Savage's indignation. Yet Johnson suggests that there was certainly fault on the potential patron's side too, as he was 'a man not indeed remarkable for moderation in his prosperity'.

The balance that Johnson attains here is obviously a personal achievement, a way of coming to terms with his own complex feelings for Savage and with the elements of Savage in his own personality, not least his strong streak of defiance and anti-authoritarianism. But the balance of sympathy and judgement is also at the heart of the book's moral teaching. Johnson rejects the elaborately unrealistic exemplary virtues and monitory vices of previous biography in favour of something much truer to life, much more human, and this is not only because he believes it wrong to conceal the truth. Savage's considerable gifts are marred by human weaknesses. Because we can sympathize with him and identify with him we can in a way *experience* his life through his biography. Moral lessons will therefore result, as they inevitably will from all genuine human experience, but they will be real ones rather than the artificial ones of the exemplary tradition of biography. The figures we find there are too far above or below us to be of use. We can only truly learn from that which we relate to:

> This relation will not be wholly without its use, if those, who languish under any part of his sufferings, shall be enabled to fortify their patience . . . or those who disregard the common maxims of life, shall be reminded, that nothing will supply the want of prudence.

From 'Life of Pope'

Most of what can be told concerning his petty peculiarities was communicated by a female domestic of the Earl of Oxford, who knew him perhaps after the middle of life. He was then so weak as to stand in perpetual need of female attendance; extremely sensible of cold, so that he wore a kind of fur doublet under a shirt of very coarse warm linen with fine sleeves. When he rose he was invested in bodice made of stiff canvas, being scarce able to hold himself erect till they were laced, and he then put on a flannel waistcoat. One side was contracted. His legs were so slender that he enlarged their bulk with three pairs of stockings, which were drawn on and off by the maid; for he was not able to dress or undress himself, and neither went to bed nor rose without help. His weakness made it very difficult for him to be clean.

His hair was fallen almost all away, and he used to dine sometimes with Lord Oxford, privately in a velvet cap. His dress of ceremony was black, with a tie-wig and a little sword.

The indulgence and accommodation which his sickness required had taught him all the unpleasing and unsocial qualities of a valetudinary man. He expected that every thing should give way to his ease or humour, as a child whose parents will not hear her cry has an unresisted dominion in the nursery.

> *C'est que l'enfant toujours est homme,*
> *C'est que l'homme est toujours enfant.*
> [the child always has something of the man in him,
> the man always has something of the child.]

When he wanted to sleep he 'nodded in company'; and once slumbered at his own table while the Prince of Wales was talking of poetry.

The reputation which his friendship gave procured him many invitations; but he was a very troublesome inmate. He brought no servant, and had so many wants that a numerous attendance was scarcely able to supply them. Wherever he was he left no room for another, because he exacted the attention and employed the activity of the whole family. His errands were so frequent and frivolous that the footmen in time avoided and neglected him, and the Earl of Oxford discharged some of the servants for their resolute refusal of messages. The maids, when they had neglected their business, alleged that they had been employed by Mr Pope. One of his constant demands was for coffee in the night, and to the woman that waited on him in his chamber he was very burdensome; but he was careful to recompense her want of sleep, and Lord Oxford's servant declared that in a house where her business was to answer his call she would not ask for wages.

He had another fault, easily incident to those who suffering much pain think themselves entitled to whatever pleasures they can snatch. He was too indulgent to his appetite: he loved meat highly seasoned and of strong taste, and, at the intervals of the table, amused himself with biscuits and dry conserves. If he sat down to a variety of dishes he would oppress his stomach with repletion, and though he seemed angry when a dram was offered, did not forbear to drink it. His friends, who knew the avenues to his heart, pampered him with presents of luxury, which he did not suffer to stand neglected. The death of great men is not always proportioned to the lustre of their lives. Hannibal, says Juvenal, did not perish by a javelin or a sword; the slaughters of Cannae were revenged by a ring. The death of Pope was imputed by some of his friends to a silver saucepan, in which it was his delight to heat potted lampreys.

That he loved too well to eat is certain; but that his sensuality shortened his life will not be hastily concluded when it is remembered that a conformation so irregular lasted six and fifty years, notwithstanding such pertinacious diligence of study and meditation.

(Hill (ed.), III, 197–200)

Context After a chronological survey of Pope's life Johnson moves on to consider his character as a man and as a poet, beginning with this account of his physique and physical difficulties – themselves, of course, of considerable psychological significance.

Criticism The first thing we are likely to notice about this passage is that the style is simpler than in much of Johnson's other work. The language is bare to the point of starkness at times, the sentences often short: 'His weakness made it very difficult for him to be clean.' This is appropriate to Johnson's sense of the decorum of biography; the critical sections of the 'Life of Pope' are more elaborate. But the *Lives of the Poets* are also plainer in style than the earlier biographies including the *Life of Savage*, which is reprinted there but dates from an earlier period. This reflects Johnson's deepened sense of the importance of the 'minute peculiarities of conduct' ('Life of

Addison'). Attention to such matters is a mark of Johnson's commitment to realism and factual accuracy in biography. But it is also in the small details of life that the distinctiveness of individual character is revealed. They remind us that human beings are contingent creatures, and dwarf the heroic pretensions classical biography sometimes embodies. They embody likewise Johnson's deep conviction, itself anti-heroic and perhaps bourgeois, that it is domestic and private life that is the true moral arena. Both the strenuous necessity of truth and this general anti-heroic moral purpose demand that even unfavourable details should not be suppressed:

> If nothing but the bright side of characters should be shown, we should sit down in despondency, and think it utterly impossible to imitate them in anything. The sacred writers (he observed) related the vicious as well as the virtuous actions of men: which had this moral effect, that it kept mankind from *despair*, into which otherwise they would naturally fall were they not supported by the recollection that others had offended like themselves, and by penitence and amendment of life had been restored to the favour of heaven.
>
> (Life, IV, 53)

In the *Life of Savage*, as we have noted, the detail is assimilated together much more into a representative account, expressed in a relatively generalizing style. Here the facts are left to speak for themselves to a greater degree, though obviously Johnson stands back from them to make general comment from time to time as well. The emphasis on Pope's 'petty peculiarities', which some contemporary reviewers found reprehensible, is apparent from the very first sentence of the extract, as is Johnson's concern for factual evidence and documentation. The details passed on by the Earl of Oxford's maid were written in a short memoir published in the *Gentleman's Magazine*, but there is some evidence to suggest that Johnson also went to the trouble of interviewing her personally. His plain rendition of her account is highly detailed and factual. We obtain a vivid sense of the indignities and difficulties Pope suffered. The more elaborate word 'invested', however, carries a slightly mock heroic note, and there are obvious touches of pathetic vanity as well: 'His legs were so slender that he enlarged their bulk with three pairs of stockings . . .'. These are made the more piquant by the ironic juxtaposition (though the irony is unstated) with the dependency that follows, 'which were drawn on and off by the maid; for he was not able to dress and undress

himself . . .'. We remember that this man was the most famous
poet of the age, notoriously proud and defensive, and that the
sense of dependency is obviously made worse by characteristic
eighteenth-century attitudes to servants and to women: 'He
was then so weak as to stand in perpetual need of female
attendance. . . .'

The next paragraph confirms and strengthens the sense of
vanity. We think of the contrast between the baldness of Pope
and the velvet cap and the tie-wig, and there is again a slightly
mock-heroic note in 'dress of ceremony' (the contrast between
the private indignities and the public pretensions). This is more
obvious in '*little* sword' (Pope was only four foot six tall). At the
same time we also remember that Pope's dining partner was,
after all, a former Prime Minister, and so we are aware of his
genuine status too.

The movement out into judgement is signalled by a certain
heightening of diction – 'indulgence . . . accommodation . . .
valetudinary . . . dominion'. Johnson, a man frequently suffering from pain and illness himself, was always fiercely determined not to give in to self-indulgence as a result. His sternness
with himself is reflected in his sternness against Pope, and the
simile about the spoilt child makes us think of his resistance
to the new permissiveness in attitudes to child rearing in the
period encouraged by the influence of Locke and Rousseau.
Johnson moves again at the end of the paragraph to a vivid and
ironic anecdote as an example of the embarrassing extremes
that Pope's self-indulgence in his weakness brought him to.

The account of the trouble that Pope's visits to his aristocratic
friends caused the servants continues the relentlessly realistic
appraisal. Johnson is very aware that it was the honour of being
on intimate terms with a man as famous as Pope that 'procured
him many invitations' and if this reminds us of Pope's greatness,
there is an irony in the trouble these invitations caused and a
certain cynicism about the motive behind them. On the whole
Johnson is not very sympathetic to Pope's demands. We note
his distance from any romantic view that the great artist is
deserving of special consideration (Pope's requests, in fact, were
often for pen and paper) as well as his continued refusal to
allow special indulgence to the sick. These errands are 'foolish
and frivolous'. At the same time there is no sentimentalizing
of the servants either. The maids use Pope as a cynical excuse
when they have been 'neglecting their business', and Johnson is
careful to be fair at the end of the paragraph in pointing out
that Pope did recompense these servants handsomely.

The mention of Pope at the beginning of the next paragraph

as one of those who suffer 'much pain' indicates compassion, sympathy and understanding, but once again this is not allowed to excuse the moral failing of greed to which the rest of the unit is devoted. Johnson's judgement is, as always, certain and unflinching: 'He was *too* indulgent to his appetite' admits of no doubt or mitigating circumstances in its expression, though the latter have already been implied. There is a rather pathetic self-deception and hypocrisy in 'though he seemed angry when a dram was offered him, did not forbear to drink it' and a weakness that permits manipulation by others in 'His friends, who knew the avenues to his heart, pampered him with presents of luxury'. There is a kind of sad irony about the fact that this should be the way to a man such as Pope's heart. The final striking classical allusion is more complex. Its whole thrust is anti-heroic, reminding us that we are at best frail creatures vulnerable to petty circumstances. Yet this, of course, applies to Hannibal as well as to Pope, and if Pope is, in this instance at any rate, more culpable, he is put on the same level as the classical hero as a 'great man'.

Characteristically, however, the scrupulous demands of truth require Johnson to take back some of what he could not resist putting in. The antithesis that begins the next brief paragraph is no empty rhetorical flourish, but enacts the necessary qualification to what has just been said. The choice of more elaborate words here also indicates a summarizing judgement at a distance from the earlier factual details of narration, 'conformation', 'pertinacious diligence'.

Johnson on Johnson

John Wain has published a whole excellent anthology under this title (Dent, 1976). There are many parts of Johnson's writing that are purely personal – fragments of autobiography, journals, prayers and meditations, as well as a large number of interesting letters. Most of this material was not intended for publication, however, and despite its great fascination it does not seem appropriate to make it part of this critical survey section. Johnson in many respects followed neo-classical tenets about the irrelevance of purely personal material in literature, but as Wain shows he is prepared to write about himself very movingly even in his work intended for publication, though he always preserves a strong sense of rhetorical decorum in so doing. It is a magnificent passage of this kind that constitutes the example below.

From 'Preface' to the *Dictionary*

In the hope of giving longevity to that which its own nature
forbids to be immortal, I have devoted this book, the labour
of years, to the honour of my country, that we may no
longer yield the palm of philology to the nations of the
continent. The chief glory of every people arises from its
authors: whether I shall add anything by my own writings
to the reputation of English literature, must be left to time:
much of my life has been lost under the pressures of disease;
much has been trifled away; and much has always been spent
in provision for the day that was passing over me; but I
shall not think my employment useless or ignoble, if by my
assistance foreign nations, and distant ages, gain access to
the propagators of knowledge, and understand the teachers
of truth; if my labours afford light to the repositories of
science, and celebrity to Bacon, to Hooker, to Milton and
to Boyle.

When I am animated by this wish, I look with pleasure
on my book, however defective, and deliver it to the world
with the spirit of a man that has endeavoured well. That
it will immediately become popular I have not promised to
myself: a few wild blunders, and risible absurdities, from
which no work of such multiplicity was ever free, may for
a time furnish folly with laughter, and harden ignorance in
contempt; but useful diligence will at last prevail, and there
never can be wanting some who distinguish desert; who will
consider that no dictionary of a living tongue ever can be
perfect, since while it is hastening to publication, some words
are budding, and some falling away; that a whole life cannot
be spent upon syntax and etymology, and that even a whole
life would not be sufficient; that he, whose design includes
whatever language can express must often speak of what he
does not understand; that a writer will sometimes be hurried
by eagerness to the end and sometimes faint with weariness
under a task which Scaliger compares to the labours of the
anvil and the mine; that what is obvious is not always known,
and what is known is not always present; that sudden fits
of inadvertency will surprise vigilance, slight avocations will
seduce attention, and casual eclipses of the mind will darken
learning; and that the writer shall often in vain trace his
memory at the moment of need, for that which yesterday he
knew with intuitive readiness, and which will come uncalled
into his thoughts tomorrow.

In this work, when it shall be found that much is omitted,

let it not be forgotten that much likewise is performed; and though no book was ever spared out of tenderness to the author, and the world is little solicitous to know whence proceeded the faults of that which it condemns; yet it may gratify curiosity to inform it, that the *English Dictionary* was written with little assistance of the learned, and without any patronage of the great; not in the soft obscurities of retirement, or under the shelter of academic boughs, but amidst inconvenience and distraction, in sickness and in sorrow; and it may repress the triumph of malignant criticism to observe, that if our language is not here fully displayed, I have only failed in an attempt which no human powers have hitherto completed. If the lexicons of ancient tongues, now immutably fixed, and comprised in a few volumes, be yet, after the toil of successive ages, inadequated and delusive; if the aggregated knowledge, and cooperating diligence of the Italian academicians, did not secure them from the censure of Beni; if the embodied critics of France, when fifty years had been spent upon their work, were obliged to change its economy, and give their second edition another form, I may surely be contented without the praise of perfection, which, if I could obtain, in this gloom of solitude, what would it avail me? I have protracted my work till most of those whom I wished to please, have sunk into the grave, and success and miscarriage are empty sounds: I therefore dismiss it with frigid tranquillity, having little to fear from censure or from praise.

Context In the first part of his Preface, Johnson discusses all the technical decisions of procedure he has had to make in his great work. He goes on to say that people may hope that he will be able to 'fix' the language, but that, since language is a human product, no final permanency can be expected of it. This does not mean, though, that we should stop trying. We should at least do what we can to slow down the pace of change. Johnson ends in what had become the traditional way of introducing great works. He prepares a defence in advance against adverse criticism and gives the usual rhetorical expression of his own unworthiness.

Criticism Despite the traditional nature of what he has to say here, Johnson, as always, revitalizes convention and makes it not only eloquent but genuinely moving. He fills it out with personal sincerity and touches of autobiography, yet generalizes the significance of the purely personal elements at the same time in so doing. All this too in such a way that the purely rhetorical functions of the passage are actually enhanced.

He begins this extract by reinforcing a point he has just made, and one that is central to his whole attitude here: nothing purely human is eternal or perfect, and this applies to language as much as anything else, yet this does not mean we should give up the attempt to preserve as much stability as we can. With characteristic logical precision he opposes the 'longevity' which it is proper to *hope* his book might give to English words against the immortality that they can never have. This not only relates to Johnson's general views about human affairs but is also the key to the rhetoric of the whole passage *as an apology*. As is entirely appropriate it combines pride in his achievement with modesty and self-depreciation. The work is far from perfect, but then nothing human is perfect, and what has been done, in the circumstances, is considerable. In particular, it is a contribution, he writes patriotically, to English national pride in that we need no longer feel inferior to those continental countries that already have a dictionary. The 'chief glory of every people', he says, in a typically authoritative aphorism, 'arises from its authors'. Whether his own writings will contribute to that glory he cannot know until time has judged them. He has always written under great pressure of circumstance, which he summarizes in three clauses that amount to something like a personal complaint, though they combine the element of self-pity and excuse – 'under the pressures of disease' – with self-condemnation – 'trifled away'. He then moves to a quasi-biblical eloquence of phrasing that generalizes his own situation into that of every human being: 'and much has always been spent in provision for the day that was passing over me'. 'Passing over me' in particular carries the traditional sense of the fleetingness of life. But his work on the *Dictionary* at least (leaving aside the other writing he refers to earlier with a mixture of modesty and pride as of uncertain status since it may or may not last) has not been useless in that it has been at the service of the great English writers. He refers to these at first in general terms with an almost missionary note of zeal on their behalf – 'propagators . . . afford light . . .' – and then in a great roll-call of noble names: a great popularizer of scientific philosophy, a great Anglican theologian, a great poet and a great scientist. The whole long sentence that constitutes the great part of this paragraph is thus carefully constructed so that it ends on a note that illustrates its firmly asserted opening, and so that the personal reference that it contains is assimilated within and made subservient to the patriotic cause of English letters.

The next paragraph is an extended apology in the technical rhetorical sense. Johnson begins with a transition: the hopes he has described in the preceding paragraph are enough to prove that he has 'endeavoured well', whatever the defects of the book. He concedes 'wild blunders' and 'risible' [laughable] absurdities, but if this seems a damaging confession he is in fact disarming the opposition in advance by saying that only fools would fail to expect them in so large a work. The thoughtful on the contrary will recognize 'desert', and he obviously invites us to be among them. The rest of the sentence (which makes up the rest of the whole paragraph) consists of a long list of clauses that explains why the defects of the book are unavoidable. He begins by attributing them to the imperfection and instability of language as such, using a beautiful metaphor of budding and falling away to capture the idea. The next clause strikes a fine balance, as throughout the rest of the 'Preface', between a sense of the dignity and yet the pettiness of language studies, depending on which view of them is taken. On the one hand, we have many different things to occupy us; on the other hand, as the Latin tag has it, 'Art is long and life is short', and we can never exhaust the study of language no matter how much time we devote to it. For our minds are limited, and the clauses that follow explain the inadequacies of Johnson's mind as revealed in his work as examples of the general limitations of fallible creatures. Again the balanced phrasing creates a fine sense of local ironies: '. . . while it is hastening to publication, some words are budding, and some falling away . . . sometimes hurried by eagerness to the end . . . sometimes faint with weariness. . . .' But the elaborate balance of the clauses also creates a dignified and sad rhythm overall that relates to a deeper sense of irony about the greatness and yet the vulnerability of the human mind. At the same time Johnson has avoided monotony by a very careful rhetorical 'variation' in the arrangement and number of syntactical units in his clauses in ways that will be obvious on examination.

The final paragraph summarizes what Johnson has been saying: that the work is imperfect but good. He is realistic enough to know that readers are not prepared to make concessions to books because of personal consideration to the author. Yet this assertion actually serves as a kind of rhetorical *praeteritio* or passing over (a device where a writer says he is not going to mention something but in fact goes on to talk about it at some length). For Johnson immediately proceeds to speak in the most moving and eloquent terms of his personal difficulties in writing the *Dictionary*. He had no academic assistance, for

181

example, and no patronage (a reference to the controversy with Lord Chesterfield). Apology, as so often here, soon reveals itself as righteous pride: he wrote in the midst of real life, and if this made things harder it also gave his work a strength of mind and realism on which he prided himself. But it has been said that Johnson's style always takes on a special resonance when he speaks of the wretchedness of his own situation and this is, of course, true here too. The cadences are dignified, the phrasing like the Anglican Prayer Book: 'Amidst inconvenience and in distraction, in sickness and in sorrow.' He returns to the idea of 'malignant criticism' (rather obsessively, despite what he says at the end) but tries once more to disarm it by repeating that no one has ever been able to produce a *perfect* dictionary. The point is then reinforced and expanded in the three long rhetorical 'if' clauses of the sentence that follows, each of which is an example of a dictionary produced in much more favourable circumstances than Johnson's that was still imperfect. Again, of course, under the guise of apology we are also being reminded of the greatness of Johnson's almost single-handed achievement compared with the 'aggregating knowledge and cooperating diligence of the Italian academicians' and the 'embodied critics of France' (we remember that when asked how one Englishman could do in the three years initially contracted for what forty Frenchmen of the Academy had taken forty years to do, he said, 'Let me see; forty times forty is sixteen hundred. As three to sixteen hundred, so is the proportion of an Englishman to a Frenchman'). But the sentence ends not where we might expect with the recognition that perfection is not to be obtained, but with a surprising note of pathos and irony. The last sentence expands this into a sad example of the 'vanity of human wishes' (he is referring primarily to his wife Tetty, who died in 1752) – 'I have protracted my work until most of those whom I wished to please, have sunk into the grave' – and a final flourish of rhetorical self-defence about the reaction to the work (not entirely convincing, of course) – I do not care *what* people say about it!

Johnson the critic

As we have seen, Johnson is active as a literary critic throughout his long career. We must not always expect, though, to find criticism in the formal modern sense. The notes in the edition of Shakespeare, for example, are not primarily literary criticism, though they contain passages of it, but are explanatory or are concerned with the correct textual readings. Similarly, the general comments at the end of the plays, the 'Concluding Notes' are sometimes too casual and general to have much objective merit as criticism, though they are of great interest, of course, for what they tell us of Johnson. The first sentence of the comment on *All's Well that Ends Well*, for example, seems no more than general assertion: 'This play has many delightful scenes, though not sufficiently probable, and some happy characters, though not new, nor produced by any deep knowledge of human nature.' Johnson continues much more interestingly in the next paragraph with the well-known personal comment 'I cannot reconcile my heart to Bertram', which shows that he shares the commonsense reaction of many people to this day.

The extract chosen for detailed discussion below is one of the best of these 'Concluding Notes' and it shows striking personal response and general commentary combining most impressively.

FROM 'Concluding Notes', *King Lear*

The tragedy of Lear is deservedly celebrated among the dramas of Shakespeare. There is perhaps no play which keeps the attention so strongly fixed; which so much agitates our passions and interests our curiosity. The artful involutions of distinct interests, the striking opposition of contrary characters, the sudden changes of fortune, and the quick succession of events, fill the mind with a perpetual tumult of indignation, pity, and hope. There is no scene which does not contribute to the aggravation of the distress or conduct of the action, and scarce a line which does not conduce to the progress of the scene. So powerful is the current of the poet's imagination that the mind which once ventures within it is hurled irresistibly along.

On the seeming improbability of Lear's conduct it may be observed that he is represented accorded to histories at that time vulgarly received as true. And perhaps if we turn our thoughts upon the barbarity and ignorance of the age to which this story is referred, it will appear not so unlikely as while we estimate Lear's manners by our own. Such preferences of one daughter to another, or resignation of dominion upon such conditions, would be yet credible if told of a petty prince of Guinea or Madagascar. Shakespeare, indeed, by the mention of his earls and dukes, has given us the idea of times more civilised, and of life regulated by softer manners; and the truth is that though he so nicely discriminates, and so minutely describes the characters of men, he commonly neglects and confounds the characters of ages, by mingling customs ancient and modern, English and foreign.

My learned friend Mr Warton, who has in the *Adventurer* very minutely criticised this play, remarks that the instances of cruelty are too savage and shocking, and that the intervention of Edmund destroys the simplicity of the story. These objections may, I think, be answered by repeating that the cruelty of the daughters is an historical fact, to which the poet has added little, having only drawn it into a series by dialogue and action. But I am not able to apologise with equal plausibility for the extrusion of Gloucester's eyes, which seems an act too horrid to be endured in dramatic exhibition, and such as must always compel the mind to relieve its distress by incredulity. Yet let it be remembered that our author well knew what would please the audience for which he wrote.

The injury done by Edmund to the simplicity of the action is abundantly recompensed by the addition of variety, by the art with which he is made to co-operate with the chief design, and the opportunity which he gives the poet of combining perfidy with perfidy, and connecting the wicked son with the wicked daughters, to impress this important moral, that villainy is never at a stop, that crimes lead to crimes, and at last terminate in ruin.

But though this moral be incidentally enforced, Shakespeare has suffered the virtue of Cordelia to perish in a just cause, contrary to the natural ideas of justice, to the hope of the reader, and what is yet more strange, to the faith of chronicles. Yet this conduct is justified by the Spectator, who blames Tate for giving Cordelia success and happiness in his alteration, and declares that in his opinion 'the tragedy has lost half its beauty'. Dennis has remarked, whether justly or not, that to secure the favourable reception of *Cato*, 'the town was poisoned with much false and abominable criticism', and that endeavours had been used to discredit and decry poetical justice. A play in which the wicked prosper, and the virtuous miscarry, may doubtless be good, because it is a just representation of the common events of human life: but since all reasonable beings naturally love justice, I cannot easily be persuaded that the observation of justice makes a play worse; or, that if other excellencies are equal, the audience will not always rise better pleased from the final triumph of persecuted virtue.

In the present case the public has decided. Cordelia, from the time of Tate, has always retired with victory and felicity. And, if my sensations, could add any thing to the general suffrage, I might relate that I was many years so shocked by Cordelia's death that I know not whether I ever endured to read again the last scenes of the play till I undertook to revise them as an editor.

Criticism   The reader of the *Preface to Shakespeare* may be surprised to find Johnson making derogatory remarks at times about the style of Shakespeare's tragedies. But there is no sign of any reservations in the noble tribute to *Lear* in the first paragraph here. Johnson has always had a strong sense that the one indispensable thing literature needs is the power of attracting our attention, and he describes unforgettably the way the action of the play catches us up. 'I must *burn* through *King Lear* again', wrote Keats. Johnson's response is of similar intensity: 'So powerful is the current of the poet's imagination that the mind which once ventures within it is hurried irresistibly along.' ('Imagination' here, as often in *literary* contexts in Johnson, clearly has positive connotations.) But if Johnson's reactions are just as personal and just as deeply felt as the romantic poet's, he obviously both feels the necessity of generalizing the expression of that response and has the requisite confidence to be able to extrapolate out from it to that of the average reader: '*our* passions and *our* curiosity . . . *the* mind'.

Johnson, we also notice, is writing at one and the same time about human psychology and about qualities inherent in the work. He conveys well the variety of the play and yet its powerful unity: 'There is no scene which does not contribute to the aggravation of the distress or conduct of the action, and scarce a line which does not conduce to the progress of the scene.' Just as he is confident that his reactions are the same as those (as he says later) of 'all reasonable beings' so he feels sure that there is a natural fit between specific literary effects and the way the human mind works: 'The artful involutions of distinct interests, the striking opposition of contrary characters, the sudden changes of fortune, and the quick succession of events fill the mind with a perpetual tumult of indignation, pity and hope.' The authoritative tone of the rhythm and phrasing here conveys the confidence Johnson feels.

The next paragraph has a certain 'Enlightenment' complacency about it that we have noticed before in Johnson's comments on Shakespeare. There is a strong sense here of the differences between historical periods and cultures, and a preparedness to take these into account as explanations and even as mitigating circumstances in judging literature. What seems improbable to us was far less so in earlier periods and different cultures. But this approach to 'historical criticism' stops far short of relativism. Johnson is quite certain of his own age's superiority not only to the mysterious period which the play is supposedly set in but also (by implication) to Shakespeare's own time. He is equally certain of his own country's superiority to that of 'Guinea or Madagascar', where they might behave like Lear.

We cannot help but also be aware though of what seems to us a kind of naïveté in evaluating Lear's initial behaviour (or for that matter Cordelia's) in terms of probability and realism in the first place. Johnson's care for probability is a neo-classical criterion akin to decorum. It seems to be strengthened in his case by what can only be termed a moral suspicion of fiction. Certainly we expect today that the events of most kinds of plays should follow on logically one from another and seem psychologically plausible in that respect. But we are also perfectly willing to accept without too much scruple an initial premise such as the one on which this play depends.

Yet these considerations lead Johnson to a striking insight about Shakespeare's lack of concern with historical verisimilitude, his mingling of periods, his anachronisms (like the introduction of Edgar as the English and Elizabethan beggar Tom o' Bedlam). This is something that Johnson not only recognizes but also seems quite willing to accept.

The model of debate in a law court is obviously in Johnson's mind as he introduces the arguments of Joseph Warton to the effect that *Lear* is too cruel a play. We may find the answer that the cruelty of the daughters was a historical fact another example of a slightly naïve literalism that fails to grasp that a play is an imaginative creation that inevitably uses some kind of exaggeration to achieve its effect. Johnson, in other words, seems not to have appreciated the full implications of his own earlier eloquent comment about the power of the poet's imagination and the way that 'the mind which once ventures within it is hurried irresistibly along'. The question of Gloucester's blinding is, of course, a more complicated one and inevitably controversial in neo-classical terms, since classical plays would not portray such events on stage but only describe them by a messenger. The authority of this is compounded by Johnson's own extreme imaginative sensitivity. The word 'extrusion' seems to try to create a distance from that extreme personal response, and we must note that 'horrid' has much stronger connotations than today (in the *Dictionary* Johnson defines it as 'hideous; dreadful; shocking', and separates off the weakened modern sense that was beginning to come in as 'womens cant'). Once again there is evidence of Johnson's historical sense in his recognition that Shakespeare's audience would have been more ready for violence, but the tone does not imply that this is any extenuation in this particular instance.

The next paragraph, however, defends the play against the suggestion that what it has become customary to call the sub-plot involving Edmund and Gloucester weakens the action. Not only is Johnson sure that this is not so, but he seems extremely perceptive about the way this sub-plot actually contributes to the play. He speaks of this admittedly in rather more moralistic terms than those to which we are accustomed, but essentially here he has anticipated the ideas of the great Shakespearian critic A.C. Bradley about the way that Shakespeare manages to *universalize* the action by this means.

As in the *Preface* though, Johnson goes on to complain that the moral teaching Shakespeare offers is only incidental and that in more important respects he has been prepared to infringe morality. Nowhere is this more true than in the case of the death of Cordelia, an innocent and virtuous victim, who dies almost by accident, it seems, when the audience hopes that she will be saved at the last moment. This was a great offence against the neo-classical idea of poetic justice, the view that drama must always show virtue rewarded and vice punished. Addison had himself infringed this tenet in his famous play *Cato*, and Johnson repeats, without completely committing himself to it, John Dennis's claim that it is for that reason that Addison defended Shakespeare's practice in *Lear*. He concedes himself, of course, that in terms of sheer realism poetic justice has little to be said for it, for it is the way of the world that injustice is often perpetrated. But here is one clear way in which the *imitation* proper to art is to be distinguished from realism. Interestingly, though, Johnson's argument here is not religious or moral as such (despite the fact that he clearly found offences against poetic justice threatening for religious reasons) but related once more to the audience's pleasure and psychology. With enviable confidence and despite his strong sense of our fallen natures Johnson still believes that there is a natural bias in our minds towards justice, and suggests that our very pleasure in a play will be disturbed if this is not regarded.

Eighteenth-century audiences in fact only ever saw the revised version of *Lear* by Nahum Tate, where the ending was altered so that Cordelia survived and married Edgar. Johnson makes this – the judgement of the public – his clinching argument, and he implies an analogy with political decisions in his use of the word 'suffrage'. He is also able once again, however, to report a reassuring overlap between the general judgement and his own personal response, though he offers the latter only very tentatively it seems and implies that it might be of no significance without that overlap, 'And, if my sensations, could add any thing to the general suffrage'. At the same time, of course, this last comment is another famous example of his own extreme (almost morbid and romantic?) imaginative sensitivity: 'I might relate that I was many years so shocked by Cordelia's death that I know not whether I ever endured to read again the last scenes of the play till I undertook to revise them as an editor.'

From 'Life of Pope'

To the praises which have been accumulated on the *Rape of the Lock* by readers of every class, from the critic to the waiting maid, it is difficult to make any addition. Of that which is universally allowed to be the most attractive of all ludicrous compositions, let it rather be now inquired from what sources the power of pleasing is derived.

Dr. Warburton, who excelled in critical perspicacity, has remarked that the preternatural agents are very happily adapted to the purposes of the poem. The heathen deities can no longer gain attention: we should turn away from a contest between Venus and Diana. The employment of allegorical persons always excites conviction of its own absurdity; they may produce effects, but cannot conduct actions: when the phantom is put in motion, it dissolves: thus *Discord* may raise a mutiny, but *Discord* cannot conduct a march, nor besiege a town. Pope brought into view a new race of beings, with powers and passions proportionate to their operation. The sylphs and gnomes act at the toilet and the tea-table, what more terrific and more powerful phantoms perform on the stormy ocean or the field of battle; they give their proper help, and do their proper mischief.

Pope is said by an objector not to have been the inventor of this petty nation; a charge which might with more justice have been brought against the author of the *Iliad*, who doubtless adopted the religious system of his country; for what is there but the names of his agents which Pope has not invented? Has he not assigned them characters and operations never

heard of before? Has he not, at least, given them their first
poetical existence? If this is not sufficient to denominate his
work original, nothing original can be written.

In this work are exhibited in a very high degree the two
most engaging powers of an author: new things are made
familiar, and familiar things are made new. A race of aerial
people never heard of before is presented to us in a manner
so clear and easy that the reader seeks no further information,
but immediately mingles with his new acquaintances, adopts
their interests and attends their pursuits, loves a sylph and
detests a gnome.

That familiar things are made new every paragraph will
prove. The subject of the poem is an event below the common
incidents of common life; nothing real is introduced that is
not seen so often as to be no longer regarded, yet the whole
detail of a female day is here brought before us invested with
so much art of decoration that, though nothing is disguised,
every thing is striking, and we feel all the appetite of curiosity
from that from which we have a thousand times turned
fastidiously away.

(Hill (ed.), III, 233–4)

Context After describing the biography of Pope Johnson moves
into a section dealing with his *general* character as a man and
then as a poet. He proceeds next to discuss each of his major
works in chronological order.

Criticism To the principle of the test of time which Johnson
proposes as the major criterion of literary greatness in the
Preface to Shakespeare he adds another here which is only implied
in the earlier work, the idea of universality of appeal, 'from
the critic to the waiting maid'. Johnson himself found the
Rape of the Lock the 'most airy, the most ingenious and the
most delightful' of all Pope's poems, and he was happy to be
able to back up his own view with what he presents as an
unassailable consensus of opinion. He thus differentiates, as
always, between a quirky subjective view and one where the
personal sincerity both confirms and is confirmed by a more
general assent. The critic, we note, for Johnson may well be
distinguished by a wider reading and knowledge, but he is
essentially an example of 'the common reader', not someone
marked out by a godlike subtlety of aesthetic taste. Yet it remains
the task of criticism to

> establish principles; to improve opinion into knowledge; and
> to distinguish those means of pleasing which depend upon

known causes and rational deduction, from the nameless and
inexplicable elegancies which appeal wholly to the fancy, from
which we feel delight, but know not how they produce it . . .
(Rambler 92)

The *Rape* is a major example of 'ludicrous composition': i.e.
lightly satiric mock-epics, and since each kind of literature has
its own sources of pleasure, it must be possible to ascertain what
its especial merits are.

Like William Warburton, Pope's friend and commentator,
and most other readers, Johnson finds the use of the sylphs
and gnomes one of the most distinctive features of the poem,
though the machinery, a parody of the use of the gods and
goddesses in classical epic, was not in fact added until the
expanded second version. But Johnson's whole discussion is
conducted in terms of the principle of decorum rather than by
focusing on the more superficial aesthetic pleasure that these
shimmering tiny creatures obviously create. As a mock-epic the
Rape of the Lock has to have some equivalent to the supernatural
agents of full-scale epic. Johnson once again reveals his distance
from the full Renaissance literary preconceptions in indicating
that it is no longer possible to write convincingly using the
classical gods. A rigorous logical sense also suggests that, while
allegorical persons like Discord may be all very well as a literary
device, they cannot be used in an extended action. But Pope
has solved the resulting problem of decorum to perfection, and
Johnson's repeated word 'proper' is a technical term to signify
this appropriateness and decorum. The sylphs and gnomes are
exactly proportioned to the physical world of the poem and to
its trivialized moral world as well.

The tactfully anonymous 'objector' to whom Johnson next
refers is Joseph Warton, whose *Essay on the Writings and Genius
of Pope* (1756) had argued that Pope was not the greatest kind
of poet because he lacked imagination. Although Warton found
more of this quality in the *Rape of the Lock* than in any of Pope's
other poems he suggested a reservation even there in that Pope
had not actually *invented* the sylphs, but found them ready to
hand in contemporary occultist writings. Johnson, we note, is
far from downgrading the importance of 'imagination' and even
originality in response. On the contrary, he is determined to
defend Pope's claim to these qualities. His point is, though,
that 'imagination' does not have to be pure invention out of
the poet's head but can be displayed in the way pre-existent
material is made use of and given 'poetical existence'. Johnson
certainly values 'originality', but, as the next paragraph goes on

to show, that originality needs to preserve a certain probability and naturalness (and this is perhaps more likely to be found when the subject-matter is itself not *complete* invention).

In his famous discussion of the metaphysical poets in the 'Life of Cowley' Johnson had presented a new definition of wit: 'If by a more noble and adequate conception, that be considered as wit which is at once natural and new, that which though not obvious is, upon its first production, acknowledged to be just; if it be that which he that never found it wonders how he missed. . . .' This is a criterion with far wider implications, of course, than its immediate context, and it has a central importance in Johnson's whole perspective on literature. What he seeks is a combination of the sparkle and interest of novelty with the sense of recognition that comes from probability and truth, the human centrality of 'nature' that we have discussed in the context of Shakespeare. It is revealing to see how Johnson works out the implications of this principle with regard to the poem under discussion, and the way he combines the theory with affectionate appreciation. The *Rape of the Lock*, he makes clear, has to an abundant degree the quality by which 'new things are made familiar, and familiar things are made new'. Pope writes of his exotic new creatures 'in a manner so clear and easy' that he creates a kind of quasi-human sympathy for them and a real sense of intimacy, and the reader soon 'adopts their interests and attends their pursuits, loves a sylph and detests a gnome'.

At the same time Pope uses his new machinery to confer an enormous mystery and glamour on the common details of domestic life, which have been 'seen so often as to be no longer regarded'. Johnson's phrasing of this point shows evidence of a certain ambivalence. On the one hand there is a neo-classical feeling that great literature demands great subject-matter, and that the 'common incidents of common life' can only have comic treatment and need all the 'art of decoration' to make them proper subjects for literature *at all*. (Clearly this is compounded by an element of sexism – it is the 'whole detail of a *female* day' from which 'we have a thousand times turned fastidiously away'.) On the other hand, we cannot help but think of Wordsworth's ambition in the *Preface to Lyrical Ballads* to bring out the true poetic significance of such common incidents. Johnson himself always argued that the real moral struggle in which we find ourselves lay not in heroic events but in private life, and he goes on in the paragraph that follows this extract to say with characteristic wisdom that Pope's moral in the poem is a genuinely important

191

one, despite its apparent light-heartedness. Family quarrels can constitute a very serious obstruction to human happiness, for it is a part of our very natures that 'the misery of life proceeds not from any single crush of overwhelming evil, but from small vexations continually repeated'.

Part Three
Reference Section

Short biographies

ADDISON, JOSEPH, 1672–1719 Essayist, poet, playwright and Whig politician. After a time in academic life Addison entered diplomatic service and politics, where he rose steadily to success, first as an MP and then as Chief Secretary of State for Ireland. He married the Countess of Warwick in 1716. Throughout this whole time he was also highly successful as a writer and a critic and as the centre of a circle of Whig writers (in which role he was satirized by Pope as Atticus in *An Epistle to Dr Arbuthnot*). He was famous for his tragedy *Cato* (1713), but far more for his collaboration with Sir Richard Steele on the two most influential literary periodicals that have ever been produced, the *Tatler* (1709) and the *Spectator* (1711–12), which set a norm for social, literary and to some extent political and religious values for a long time to come.

BACON, FRANCIS, BARON VERULAM, 1561–1626 Lawyer, politician and philosophical writer. After a time as an MP Bacon rose between 1607 and 1618 from Solicitor-General to Attorney-General and then to Lord Chancellor. In 1621 he was found guilty of bribery and removed from office, though to this day differing opinions about the degree and nature of his guilt remain. He published his famous *Essays* in 1597, with an augmented edition in 1625. Here, in a terse aphoristic style that has some influence on Johnson, he recommends a characteristic worldly wisdom. His most important writings are English and Latin works on science and philosophy, especially *The Advancement of Learning* (1605) and the *Novum Organum* (1620) where he discusses the obstacles the human mind puts up to knowledge of the truth and proposes a collaborative scientific effort to improve the human lot.

BANKS, SIR JOSEPH, 1743–1820 Naturalist. Beginning a life-long commitment to natural history at Eton, Banks went to Oxford and then visited Newfoundland to study botany. Banks and the Swede Dr Solander then accompanied Captain James Cook around the world to study nature (1768–71). In Australia they discovered the kangaroo, to Johnson's great interest (as a famous anecdote of the Hebrides trip reveals). Banks was made President of the Royal Society in 1778 and received many other honours. He was elected to 'The Club' in 1778.

BOSWELL, JAMES, 1740–95   Biographer and diarist. The son of a Scottish judge, Lord Auchinleck, Boswell studied law in Scotland but came to London in the hope of fame and contact with great men. He suffered himself from depression and a tendency to alcoholism and, despite high religious and moral aspirations, he compulsively resorted to prostitutes, resulting in several serious bouts of venereal disease. Boswell found Johnson, whom he met in 1763, a moral mentor, and he soon conceived the project of his great biography, which did not appear until 1791. He toured the continent in the 1760s, where he met Rousseau, Voltaire and the liberator of Corsica, General Paoli. He practised law in Edinburgh on his return, but with frequent visits to London. He was elected to Johnson's 'Club' and went to the Hebrides with him in 1773. His problems with alcohol increased in his later years. The discovery of his brilliant manuscript journals at Malahide Castle has been one of the great scholarly and publishing events of this century.

BURKE, EDMUND, 1729–97   Politician and writer. A member of an Anglo-Irish Protestant family, Burke's earliest writing of significance is on aesthetics, *A Philosophical Enquiry into the Origin of our Ideas of the Sublime and the Beautiful* (1756). He became a member of 'The Club' in 1763. In the same year he became an MP and Private Secretary to the Prime Minister. He later opposed the government's attitude to the American colonists, and worked in the cause of Ireland and Catholic emancipation. His most famous work, however, was his *Reflections on the Revolution in France* (1790) where he opposed the Revolution with great eloquence in the name of tradition. He broke with the liberal Whigs under Charles James Fox as a result, and has been regarded ever since as one of the greatest 'Conservative' thinkers.

BUTLER, JOSEPH, 1692–1752   Theologian and moral philosopher. Born into a dissenting merchant family, Butler became an Anglican, studied in Oxford and was ordained. His *Fifteen Sermons* (1726) mediate between self-love and benevolence in the moral philosophy of the time. In his *Analogy of Religion* (1736) he showed that nature alone could hardly be regarded as a reliable source of revelation. He became Bishop of Bristol in 1738 and Bishop of Durham in 1750.

CARTER, ELIZABETH, 1717–1806   Writer. Her mother dying early, Elizabeth was educated by her clergyman father and by intense study learned Latin, Greek, Hebrew, Arabic and other languages. She met Johnson through her work on the *Gentleman's Magazine* and later contributed two essays to the *Rambler*. She became a member of the 'Bluestocking' circle around Elizabeth Montagu, and wrote poetry, memoirs and a translation of the Stoic Epictetus.

CAVE, EDWARD, 1691–1754   Printer and editor. Expelled from grammar school in Rugby, Cave went to London and became apprenticed to a printer. He eventually purchased a printing establishment at St John's Gate in Clerkenwell. In 1731 he began the *Gentleman's Magazine*. Johnson produced work for this when he first came to London and became Cave's assistant. Cave also printed Johnson's *Irene*, his *Life of Savage* and *London*. He became prosperous through the success of the magazine, and painted the Gate at Clerkenwell as a crest on his coach.

CHESTERFIELD, PHILIP DORMER STANHOPE, EARL OF, 1694–1773   Politician, wit and writer. Chesterfield had a distinguished diplomatic and political career. He was Ambassador to the Hague and Lord Lieutenant of Ireland. He was a generous patron of writers, and it is ironic therefore that he is now remembered in this context mainly for Johnson's stinging letter of rebuke for recommending the *Dictionary* just before publication after apparent years of neglect. Chesterfield's own most famous works are the letters to his son and his godson preaching manners and the way of the world.

COLLINS, WILLIAM, 1721–59   Poet. Collins published his *Persian Eclogues* while still an Oxford undergraduate. Thereafter he has a central role in the new poetry of his time, producing lyrical work about nature and the role of the inspired poet in *Odes* (1746) and writing *Ode on the Popular Superstitions of the Highlands of Scotland* in 1749. He suffered from nervous depression and was at times insane.

DODD, REV. WILLIAM, 1729–77   The son of a clergyman, Dodd sought eagerly for fame and popularity after his own ordination. He became a fashionable preacher and author, cultivated the rich and lived extravagantly. Eventually he forged the name of his old pupil, Lord Chesterfield on a £4200 bond, believing no doubt that he would never be brought to prosecution. George III refused to exercise the royal prerogative of mercy, despite many appeals on Dodds's behalf, of which the most distinguished were Johnson's, and the clergyman was duly hanged.

DRYDEN, JOHN, 1631–1700 Poet, playwright and critic. After writing in praise of Cromwell Dryden celebrated the Restoration of Charles II in verse and became a popular playwright both in heroic tragedies and Restoration comedies. Defence of his own dramatic principles led him into literary criticism, especially the *Essay of Dramatic Poesy* (1668), and he is a major influence on Johnson as a critic. In 1668 he became Poet Laureate, and much of his brilliant verse satire in heroic couplets arises out of the need to defend and justify the court against opposition, *Absalom and Achitophel* (1681–2) in particular. In 1686 he became a Roman Catholic, and he lost his court offices on the fall of his master James II in 1688. In his last years he produced a wide range of translations, fables, odes and critical essays.

FIELDING, HENRY, 1707–54 Dramatist, novelist and magistrate. A relatively impoverished member of a distinguished family, Fielding studied law and then became a successful playwright. This career ended abruptly with Walpole's censorship laws in 1737. He became a novelist with *Joseph Andrews* (1742), which began as a parody of Richardson's *Pamela*, and then with the comic epic *Tom Jones* (1749). Johnson always disapproved of the apparent laxity about sexual morality in these works, but Fielding has very serious moral concerns of his own. He was also active in the suppression of crime as Justice of the Peace for Middlesex.

FOX, CHARLES JAMES, 1749–1806 Politician. A member of a wealthy Whig aristocratic family, Fox was always noted for his drinking and gambling debts as well as for his great oratory and political talents. He became MP for Midhurst and soon won applause for his speeches. In 1770 he was appointed one of the Lords of the Admiralty, and then a junior Lord of the Treasury. But George III disliked him, and opposition to the political power of the King was to become the main theme of the rest of Fox's career. He was leader of a Whig faction that opposed the government's treatment of the American colonists and he supported the French Revolution. The King was able to prevent him from holding high office for long, even when he entered into coalition with the conservative politician Lord North. Despite their political differences Johnson admired him and he joined 'The Club' in 1774.

GARRICK, DAVID, 1717–79 Shakespearian actor and theatre manager. Garrick had attended Lichfield Grammar school and also been taught by Johnson during the latter's own brief venture of running the school at Edial Hall. The two travelled to London together in 1737, but Garrick was a much more rapid success story than Johnson. After his stunning performance as Richard III in 1741 he was by the next year receiving at Drury Lane the highest annual salary any actor had ever been given. Equally successful as Shakespeare's greatest tragic heroes, Garrick re-opened Drury Lane in 1745, and oversaw a great Shakespearian revival. Johnson was in some ways jealous of his old pupil's success, but his famous remark that Garrick's death had 'eclipsed the gaiety of nations' was placed over the latter's grave.

GEORGE III, KING, 1738–1820   Succeeding his grandfather George II on the throne at the age of twenty-two in 1760, George III seemed likely to make an auspicious monarch. But he was badly advised and under the thumb of his former tutor, Lord Bute, who became Prime Minister shortly afterwards. George was unlucky in that his long sixty years reign saw the loss of the American colonies and political disaffection at home with the controversies about Wilkes and later agitation for parliamentary reform. He also showed signs of temporary madness as early as 1788 (now known to be the symptoms of the illness porphyria). In 1810 he became totally incapacitated, and his eldest son was appointed Regent. Yet the historical consensus now is that he was well intentioned politically and he was popular with the public as 'Farmer George' for his simple tastes and domestic virtues. On a famous occasion in 1767 he came to meet Johnson in the Buckingham House library when the latter was using it, and the two spoke respectfully together.

GIBBON, EDWARD, 1737–94   Historian. After an 'unprofitable' time at Oxford Gibbon engaged in prodigious reading, and devoted the main part of his life to his great *Decline and Fall of the Roman Empire*, though he was also an MP for a time. The first volume of his great work appeared in 1776, and he was soon forced to defend himself against attacks on his ironic and hostile attitude to Christianity. The work was finally completed in 1788. He had become a member of 'The Club' in 1774, but no major clashes with Johnson are recorded.

GOLDSMITH, OLIVER, 1728–74   Poet, essayist, dramatist. A man of great charm, one of the foremost contemporary writers and one of Johnson's closest friends. Goldsmith was from an Anglo-Irish family. He studied medicine and then led a wandering life in Europe. On his return he failed as a physician, chemist's assistant and schoolmaster and began to make a living as a literary hack. His reputation increased; he met Johnson and was one of the original members of 'The Club'. Despite the fame of such works as *The Chinese Letters (The Citizen of the World*, 1760–62), the poem *The Deserted Village* (1770), and the immensely successful play *She Stoops to Conquer* (1773) Goldsmith was always improvident, and there is the famous story of Johnson finding the manuscript of *The Vicar of Wakefield* and arranging for its publication (1766) when Goldsmith was arrested for debt. Johnson's Latin tribute 'He touched nothing that he did not adorn' was placed on Goldsmith's memorial in Westminster Abbey.

GRAY, THOMAS, 1716–71   Poet, scholar and letter-writer. After school at Eton, Gray studied at Cambridge and travelled abroad. He lived virtually the whole of the rest of his life as a Cambridge don apart from a period in London studying at the British Museum. He had elaborate antiquarian and botanical interests as well as literary ones. The volume of his poetry was small, but it was immensely influential. Johnson had great admiration for his famous *Elegy Written in a Country Churchyard* (1751), in which romantic sentiment is contained within moral generalization. Gray's other important poems, however, are more extravagant in their bardic tone and elaborate stanzas and dictions, and Johnson strongly opposed the vogue.

HOBBES, THOMAS, 1588–1679   Philosopher. After graduating from Oxford Hobbes spent much of his time as a private tutor to the sons of English noblemen. During an extended continental tour from 1634–7 he met European philosophers such as Descartes and Galileo and began to develop his own version of a mechanical philosophy that would explain the human world as well as the universe by the laws of the motion of matter. This was explained in *The Elements of Law Natural and Politic*, which was circulated in manuscript and published in part in 1650. Here Hobbes presents human beings, startlingly, as the product of complete determinism and relativism, dominated by desire and the drive to self-preservation. The political implications of this are developed in *Leviathan* (1651), where Hobbes defends monarchy in purely secular terms as the one agent that can keep the peace. Hobbes's cynicism and materialism made him a great bugbear, and much of the thought of the seventeenth and eighteenth centuries is devoted to the attempt to refute him.

HOOKER, RICHARD, 1554–1600   Theologian. Educated at Oxford and ordained in the Church of England, Hooker thereafter accepted only quiet rural parishes so that he would be free to write his great work, *Of the Lawes of Ecclesiasticall Politie* (Books I–IV, 1594; V, 1597; VI and VIII, 1648; VII, 1662: the last three books may not be fully authentic). This is the definitive statement of the central Anglican position against Roman Catholics and especially the Puritans. It defends bishops, but does not regard them as indispensable, and argues throughout for respect for reason, nature and tradition as well as the Bible.

HUME, DAVID, 1711–76 Philosopher and historian. Educated in Edinburgh Hume became a leading figure in the Scottish Enlightenment. His scepticism produced ecclesiatical opposition to his appointment as a professor at Glasgow. He was secretary to the British embassy in Paris from 1763 to 1766, and brought Rousseau on a tour of Britain, though the two quarrelled. He was Under Secretary of State from 1767 to 1768. His major philosophical works such as *Treatise of Human Nature* (1739), *Philosophical Essays concerning the Human Understanding* (1748) and *Enquiry concerning the Principles of Morals* (1751) take scepticism to the point of questioning causation and undermine confidence in reason, but they do so with an optimistic and almost complacent confidence in human common sense and virtue. The same 'Enlightenment' tone is apparent in *History of England* (1754–61), the first to embrace all English history and to include manners, arts, sciences and economics. In his own period Hume was notorious for questioning the testimony of miracles in an essay included in an *Enquiry concerning Human Understanding*.

JENYNS, SOAME, 1704–87 Minor politician and miscellaneous writer. An MP for many years and Commissioner of the Board of Trade, Jenyns was also a liberal intellectual and voluminous writer whose works include a poem on *Dancing* as well as a variety of controversy. His complacent *A Free Inquiry into the Nature and Origin of Evil* (1757) incurred Johnson's devastating review. Jenyns later composed a mock epitaph beginning, 'Here lies poor Johnson! Reader, have a care,/Tread lightly, lest you move a sleeping bear.'

JOHNSON, ELIZABETH JERVIS PORTER, 'Tetty', 1689–1752 Johnson's wife. Daughter of a Warwickshire squire and widow of Harry Porter, mercer and woolen draper. She married Johnson in 1735 when she was forty-six and he was twenty-five. She brought with her a reasonable dowry, but this was soon exhausted on the expenses of Edial Hall school. There were many problems in the marriage and she became an invalid and probably a laudanum (opium) addict in later years. But Johnson was always grateful for her acceptance of him and mourned her deeply after her death.

LAW, WILLIAM, 1686–1761   Devotional and mystical writer. After being ordained and becoming fellow of his Cambridge college, Law refused to take the oath of allegiance to George I and thus lost his position. He became a tutor for a time in the family of Gibbon's father and later lived a retired life of good works and piety. A strong high-churchman, his works include controversy against deists and against those who held a low or purely functional sense of the role of the Church. In his later career he was influenced by less orthodox mysticism. But his most influential work was *A Serious Call to a Devout and Holy Life* (1728), an incitement and invitation to deep spiritual conversion and commitment, of which Johnson wrote that he took it up 'expecting to find it a dull book, as such books generally are, and perhaps to laugh at it. But I found Law quite an over-match for me; and this was the first occasion of my thinking in earnest of religion . . .'

LOCKE, JOHN, 1623–1704   Philosopher. Son of a lawyer who fought for the parliamentarians in the Civil War, Locke became an Oxford don and then secretary and physician to the first Earl of Shaftesbury, leader of the Exclusion movement to keep James II from the throne. After the collapse of the movement Locke fled to Holland and worked on the philosophical and political writings he published after the 1688 Revolution made it safe for him to return to England. The most influential of these were the *Letters Concerning Toleration* (1689–90); *Two Treatises on Government* (1690); and the *Essay concerning Human Understanding* (1690). The last in particular made him the most famous philosopher of the age. He later wrote *Some Thoughts Concerning Education* (1693) and *The Reasonableness of Christianity* (1695).

MACPHERSON, JAMES, 1736–96   'Translator' of Gaelic poems. The son of a farmer in the Scottish Highlands, Macpherson became a schoolmaster after attending Aberdeen and Edinburgh universities. His *Fragments of Ancient Poetry . . . translated from the Gaelic or Erse Language* (1760) was followed by his epic prose 'translations' of a Gaelic poet, *Fingal* (1762). These appealed not only to Scots patriotism but also to the growing romantic interest in primitivism, and Goethe and Napoleon are among the distinguished Europeans impressed with Macpherson's work. Johnson always refused to believe in the authenticity of these poems until the original manuscripts were produced, and this occasioned Macpherson's famous threatening letter, which Johnson replied to in suitable style and provided himself with a stout oak cudgel. But the question of whether Macpherson was a fraud or not has recently been reopened.

MANDEVILLE, BERNARD, 1630–1733 Controversialist and writer on economics. Born in the Netherlands, Mandeville became a physician there and then practised in London. His poem *The Grumbling Hive* (1705) was republished and augmented with notes and a prose *Inquiry into the Origin of Moral Virtue* as *The Fable of the Bees* (1714). It was reissued once more with the addition of an essay on charity schools and *A Search into the Nature of Society* in 1723. Mandeville's apparently Hobbesian attitudes and his argument that commercial society *depends* upon vice were attacked by a variety of authorities. Johnson once said though that Mandeville had 'opened [his] views into real life very much'.

MONBODDO, JAMES BURNETT, LORD, 1714–99 Lawyer and writer on language. After study at Aberdeen and Edinburgh Universities, Monboddo was called to the Scottish Bar and in 1767 became a judge as Lord Monboddo. His two main works, *Of the Origin and Progress of Language* (1773–92) and *Antient Metaphysics, or the Science of Universals* (1779–99) are full of admiration for Greek 'simplicity'. The former has especial importance in its ideas on the evolution of language from animal communication. Johnson was not impressed with his ideas, but the two got on well together when Johnson visited Monboddo on his tour of Scotland.

MONTAGU, ELIZABETH, 1720–1800 Writer and society hostess. Daughter of a northern squire, Elizabeth Robinson married the wealthy Edward Montagu, who was many years older than her, in 1747. Spending her later life in London she became the centre of a group of writers, men of influence such as Lord Lyttelton and female intellectuals, the 'Bluestockings'. She published *An Essay on the Writings of Shakespeare* in 1769 in which she defended the dramatist against the strictures of Voltaire. Johnson spoke highly of her intellectual powers, though there was a coolness in their relationship in later years.

NEWTON, SIR ISAAC, 1642–1727 Scientist. A brilliant mathematician from early youth, Newton had by 1666 begun his optical experiments, thought out his theories of colour, discovered the elements of the calculus and conceived part of his work on gravitation. He was elected Fellow of Trinity College, Cambridge in 1667 and Professor of Mathematics at Cambridge two years later. In 1672 he became a Fellow of the Royal Society and later President. His most influential work was in the theory of the general laws of motion and universal gravitation and his application of this to the movement of the planets. This made him far and away the most famous scientist of his time throughout Europe and he exercised a considerable influence both on literature and theology as well as science. He took an active part in public life as MP for Cambridge University and as Master of the Royal Mint (1699). He also devoted much of his time to the study of biblical chronology.

PERCY, BISHOP THOMAS, 1729–1811   Editor and poet. A clergyman who became Bishop of the Irish diocese of Dromore in 1782, Percy was interested in early literature. He discovered and edited a selection from an old manuscript of poems as *The Reliques of Ancient English Poetry* (1765). This had a tremendous influence on the revival of interest in the middle ages and medieval literature. He became a member of 'The Club' in 1765.

POPE, ALEXANDER, 1688–1744   Poet. The son of a prosperous Catholic linen-draper, Pope's health was ruined by childhood illness, and he was only four foot six inches high when fully grown. He was an early friend of Addison's, though the two soon quarrelled. *Essay on Criticism* (1711) and *Rape of the Lock* (1714) were early successes, and his translations of Homer (1715–26) brought him fame and wealth. Involvement in a series of personal, literary and political controversies turned him towards satire, especially *Moral Essays* (1731–5), *Imitations of Horace* (1733–8) and *The Dunciad* (1728; 1742). He also wrote the philosophical poem *Essay on Man* (1732–4). He was undoubtedly the greatest poet of the whole period.

REYNOLDS, SIR JOSHUA, 1723–92   Painter. Apprenticed early as an artist in London, Reynolds then studied abroad. According to Ruskin he is the 'prince of portrait painters' and his reputation soon grew on his return to England. His portraits of Johnson, who was a very close friend, are among his best known works. He was one of the original members of 'The Club' (1764). As first President of the Royal Academy in 1768 he wrote influential *Discourses* (1769–90) which present broad neo-classical principles.

RICHARDSON, SAMUEL, 1689–1761   Printer and novelist. The son of a joiner (carpenter), Richardson had little formal education.

He became apprenticed to a London printer, and then set up his own printing business. He compiled a manual of letter-writing for those uncertain of the proper modes. This led into his experiments in epistolary novels, beginning with *Pamela* (1740–1), the extremely successful story of a pious servant girl whose master tries to seduce her. His greatest work is the lengthy Christian tragic novel *Clarissa Harlowe* (1747–8). He helped Johnson when the latter was arrested for debt. Johnson admired his work for its moral seriousness and psychological insight.

SAVAGE, RICHARD, 1698–1743   Poet. Savage claimed to be the illegitimate son of Lord Rivers and Lady Macclesfield. Recent scholarship has suggested that he genuinely believed the story, but had been misinformed by those who had brought him up. His supposed mother always refused to acknowledge him and worked actively against his interests. Her nephew Lord Tyrconnell gave Savage patronage for a time, but a quarrel ended the arrangement. Thereafter Savage was often in financial difficulties and on one occasion convicted of murder, though later pardoned when the circumstances became clearer. He wrote plays, poems and prose, his best-known piece being the poem *The Bastard* (1728). He met Johnson when both were in difficult circumstances, and after his death in debtors' prison in Bristol Johnson wrote his life (1744).

SHAFTESBURY, ANTHONY ASHLEY COOPER, THIRD EARL OF, 1671–1713   Moral philosopher. Pupil of Locke, though he rejected the more empirical aspects of his philosophy. After travelling in Europe Shaftesbury became an MP, and assumed the earldom in 1699. He gave up public life because of ill-health, and devoted himself to philosophy. His influential *Characteristicks of Men, Manners, Opinions* (1711) proposed a genteel and harmonious philosophy of ideal nature, the natural goodness of human beings, virtue and an innate moral sense.

SHERIDAN, RICHARD BRINSLEY, 1751–1816   Playwright and orator. Born in Dublin, the son of Thomas Sheridan, actor, teacher of elocution and author of a pronunciation dictionary, Richard began a brilliant theatrical career as playwright and manager of Drury Lane with the comedies of manners *The Rivals* and his masterpiece *The School for Scandal*. He entered parliament in 1780, where he had another brilliant career as an orator and associate of Burke and Fox. Elected to 'The Club' in 1777.

SMITH, ADAM, 1723–90   Political economist. Smith became Professor of Logic and then of Moral Philosophy at Glasgow. A friend of Hume's, he published *Theory of Moral Sentiments* in 1759. He travelled on the continent for several years and then devoted himself to his great work *An Enquiry into the Nature and Causes of the Wealth of Nations*, which finally appeared in 1776 and revolutionized thinking about trade, commercial society and capitalism. He became a member of 'The Club' in 1775, but he and Johnson were never close.

SWIFT, JONATHAN, 1667–1745   Satirist. From an Anglo-Irish family, Swift, after university, entered the household of the distinguished retired diplomat Sir William Temple and defended him against the 'moderns' in *The Battle of the Books* (1704). His *Tale of a Tub* (published 1704) is itself a powerful satire against 'modern' religion, pseudo-learning and the commercialization of literature ('Grub Street'). Became a vicar in Ireland, but returned to England on an extended visit where he became friends with Addison and Pope. He grew disillusioned with the Whigs and became a leading propagandist for and advisor to the 'Tory' administration of Harley (Lord Oxford) and St John (Bolingbroke). On the fall of the Tories he returned, embittered, to Ireland as Dean of St Patricks, Dublin. He wrote on behalf of the Irish in works such as *Drapier's Letters* (1724). His greatest satire was *Gulliver's Travels* (1726). In his last years he suffered from senile dementia. Swift fascinated Johnson, who shared much of his view of human nature but without the same bitterness.

TAYLOR, REV. JOHN, 1711–88   Clergyman. One of Johnson's oldest friends from Lichfield Grammar School, Taylor became rector of several parishes and canon of Westminster, but resided in a fine house at Ashbourne, Derbyshire, where Johnson often visited him in later years. Taylor spent much of his time on cattle-breeding, but Johnson drew on his spiritual counsel on the death of his wife and Taylor conducted Johnson's own funeral service.

THOMSON, JAMES, 1700–48   Poet. A Scotsman educated at Edinburgh University, Thomson moved to London and worked at first as a tutor. *The Seasons* (1726–30), blank verse meditations on nature, liberal theology and politics made him famous. After travelling on the continent he wrote *Liberty* and several tragedies and then retired on a pension to Richmond where he wrote the Spenserian *Castle of Indolence*.

THRALE, HENRY, 1724–81   Brewer and MP for Southwark. The third generation of the family to be connected with the Anchor

Hester Thrale and Queeney by Sir Joshua Reynolds

Brewery in Southwark, Henry Thrale was educated at Eton and Oxford before entering the business. His marriage to Hester was without love on either side, though the couple had twelve children. In 1765 Johnson was introduced to the Thrales, and very soon became an intimate of the family with his own apartment in their fine house at Streatham Park. He also accompanied them on trips to Wales and France. Although closer to Hester, Johnson always spoke with great respect of her husband and wrote political addresses and pamphlets on his behalf.

THRALE, HESTER LYNCH PIOZZI NÉE SALUSBURY, 1741–1821 From a Welsh family, Hester Salusbury married Henry Thrale in 1763. The match was a loveless one, though she bore him twelve children. Vivacious and intelligent, Hester became Johnson's main emotional support for many years after the couple were introduced to him in 1765 and provided him his own apartment in their house. Johnson was devastated when, after Thrale's death, she married the Italian musician Gabriel Piozzi in 1784. Hester wrote the highly readable and informative *Anecdotes of the Late Samuel Johnson* (1786) and other works.

WALPOLE, SIR ROBERT, FIRST EARL OF ORFORD, 1676–1745 Politician. Born at Houghton near King's Lynn, Norfolk, Walpole became the MP for King's Lynn after studying at Eton and Cambridge and continued to represent it for the whole of his political career. He was Whig First Lord of the Treasury (a post broadly equivalent to the modern Prime Minister) from 1715 to 1717 and then for more than twenty years from 1721 to 1742, having been returned to power to sort out the political mess of the South Sea Bubble, a fraudulent government share scheme in which many were ruined. He stayed in power through a careful manipulation of the patronage system, and the saying 'every man has his price' was attributed to him. He incurred the powerful opposition of many writers, Pope and Swift in particular. Johnson, too, satirized him in his early political pamphlets but later spoke highly of his peace policy.

WARTON, JOSEPH, 1722–1800 Poet and critic. After his ordination as a clergyman Warton became chaplain to the Earl of Bolton and eventually Headmaster of Winchester College. He was notoriously unsuccessful in the latter role, despite his long tenure and finally resigned after an insurrection by the boys in 1793. His *Odes* (1744, 1746) show all the fashionable 'pre-romanticism'. His *Essay on the Genius and Writings of Mr Pope* (1756, second vol. 1782) praises Pope, but still considers his satires not the highest kind of poetry. A friend of Johnson's, he joined 'The Club' in 1777.

WARTON, THOMAS, 1728–90 Critic, poet and scholar. Fellow of Trinity College, Oxford, for forty years, Warton was a poet like his brother, and produced the 'pre-romantic' *Pleasures of Melancholy* in 1747. He became Poet Laureate in 1785. His scholarly and critical work is of more importance – *Observations on the Faerie Queene* (1754) and the first *History of English Poetry* (1774–81). A friend of Johnson's, he became a member of 'The Club' in 1780.

WESLEY, JOHN, 1703–91 Son of the poet Samuel Wesley, John was ordained in the Church of England in 1725 and was elected a fellow of Lincoln College, Oxford in 1726. He became the leader of a group of devout young men, including his brother Charles, who practised austerities and regular devotions and were nicknamed 'Methodists'. Missionary work in Georgia led to contact with the pious Protestant Moravians, and John experienced his great conversion in 1738. Thereafter he devoted himself to evangelizing England, travelling a quarter of a million miles and preaching over forty thousand sermons. He wished to remain within the Church of England, but was forced to preach out of doors because of that Church's hostility. Thousands, mainly among the poor, were converted, and Methodism grew into a separate denomination by the time of Wesley's death. Wesley also wrote prolifically and produced influential volumes of hymns with his brother. Loyalty to the Church made Johnson express the usual prejudices about Methodism, but he spoke with respect of Wesley himself.

WILKES, JOHN, 1727–97   Politician and journalist. Son of a wealthy malt-distiller, Wilkes read classics with a private tutor and studied at Leyden University. He became High-Sheriff of Buckingham-shire and MP for Aylesbury. His real genius lay in political journalism, and his attacks on the Government and the King in *The North Briton* led to fines and even imprisonment. He was expelled from parliament in 1764 for an obscene version of Pope's *Essay on Man* called *Essay on Woman*. He became a symbol of radicalism and political resistance when he was elected Member for Middlesex, refused entry to the House and then re-elected several times. He was supported by the brilliant anonymous political writer 'Junius' and by popular petitions and rioting. He was also elected Lord Mayor of London. Although Wilkes was himself an opportunist the final result of the long controversy was to strengthen legal liberties.

Places to visit

Of especial importance to students and admirers of Johnson are his two former residences, which are now open to the public:

The Dr Johnson Birthplace Museum, Breadmarket Street, Lichfield (tel. 0543 264972) and

Dr Johnson's House, 17 Gough Square, London (tel. 071-353–3745).

Both have wonderful atmospheres and a wide range of Johnsonian exhibits.

Lichfield naturally enough has other Johnson associations, and the Cathedral and the Old Grammar School are interesting to visit. Johnson's Oxford college, Pembroke, is also well worth a visit, despite the brevity of his stay. Some hardy souls have traced the steps of Boswell and Johnson in Scotland and the Hebrides.

Gough Square, The Garret where Johnson compiled the Dictionary

But it is London, of course, especially the area around The Strand, that has the largest number of Johnsonian associations, only a few of which can be briefly mentioned here. Apart from the Gough Square house, Johnson also lived at Johnson's Court (the name is just a coincidence), the site now marked with a plaque, and at 8 Bolt Court. 'The Cheshire Cheese' in Wine Office Court claims Johnson as a former customer, though it is not mentioned in Boswell, and there is a portrait and plaque over his 'favourite seat'. Boswell frequented the Somerset Coffee House in The Strand (No. 166). St Clement Dane's Church, rebuilt after the blitz, was the church in which Johnson had his own pew, and the site of this is marked with a plaque. Johnson's tomb, with a bust by Nollekens, is in Westminster Abbey. At Kenwood House, Hampstead, may be found his summerhouse, which formerly stood in the grounds of the Thrales's house at Streatham Park, now destroyed. The Museum of London, London Wall, EC2, contains much interesting material on the social history of the capital in Johnson's time.

Details from maps of Johnson's and Boswell's London, redrawn from a map published in 1761 by R. and J. Dodsley

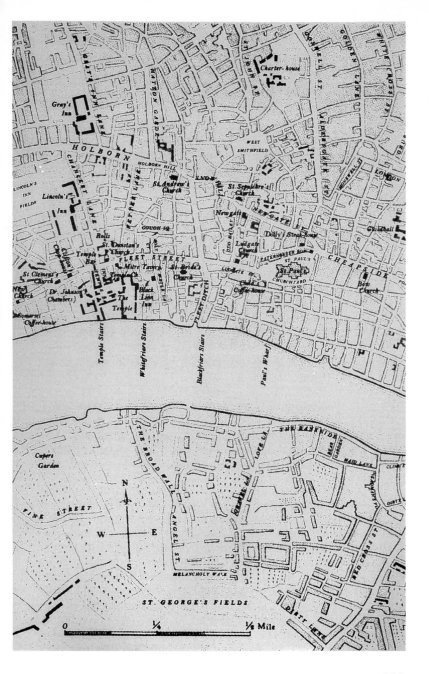

Further reading

Primary texts

The standard edition is *The Yale Edition of the Works of Samuel Johnson*. General Editor ALLEN T. HAZEN, later JOHN H. MIDDENDORF, New Haven, USA, Yale University Press. This has been the basic reference text here.

I	*Diaries, Prayers, Annals*, ed. E.L. McADAM, JR, with DONALD and MARY HYDE, 1959.
II	*The Idler and The Adventurer*, eds W.J. BATE, J.M. BULLITT and L.F. POWELL, 1963.
III, IV, V	*The Rambler*, eds W.J. BATE and ALBRECHT B. STRAUSS, 1969.
VI	*Poems*, ed. E.L. McADAM, JR, with GEORGE MILNE, 1964.
VII, VIII	*Johnson on Shakespeare*, ed. ARTHUR SHERBO, with an introduction by BERTRAND H. BRONSON, 1968.
IX	*A Journey to the Western Islands of Scotland*, ed. MARY LASCELLES, 1971.
X	*Political Writings*, ed. DONALD GREENE, 1977.
XIV	*Sermons*, ed. JEAN H. HAGSTRUM and JAMES GRAY, 1978.
XV	*A Voyage to Abyssinia*, ed. JOEL J. GOLD, 1985.
XVI	*Rasselas and Other Tales*, ed. GWIN J. KOLB, 1990. Other volumes in progress.

The Works of Samuel Johnson, LL.D, 11 vols, 1787, was reprinted various times and remains the only accessible text in some cases for works that have not yet appeared in the Yale edition, but it is unreliable in certain respects. Other good texts of selected works include, *The Lives of the English Poets*, ed. GEORGE BIRKBECK HILL, 3 vols (Clarendon Press, 1905) – this has been used for reference here; *Life of Savage*, ed. CLARENCE TRACY (Clarendon Press, 1971) – used here; *The Poems of Samuel Johnson*, ed. DAVID NICHOL SMITH and E.L. McADAM, JR (Clarendon Press, 2nd edition, 1972); *The Poems of Samuel Johnson*, ed. J.D. FLEEMAN (Penguin, 1986); *Johnson as Critic*, ed. JOHN WAIN (Routledge, 1973); *Samuel Johnson on Shakespeare*, ed. H.R. WOUDHUYSEN

(Penguin, 1989); *The Letters of Samuel Johnson, with Mrs. Thrale's Genuine Letters to Him*, ed. R.W. CHAPMAN, 3 vols (Clarendon Press, 1952); now being superseded by the edition by BRUCE REDFORD (Clarendon Press) of which 3 vols appeared in 1992. The most comprehensive anthology is *Samuel Johnson* in the Oxford Authors series, ed. D.J. GREENE (Oxford University Press, 1984). Also useful is BERTRAND BRONSON, *Samuel Johnson: Rasselas, Poems and Selected Prose* (Holt–Rinehart, rev. edn, 1971). The Dictionary appears in a facsimile edition in two volumes, *Johnson's Dictionary of the English Language* (Longman, 1990).

Biographies

Among early biographies of Johnson, the most important are: MRS THRALE (PIOZZI), *Anecdotes of the Late Samuel Johnson*, 1786; SIR JOHN HAWKINS, *Life of Samuel Johnson*, 1787 and JAMES BOSWELL, *Life of Johnson*, 1791. The edition of the latter by GEORGE BIRKBECK HILL, revised by L.F. POWELL, 6 vols (Clarendon Press, 1934; 2nd edition of last 3 vols, 1964) is the standard one (used for reference here).

The best modern biography is WALTER JACKSON BATE, *Samuel Johnson* (Harcourt, Brace, Jovanovich, 1977). JAMES CLIFFORD, *Young Samuel Johnson* (McGraw-Hill and Heinemann, 1955) and *Dictionary Johnson* (McGraw-Hill and Heinemann, 1975) are also very good. A shorter, lively biography is JOHN WAIN, *Samuel Johnson: A Biography* (Macmillan, 1974).

Criticism and studies of Johnson's thought

The best introductions to Johnson are by D.J. GREENE, *Samuel Johnson* (Twayne, 1970, rev. edn, 1989); PAUL FUSSELL, *Samuel Johnson and the Life of Writing* (Chatto and Windus, 1972) and J.P. HARDY, *Samuel Johnson: A Critical Study* (Routledge and Kegan Paul, 1979). For Johnson as a moral thinker, PAUL K. ALKON, *Samuel Johnson and Moral Discipline* (Northwestern University Press, 1967); WALTER JACKSON BATE, *The Achievement of Samuel Johnson* (Oxford University Press, 1955); ARIEH SACHS, *Passionate Intelligence: Imagination and Reason in the Work of Samuel Johnson* (Johns Hopkins University Press, 1967); and ROBERT VOITLE, *Samuel Johnson the Moralist* (Harvard University Press, 1961) can be recommended. The two major studies on Johnson's religion, CHESTER CHAPIN, *The Religious Thought of Samuel Johnson* (University of Michigan Press, 1968) and MAURICE QUINLAN, *Samuel Johnson: A Layman's Religion* (University of Madison Press, 1964) can be supplemented by JAMES

GRAY, *Johnson's Sermons: A Study* (Clarendon Press, 1972) and by NICHOLAS HUDSON, *Samuel Johnson and Eighteenth-Century Thought* (Clarendon Press, 1988) a work of interest on other topics too, though less comprehensive than its title might suggest. A selection of other valuable studies on various aspects of Johnson's work and thought follows below:

BERTRAND BRONSON, 'The Double tradition of Dr. Johnson', *ELH: A Journal of English Literary History* 18 (June 1951): 90–106.

LEOPOLD DAMROSCH, JR, *The Uses of Johnson's Criticism* (University Press of Virginia, 1976).

T.S. ELIOT, 'Introduction', *London* and *The Vanity of Human Wishes, English Critical Essays*, ed. PHYLLIS M. JONES, (Worlds Classics, 1933).

ROBERT FOLKENFLIK, *Samuel Johnson: Biographer* (Cornell University Press, 1978).

D.J. GREENE, *The Politics of Samuel Johnson* (Yale University Press, 1960; 2nd edn. University of Georgia Press, 1989).

JEAN H. HAGSTRUM, *Samuel Johnson's Literary Criticism* (University of Minnesota Press, 1952; 2nd edn, 1967).

M. LASCELLES, JAMES L. CLIFFORD, J.D. FLEEMAN and J.P. HARDY (eds), *Johnson, Boswell and Their Circle: Essays Presented to L.F. Powell* (Clarendon Press, 1965).

W.R. KEAST, 'The Theoretical Foundations of Johnson's Criticism', *Critics and Criticism*, ed. R.S. CRANE (University of Chicago Press, 1952).

ALVIN KERNAN, *Printing, Technology, Letters & Samuel Johnson* (Princeton University Press, 1987); reprinted in pbk as *Samuel Johnson and the Impact of Print* (1989).

LAWRENCE LIPKING, *The Ordering of the Arts in Eighteenth-Century England* (Princeton University Press, 1970), especially for the *Lives of the Poets*.

F.W. HILLES (ed.), *New Light on Dr. Johnson* (Yale University Press, 1959).

ALLEN REDDICK, *The Making of Johnson's Dictionary* (Cambridge University Press, 1990).

DAVID RICHTER, *Fable's End: Completeness and Closure in Rhetorical Fiction* (University of Chicago Press, 1974) – for *Rasselas*.

NIALL RUDD, *Johnson's Juvenal* (Bristol Classical Press, 1981).

RICHARD SCHWARTZ, *Samuel Johnson and the New Science* (University of Wisconsin Press, 1971) and *Samuel Johnson and the Problem of Evil* (University of Wisconsin Press, 1975).

JAMES H. SLEDD and GWIN J. KOLB, *Dr. Johnson's Dictionary: Essays in the Biography of a Book* (University of Chicago Press, 1955).

216

R.D. STOCK, *Samuel Johnson and Neoclassical Dramatic Theory* (University of Nebraska Press, 1973).

W.K. WIMSATT, *Philosophic Words: A Study of Style and Meaning in the Rambler and Dictionary of Samuel Johnson* (Yale University Press, 1948) and *The Prose Style of Samuel Johnson* (Yale University Press, 1941).

Background studies

Good general introductions and guides are A.R. HUMPHREYS, *The Augustan World* (Methuen, 1954) and PAT ROGERS (ed.), *The Context of English Literature: The Eighteenth Century* (Methuen, 1978).

INTELLECTUAL HISTORY

BASIL WILLEY, *Eighteenth-Century Background* (Chatto and Windus, 1940) is a useful introduction. Helpful surveys will also be found in ROY PORTER, *The Enlightenment* (Macmillan, 1990) and JAMES SAMBROOK, *The Eighteenth Century: The Intellectual and Cultural Context of English Literature 1700–1789* (Longman, 1986). On the religious background GORDON RUPP, *Religion in England 1688–1791* (Clarendon Press, 1986) is the most readable survey, and it includes a short section specifically on Johnson.

SOCIAL AND POLITICAL HISTORY

J.H. PLUMB, *England in the Eighteenth Century (1714–1815)* (Penguin, 1950 and reprints) is a classic brief study. For a more detailed and more recent survey see PAUL LANGFORD, *A Polite and Commercial People: England 1727–1783* (Clarendon Press, 1989). Very useful on attitudes to commerce are JOHN SEKORA, *Luxury: The Concept in Western Thought from Eden to Smollett* (John Hopkins University Press, 1977) and NEIL McKENDRICK, JOHN BREWER and J.H. PLUMB, *The Birth of a Consumer Society: The Commercialization of Eighteenth Century England* (Hutchinson, 1984).

LITERATURE AND LANGUAGE

On the literary scene see the general surveys above, and PAT ROGERS, *The Augustan Vision* (Weidenfeld and Nicolson, 1974) and BORIS FORD (ed.), *From Dryden to Johnson: New Pelican Guide to English Literature, Vol. 4* (Penguin, 1991). For literary criticism see: W.K. WIMSATT and CLEANTH BROOKS, *Literary Criticism: a Short History* (Vintage Books, 1957); PATRICK PARRINDER, *Authors and Authority: A Study of English Literary Criticism and its Relation to Culture 1750–1900* (Routledge, 1977; rev. edn, Macmillan, 1990); and R.S. CRANE, 'English Neoclassical Criticism: An Outline Sketch', *Critics and Criticism* (University of Chicago

Press, 1952). On biography, DONALD STAUFFER, *The Art of Biography in Eighteenth Century England*, 2 vols (Princeton University Press, 1941) remains useful. There is a good survey of 'Language 1660–1784' by A.S. COLLINS in FORD above, and a more general study by MURRAY COHEN, *Sensible Words: Linguistic Practice in England, 1640–1785* (Johns Hopkins University Press, 1977).

General index

Index to Johnson's works